ATLANTIC STUDIES ON SOCIETY IN CHANGE

No. 74

War and Society in East Central Europe

Volume XXIX

HUNGARIAN ECONOMY AND SOCIETY DURING WORLD WAR II

Edited by György Lengyel

Translated from the Hungarian Original by Judit Pokoly

Social Science Monographs, Boulder, Colorado
Atlantic Research and Publication, Highland Lakes, New Jersey

Distributed by Columbia University Press, New York
1993

EAST EUROPEAN MONOGRAPHS, NO. CCCLXII

Typesetting and Design by Stuart Ian Bernath

Library of Congress Catalog Card Number 92-84123
ISBN 0-88033-259-X
Printed in the United States of America

TABLE OF CONTENTS

III. WAR CASUALTIES

List of Tables

Preface to the Series

The present volume is a component of a series that, when completed will constitute a comprehensive survey of the many aspects of East European society. The books in the series deal with the peoples whose homelands lie between the Germans to the west, the Russians to the east and the Mediterranean and Adriatic Seas to the south. They constitute a particular civilization, one that is at once an integral part of Europe, yet substantially different from the West. The area is characterized by a rich variety in language, religion and government. The study of this complex subject demands a multidisciplinary approach and accordingly, our contributors to the series represent several academic disciplines. They have been drawn from the universities and other scholarly institutions in the United States and Western Europe, as well as East and Central Europe. The editor of the present volume is a distinguished sociologist and Chairman of the Department of Sociology of the Budapest University of Economic Sciences.

The editors take full responsibility for ensuring the comprehensiveness, cohesion, internal balance and scholarly quality of the series. We cheerfully accept this responsibility and intend this work to be neither a justification nor condemnation of the policies, attitudes and activities of any persons involved. At the same time, because the contributors represent so many disciplines, interpretations and schools of thought, our policy in this, as in past volumes, is to present their contributions without major modifications.

Foreword

This publication aims to present a cross section, within the limited scope of this volume, of Hungarian research into wartime economy and society carried out in the past decades. Though written at various points of time, the studies share the common feature of objective analysis based on empirical research results.

The earliest study in this collection is that of Professor Berend. He was somewhat reluctant when I asked him to offer a chapter of his unpublished doctoral dissertation for this volume, but thankfully, he accepted my reasoning. The examination of the wartime social structure would not have been complete without a study about the workers. This special area had been neglected by research during the communist era, either because it elicited excessively dogmatic associations among the younger generations of researchers or because it was heavily controlled by party ideology. Much could have been and still needs to be explored in this area through local historical research and through life-course interviews.

In recent years, the appeal of works tackling the social history and sociology of 1956 has greatly increased. It can only be hoped that this interest in the former taboo topic will not evaporate when it comes to the analysis of broader social-historical processes. Professor Berend deemed it necessary to note that the chapter cannot be regarded as a comprehensive treatment of the subject since he has not carried out more recent investigations in this area. Nevertheless, the analysis of the statistical and archival sources is a good starting point for further research.

The contribution of Iván T. Berend and György Ránki to the historiography of the Hungarian economy in the past decades has been decisive. There are, however, areas of interest that were beyond, or on the periphery, of their research. One such area is Lóránd Dombrády's investigations concerning the relationship between the army and the economy, based chiefly on the source material preserved in the Archives of the Institute for Military History. Another area of this kind is elite research, a new area of interest in Hungary. One of the first outcomes of this endeavor by sociologists and historians was Sándor Szakály's paper on the Hungarian military elite of the World War II.

Several social science researchers in the middle age bracket had gained inspiration to carry on archival research in the seminars of Professors Berend or Ránki. But Károly Szabó and László Virágh have been guided in their first research attempts by this middle generation. They decided to analyze the changes in the institutional system of forced delivery of supplies during the war and in the initial period of the planned economy. For this work they also tried to utilize the material of archives throughout the country. Like so many of their colleagues, they have been carried off by the whirl of recent political changes — abandoning their promising academic careers — assuming senior posts in the administration. Their thesis, whose chapters on the war economy are reproduced here is in an abridged form.

Another contributor is Tamás Stark, one of the authorities on an issue that stirred tempestuous debates on the war casualties. Some will question some of the research results, but one thing is certain: the legitimacy of his method — implying the meticulous, objective registration of facts and a comparison of data — can hardly be disputed.

We wish to thank Judit Pokoly for translating the manuscripts from Hungarian into English and Stuart Bernath for smoothing out the inconsistencies of the text.

Finally, allow me to say a few words about the peculiar circumstances of the genesis of this volume. When I first discussed the plan of this volume with Professors Béla K. Király and Peter Pastor, they agreed to proceed with the project on the condition that one of the academician authors of the volume be the editor. Since, at that time, Iván Berend was president of the Hungarian Academy of Sciences, György Ránki was the obvious choice. He was a highly respected scholar with great professional experience not to mention his congenial personality. I saw him as someone I could learn from. We agreed on the topics and the authors to be commissioned. Ránki wished to give the closing chapter of his book that he was working on for this collection, although he was also considering the idea of writing a separate study, but his unexpected death foiled those plans. Therefore, the job of editing this volume was again placed on me, but from that time on, it was a bitter task. The contributors of this volume and I wish to dedicate these studies to the memory of György Ránki.

The Editor

I. COORDINATES

INSTITUTIONS, ELITES, IDEOLOGIES: FROM CONTROLLED ECONOMY TO WAR ECONOMY

György Lengyel

When searching for the historical roots of the Hungarian economy during World War II, one finds the early instances of state intervention as the most general precondition. Modern redistributive interventionism and a war economy have two similarities. One is the emergence of the institutional network of economic control and the spread of the pertinent mentality. The other is a triple division within the structure of the business elite into the political elite of landowners-aristocrats, the leaders of private economy and the elite of the special bureaucracies. In one respect, however, there is a fundamental difference between the two economic time periods. Early interventionism was supportive, promoting the transactive market economy and the liberal political system.[1] By contrast, the war economy was based on restrictive principles, eventually resulting in the abolition of these institutions.

It was during the course of World War I that the positive and negative experiences of the controlling and redistributive techniques emerged.[2] That was when price control was worked out together with the institutions of raw material distribution patterned after the German model. This included the network of state-controlled raw material committees set up by officials of the central authorities and interest-protecting organs and the raw material centers organized as joint stock companies. At the same time, the shortage of raw materials led to the retention of stocks, stockpiling and the expansion of the black market, which the administration tried to eliminate by maximizing the prices of new purchases and setting up new committees of combined powers. Similarly ineffective was the attempt to control the labor market. The order for compulsory labor and the gradual increase in the number of factories under military supervision — exceeding 600 by the end of the war — made it easier for private capital to pass on the social burdens of the war. The labor grievance committees designed to quell growing social tensions were unable to integrate the dynamically expanding trade unions and the series of strikes organized to press for pay-raise demands. Since the industrial management of the Hungarian Soviet Republic in 1919 was based on the war institutions,[3] when the war was over employment of the industrial masses swollen by the war boom caused serious problems. All in all, the techniques of economic control worked out during World War I as a series of emergency measures intensified the conflicts of the transactive system. In the twenties, the newly consolidated ruling elite gave way to supportive, indirect interventions until the economic depression.

The image of a stable market economy was swept away by the economic crisis which added to the growing importance and longevity of state intervention.[4] They had to choose between two supportive interventions. The first would stimulate domestic demand within a liberal economic framework. The second would stimulate investment and reduce demand for consumer goods. The second coincided with the choice of territorial expansion which would crush the liberal system of rule. In Hungary, too, institutional changes were induced by the economic crisis. Here, however, the search for alternatives was not necessitated by the exhaustion of the resources of extensive growth. The alternative to a controlled economy in Hungary was derived from an aspiration toward territorial revision, requiring a specific foreign policy orientation and the modification of internal power constellations. The importance of the crisis lay primarily in the fact that it shattered the consensus of interests in the ruling elite based on compromise and catalyzed the modification of power relations. After Gyula Gömbös' appointment as premier, several key power positions in control of the special bureaucracies were seized by the political exponents of the bureaucratic elite which was comprised of the Hungarian intellectuals with a Christian middle-class background. The ideological basis for the new type state intervention and the offensive against economic liberalism by the bureaucratic elite was a direct result of the economic conditions that they experienced. A massive shift toward the political right took place within the ruling party and Gömbös' followers gained ground in the legislation as well. There was an immense increase in the faction representing the bureaucratic interests in support of the political right-wing reformists and the change of government. The influence of the agrarian group embodying related interests of the middle-size estate holders grew at a similar pace. In contrast to that, the proportion of the fraction allied with István Bethlen and representing the political elite of landowning aristocrats and the business elite became reduced.[5] Owing to the social changes generated by the crisis, major changes occurred within the business elite, too: 40% of the elite had been replaced between 1927 and 1937 and the rate of Jewish business leaders in top positions began to decrease.

With the growth of state intervention and the ascendancy of the bureaucratic elite, the battle was not yet decided as to the type of intervention. The business elite and the landowning aristocrats preferred the indirect, supportive measures as reflected in the savings-centric views of political leaders like István Bethlen and Gyula Károlyi.[6] But Gömbös' conception implied an unambiguous drive at a rightist corporative model. His views relied heavily on the transition from governing by decrees to extending the jurisdiction of those decrees.[7] Although these ideas were not fully realized in the economic policy, they proved to have far-reaching effects later.

One of the central concerns at the time was that of unemployment and the workers organizations. In this regard, Gömbös was an outspoken proponent of a "national work plan" which was a political program designed to achieve popular support. Gömbös' national work plan claimed to be "opposed to the idea of the so-called unemployment benefit (and benefit in cash) for those who do not work as demanded by the Social Democratic Party, because once on this road, there will be no stopping: the unemployment benefit destroys the sacred notion of work..."[8] Around this time proposals were raised to eliminate the labor market and create a uniform labor organization.[9]

These proposals, however, did not find their way to practice. Though the National Labor Center was set up whose leadership originally aspired to have the sole right of labor exchange, a later petition to Regent Miklós Horthy described its work as futile and harmful: "organizing the traveling in Europe of 200 workers spruced up in national costumes led by President Béla Marton..."[10] The Price Analyzing Committee was reshuffled and entrusted with the preparation of the anti-trust law and the examination of prices and production costs.[11] The alternative of controlled economy was also considered in some of the ministries.[12] Yet, the concrete steps and institutional changes were still moderate compared to what the political right envisaged. But what had a far wider-reaching effect than the actual measures was the change in ideology, the modification of the administrative system and a shift in foreign policy.

In view of the pace of armament in the European countries, the Hungarian high command concluded in the mid-1930s that by the end of the decade the Axis powers would increase their lead considerably. That would greatly increase the chance of a European war in which Hungary would inevitably be involved by her mere geographical location and by virtue of her aspiration to territorial revision. In a memorandum the chief-of-staff's estimate for the necessary military development was a total of 1.7 billion pengős. In late 1937, Regent Miklós Horthy discussed the document in a closed meeting. The finance minister declared that the financial requirement of the plan was simply impossible to satisfy, while Béla Imrédy, then the president of the bank of issue, thought an even a larger amount could be afforded. No concrete decision was taken at the meeting, but the economic and political power relations clearly pointed towards the so-called "Győr Program." Imrédy invited the Swedish economist Bertil Ohlin to prognosticate the extent of state investment without the danger of inflation. Ohlin and his associates opined that state investment worth 1 billion pengős in five years was possible in the interest of full employment. In February 1938, some news was leaked about the prospective program.[13]

But the plan was kept secret until the last moment since there were fears that its airing might upset the economic conditions.[14] Even so, Prime Minister Kálmán Darányi's speech in Győr on March 5, touching on the outlines of the program incurred much speculation and criticism. Though the industrial press was looking forward to the boom, it was afraid that the resources drained from agriculture and put into state investment would reduce the productive possibilities and jobs in consumer industries reinforcing the etatist tendencies through the increase of direct control. It voiced its dissatisfaction also because under the plan a disproportionately high rate of the extraordinary property tax covering 60% of the investment would be burdened on the joint stock companies.[15] The bill on investment was only tabled by the finance minister a month later, on April 8th and the debates dragged on until mid-May.

The first point of the act laying down the overall objectives was formulated as the basis of an extensive program of economic development:

> The ministry is herewith authorized to spend 1 billion pengős in excess of the appropriation of the state budget on military and defense aims, the construction of roads and bridges, the development of the railways and water-ways as well as the equipment of the post, telegraph and telephone network. Money should be spent on the promotion of agricultural production and sales, on the planned implementation of works laid down in Article XX/1938 to promote irrigation and on other hydrological investment, on constructing and equipping schools, conference rooms and other institutions for agricultural training and public education, on providing villages with health centers and healthy drinking water to raise the sanitary and social level of the rural population, on mining and raw material research and the promotion of the utilization of raw materials, as well as other public utility works and finally, on boosting agricultural credit.[16]

It is noteworthy that the program included several kinds of social investment but the concrete division of the 1 billion pengős was not fixed in the act. The other sections of the act provided for the raising of the sum, notably that 600 million pengős was to be collected as investment contribution in the form of property tax, while 400 million pengős was to be gathered from domestic loans. 60% of the 1 billion pengős was put into military development, while another 210 million was meant for the development of transportation in connection with the war aims.[17]

The Győr Program was a five-year plan. In the first two years of its implementation it brought about an economic boom. The preparation of the defense act was announced in autumn 1938 and the proclamation of universal conscription was expected to boost the economy again. During this period of upswing the concrete problem was the securing of the consumers market through military and state orders. In 1939, a decision was made to attain the goals of the five-year plan in two years. With this decision, the central problem of economy shifted from the fight for consumer markets to the distribution of scarce capital goods. This shift marked a qualitative change in the character of state intervention. From 1940, when the possibility of entering the war was growing more and more imminent, the terms under which private capital was working were tightened up, the production of a part of the consumer industries was restricted with the parallel increase of heavy industries and the issuing of credits was centralized. The economy turned into an economy of scarcity and remained that way for a long time. The members of parliament protested, but even a new finance minister and the minister of agriculture could not affect the direction of the economy.[18] In 1940, the finance minister projected the perspective of investment worth 2.8 billion pengős, raised to 4.5 billion pengős in 1941, 2.3 billion pengős of which was paid by the end of 1941.[19]

This meant that ever larger sums were drained by the redistributive channels of the state budget: in 1938-1939 one-third and in 1941 half of the national income was devoured by central expenditures.[20] The structure of state spending was also considerably changed. Between 1936-1937, two-fifths of the expenses were spent on the stabilization of power and three-fifths on social, cultural and production goals. In the tripled budget of 1939-1940 the proportion was exactly the inverse of the above.[21]

Structural Changes

The growing importance of redistribution was indicated by the fact that against the 60% rise of global economic investment, budgetary investment nearly doubled between 1924-1925 and 1938-1939, in the latter years, 90% of all the investment being financed by the state.[22] Compared to the average 4% of the previous years, in 1938 investment amounted to 12% of the national income and at this time almost half of the military investment was to build the infrastructure.[23]

When the war economy began, the Hungarian economy had arrived at threshold values in the structure of production and occupation. As against the Balkan countries where more than half of the national income derived from agriculture and four-fifths from industry, in 1938 the agriculture's share was 37% and industry's share was 36%.[24] By the end of the war the share of agriculture dropped to 28% and that of industry rose to 43%.[25] The extraction of some industrial raw materials picked up immensely. Between 1938 and 1943 oil mining grew 20-fold, natural gas production grew 9-fold and bauxite mining almost doubled.[26]

As regards agricultural and industrial employment, in 1930 Hungary was just touching the limit of agrarian countries characterized by a rate of 50-80% of the population employed in agriculture: in 1930 51% of the active population worked in agriculture and 48% in 1941. Labor mobility between the economic sectors were stuck at this level and after the war there was a slight shift towards pre-war rates.[27] All this resulted in the tension-generating phenomenon that at the time of the war economy approximately half of the active population produced a quarter of the national income and a quarter of the population produced about half the national income.

In the early 1920s, the sectorial structure of industry was predominated by the food industry at 47%, with a production rate of 37% for heavy industry and 16% for light industry. By 1938, the growth rate of the food industry had significantly decreased, while light industrial production grew dynamically, with a slower growth in heavy industry. In 1938, 42% of industrial production came from the heavy industry where 51%

of the industrial labor force was employed. In the period of the war economy, heavy industry clearly became the most dynamic industrial branch, in keeping with the objectives of the economic policy. In 1942, heavy industry turned out nearly half of all the industrial products, employed 62% of the industrial workers and concentrated three quarters of the industrial machinery. Within heavy industry, machine production grew most dynamically: between 1938 and 1943 the labor force almost tripled, while the production value at current prices grew nearly five and a half times. In 1943, machine industry employed 48% of the workers and turned out 42% of production within heavy industry.[28]

In comparable areas and at comparable prices, the production value of industry grew by 26% between 1938 and 1943, while the labor force increased by 33%, the number of plants by 9%, the machinery power by 30%. In the actual national area and at comparable prices, industrial production was up by 57% in 1943 from 1938, while the labor force rose by 56% and machine capacity and number of plants were one and a half times higher. Due to the territorial expansion between 1939 and 1941, 1,700 small and medium-size plants were added to the number of industrial plants. The productivity of factory work grew by an annual 4.4% on the average between 1938 and 1943. This growth resulted from a significant 11. 1% rise of capital productivity and a moderate 2.7% rise of work productivity.[29]

The concentration of Hungarian industry with a traditionally uneven plant structure grew significantly during the war economy. This type of economy foreshadowed the communist tendency of increasing the concentration of enterprise, promoting heavy industry and machine manufacturing at the cost of restricting agricultural development. Therefore, the war economy brought about the typical symptoms of quasi-advanced economies.[30]

Institutions and Resources

Parallel with the program of investment, the administrative system of the economy also underwent radical changes. A minister and government commissioner of economy and a minister of public food supply were appointed, various committees and centers were set up. These changes were designed to build up a functionally divided, redistributive economic hierarchy based on private property. There was practically no institution or instrument created during the war economy years that functioned properly. The alterations in the political power relations and economic conditions forced the controlling apparatus to change constantly, too. However, these changes all pointed in one direction: toward central control based on mobilization and working with dysfunctional overlappings.

The role of the Ministry of Defense and the General Staff in control of the economy increased enormously. With the growth in the number of war factories, the Ministry of Defense more and more often interfered with the matters of other ministries: it controlled the raw material requirements, exports and imports of war factories, the building and demolition of their industrial railways and plants and at times directly influenced the prices of certain industrial raw materials. All this led to a peculiar doubling of the controlling apparatus. A typical plant extension, for example, had to be supervised by the Ministry of Defense and the Ministry of Industrial Affairs.[31] As Pál Teleki expounded in a letter to Regent Miklós Horthy, this duality was the source of grave conflicts.[32]

The military administration ordered investments without the knowledge and the consent of the finance minister, interfered with social matters, refused to give the prime minister and the relevant ministries certain information and hindered the work of the civil administration at lower levels as well. It was another typical feature of the period that capitalist interest groups were gradually squeezed out of the decision-making. They turned to the state less frequently to arbitrate in their conflicts with the trade unions since their interests more often crashed with those of the controlling agencies. They tried to stretch the net of the redistributive hierarchy covering the private economy with stacks of memoranda and petitions.

The decree regulating the management of raw materials was first released in autumn 1938, making it obligatory to register

400 products and encompassing all the basic materials.[33] A year later it was replaced by another order providing for over 600 products. Similar to the organization of commodity management during World War I, committees for commodities management were set up to control and allocate the raw materials.[34]

The presidents and vice presidents of the committees had to be ministerial officials and their members coopted from competent circles were appointed by the minister of industry. Offices were fitted up for the committees whose maintenance was the duty of the sectorial interest protecting organs. The coordinating organ of the committees was the Central Committee of Industrial Material Management whose membership was comprised of the presidents of the various committees and whose duties included the fostering of ties with the Hungarian National Bank, the Foreign Trade Office and the Government Commissioner for Price Control. In 1939, the sequestration of material stocks began, at first affecting 380 products.[35] At this time, in Germany and in Great Britain the registration of material stocks was compulsory and in most of the South European states hoarding was punished by severe sanctions.[36] The Hungarian authorities were very well informed of these measures. Only the post and some transportation companies were entitled to buy from the frozen materials without extra permission, but the amount could not exceed 200 pengős. The sequence of urgency among the orders for larger shipments was decided by the minister of industry.[37] In the summer of 1940, the list of sequestered items included over 500 products and any kind of utilization of them was conditional upon the permission of the competent committee.[38] This was necessary because the shortage of raw materials was increasing from 1940. Several factories fell behind schedule in production because of delays in coal deliveries with one restriction inevitably leading to the next.[39] Soon control was extended over the traditional business relations as well.[40]

The enterprises resorted to a tactics based on personal contacts playing different interest groups of the controlling apparatus against one another. The maneuvers gave rise to further measures. In 1942, the special committees were abolished and the institution of the Office of Industrial Material took their place. Its employees working for fees were authorized to check the running of any industrial or commercial enterprise. An advisory board in support of the Office was set up under the name Council of Industrial Material Management. Only half of the council's membership came from the sectorial interest-protecting organs.[41] A year later, the rate of members from interest-protection was reduced to one-third.[42] In 1943, another two decrees tightened the measures on the registration and freezing of material stocks and the validity of a permit to use sequestered materials was reduced to one year.[43] By 1944, the raw material shortage was so acute that several factories had to reduce their production to a fraction of their capacity or to close down.[44]

Actually, the restriction of production and trade began with an order providing for the unobstructed operation of factories producing war-related goods.[45] Compulsory delivery to the army for defense came before all other deliveries. If an entrepreneur failed to satisfy his obligations, he was punishable with up to one year in prison.[46] The foreign trade of war materials was conditional upon a license issued jointly by the minister of defense and the minister of trade and transportation. A national supervisor of war material production was appointed who was entitled to check the trade of all the military industries.[47] An order decreed in 1940 authorized the minister of trade and transportation to oblige the private businessmen to sell their non-sequestered reserves.[48] To restrict and control public consumption at first purchase books were introduced only to be followed by coupon sheets for food in 1942.[49] Similar institutions had been introduced earlier in Germany and Italy. In this respect, the general features of a war economy were the restriction of trade in agricultural products and the constraint of raw material exports.

In place of the Price Analyzing Committee, a government commissioner was appointed in 1938 for the control of prices. He had the authority to set informative and maximized prices.[50] At first the government commissioner worked under the supervision of the minister of economy. Shortly after Béla Imrédy's appointment to the prime minister's chair, he was subordinated to the premier and in September 1939, he came under the supervision of the minister of trade and transportation. As the key figure of economic policy, Imrédy kept the controls in his hands. It was quite clear that the state's policy capital accumulation which was aimed at an economic boom would result in higher inflation. The loan of 400 million pengős did in fact cause higher inflation and the investment contribution imposed on private capital further enhanced this effect. In the years of the war economy, the volume of Hungarian bank notes in circulation grew 14-fold and the inflation rate exceeded that in Germany. In 1941, the Council of Ministers approved of the finance minister's proposal that the treasury should undertake a guarantee up to 25% of the 20 million pengős credit given by the three largest banks to non-creditable Christian merchants who were unable to get loans.[51] The pace of inflation quickened from 1941 because of the abolition of fixed prices.[52] The traditional outlook calling for "less consumption and putting the savings at the disposal of the war economy" was not an effective remedy in this spiral.[53] Growing taxes were unable to counterbalance the growing volume of investment. Under the circumstances of a chronic economy of scarcity, the centralization of credits was only able to moderate the resulting growth in the volume of money circulation, but at the same time it led to severe disproportions.[54] Due to an increased demand for staples and raw materials, inflation was immanent in the war economy. The only countermeasure attempted was price freezing.

As a result of the nature of the controlling institutions, sharp conflicts broke out between the controlling apparatus and private capital over prices. Private capital argued that it had to raise consumer prices or else the national property invested into the industry would dissipate. A similar argument quoted the higher general level of prices in the surrounding countries, which resulted in considerable illegal exports by smuggling.[55] As contemporary records reveal, much hesitation was caused in the management of enterprises because they had to include the personal judgment of the authorities.[56] In all the European war economies where the system of price control was introduced, its supervision was entrusted to special committees, the commercial administration or the police.[57] In 1941, the function of the price commissioner was eliminated and the regulation of economic processes was placed into the hands of the minister of public supply without portfolio who was in charge over the allocation of the more and more scarcely available goods.[58]

The growing disruptions of supplies required the repeated reorganization of the public food supply.[59] Government commissioners were appointed to organize public supplies regionally with the power to issue orders on key questions without consulting the local authorities.[60] The dual task of agricultural management meant the regulation of the production rates of various groups of crops as well as the redistribution of the ever shorter supply of produce. To this end, production quotas and compulsory delivery were introduced and separated in the sectorial and functional organizations. The duality and contradiction between the agencies of production and distribution hint at a deeper contradiction. The regulation of production with emergency measures was expressly temporary in nature while the regulation of distribution tried to consolidate more durable formations according to the dictates of the corporate ideology. The former wished to work out compromises in the interest of production; the latter aimed at stifling these interests.

In the first year of controlled economy, no attempts were made yet to abolish the labor market. It was not necessary because the labor requirement of the upcoming boom could be satisfied by the unemployed masses of about 100,000. The right of labor exchange was still exercised by the trade unions and wage disputes were still solved by strikes. But the extension of working hours was conditional upon the permission of the minister of industry. The change came with Article 2 of the Defense Act of 1939 which entitled the factories producing war materials to bind their employees to their workplace. Though without radical institutional reforms, the constraining and elimination of the labor market was gradually going on.[61]

When military conscriptions increased rapidly from summer 1941, a labor shortage ensued. All limitations on working hours were lifted, compulsory overtime work became regular and the employers' obligation to let the workers take paid vacations was suspended.[62] The luring of workers went on a massive scale, though the minister of industry warned the war factories in a rescript that no worker could be dismissed without permission by the factory military commander.[63]

In accordance with the economic preferences of the investment program significant differences arose in wages between heavy and consumer industries. As a memorandum reveals, this caused several workers in light industry to deliberately work ineffectively in order to get laid off and have a chance to take on a job in heavy industry.[64] As there was a considerable shortage of labor in agriculture as well, the ministries of agriculture and industry jointly established the Central Committee of Labor Exchange for central labor management and set up a so-called National Labor Inspectorate to ease social tensions.[65]

In April 1944, a decision was taken to turn the labor exchange into a state monopoly: private labor brokering firms working free of charge were to be closed down until the end of the year. In June, the minister of industry shut down over seventy labor exchange firms, including the regional bureaus of the National Labor Center.[66] A week later, an order was issued to set up a worker-protecting organization called the "National Association of Hungarian Industrial Workers" under the supervision of the minister of industry who had the power to dissolve any labor organization and decide on their property and leadership.[67] In early September, a National Labor Management Committee was set up whose president was appointed by the defense minister. The duties of the committee included deciding upon the labor requirements of foreign countries. Two weeks later, a national commissioner for personnel management was appointed "to reduce to the narrowest possible circle the incumbents of civil occupations."[68]

The working mechanism of the market was integrated in the hierarchical institutions of control during the years of the war economy. A part of the economic institutions were also formally incorporated in the controlling hierarchy, while the other part adjusted to the new working conditions retaining their autonomy formally. In a remark by Finance Minister Lajos Reményi-Schneller about foreign trade associations, he said that although they work in the form of association or society, they are undoubtedly part of the state administration as most of them are in monopoly position and can impose sanctions.[69] This shed light on an important aspect of the institutional changes. Under the circumstances of the war economy the formal and informal operation of a significant part of the economic organizations were separated for quite some time.

Elites

The disrupted consensus of the ruling elite caused by the economic depression of the 1930s was directed into new grooves by the political and institutional changes of the war. In the traditional network of relations within the elites, new cohesive and disruptive elements emerged.

What remained to be a constant component of the potential consensus was the elimination of conflicts based on class differences. Another point of agreement was the drive for Hungary's territorial revision. This aspiration was the main basis for the support of the regime's wartime policies. Reinforcing a potential consensus was the positive effect of the militarized economic policy on the business cycle.

What primarily caused clashes within the elite was the series of institutional changes that ensured the domination of politics over the economy and increased the role of the administration at the detriment of legislation. As a result, the importance of the bureaucratic elite grew against the traditional aristocratic landowners and business elite. All this came up during the Upper House debate of the Győr Program where the objection was made that the prime minister had announced the investment plan at a party meeting instead of informing the legislation first.[70] In general, the House members criticized the practice of giving full authority to the government in key questions through skeleton laws.

The institutional-political changes brought about a decline in the importance of the landowning-aristocratic elite and the business elite resulting in a radical transformation in the personnel composition of the business elite. In the group of landowners comprised of forty families with estates over 10,000 cadastral yokes*, compositional changes were effected by death,

* a cadastral yoke is equal to 6,823.95 square yards or 1.41 acres

inheritance and the fragmentation of the estates. Between 1935 and 1943, only a fourth of the group was replaced, but this did not affect any of the main features of the group's composition. The landowning elite consisted almost exclusively of aristocrats, principally from families of the historical aristocracy.[71]

The very rigid criteria of recruitment by origin into this group, two-thirds of which had higher education and 60% were Catholics, did not change during the war. Some 60% continued to take part in legislation, with a wide range of political views from opposition to anti-Semitic laws to extreme political right-wing activity. All three groups of the elite adopted the political right-wing policy based on so called "Christian and national values," but highly divergent interpretations can be discerned underlying the seemingly enthusiastic reception. The landowning aristocracy elite lent its support to a basically conservative variant, standing aloof of the rightist mass movements as well. As stated, the political influence of the group largely decreased due to the institutional changes and the shift to the political right. Though the elite's political proponents retained their informal influence on Regent Miklós Horthy, they had moderate success in "taking the wind out of the sails" of the political right.[72]

Prior to the Győr Program, the business elite numbered 1,000 leaders.[73] However, nearly two-thirds of the numerous elite group had only one position and another one-fifth had two. The upper 15% with three or more positions, the so-called "multipositional elite," held 35% of all the elite positions. Between 1935 and 1943, 55%, of the private economy including enterprise and bank leaders as well as heads of employers' interest-protecting organizations were replaced. While up to 60% of the majority with one or two positions were ousted, fluctuation among the multipositional elite was far lower though not insignificant at 32%. Fluctuation among the enterprise leaders was somewhat above average at nearly 60%, while the figure for bank directors and heads of employers' interest-protecting organs was below average at 50%. It is noteworthy that changes of similar proportions had taken place during the economic crisis between 1927 and 1937 when half of the business elite had been exchanged. At that time, however, the pace of replacement among bank and enterprise leaders did not diverge, coming to an above average 56%, while in the leadership of organizations representing the employers' interest, a significantly lower 40% fluctuation rate was typical. Only 29% of the multipositional elite had been changed in that period.

In view of the fact that the composition of the elite was effected not only by anonymous economic forces but also by radical political interference, the figures reveal the "inner group" character of the multipositional elite. 38% of the multipositional elite of enterprises, banks and employers' interest-protecting bodies had positions in organizations issuing economic legislation or were on the advisory boards of ministries in 1937; this rate rose to 42% by 1943. The ethnic composition of the elite underwent a significant change: the rate of Jewish business leaders plummeted from 34 to 18%. This decline began at the turn of the 1920s and 1930s and continued as the anti-Semitic Second Jewish Law of 1939 limited the Jewish business elite to 12% of the total. Under various exemptions, the rate of Jewish leaders exceeded the enacted limit. Therefore, one of the key elements of the disrupted consensus was the forced replacement of the elite — the so-called changing of the guard — because of ethnic considerations. That is what the Jewish industrialist, Ferenc Chorin, referred to when noting that "Reményi-Schneller along with Lajos Szász, Jurcsek, his state secretarial staff, Kulcsár and Szlamoray did their best to oust the Jews from their few remaining positions."[74]

The changing of the guard and the system of straw men in leading positions radically modified the ethnic composition of the elite.[75] Besides, the composition of the business elite as to origin, education and career-pattern also considerably changed during the war years. In the latter half of the 1930s, two-thirds of the business elite had higher education, half of which had degrees in law. During the war years, the rate of higher education graduates grew to five-sixths, with a massive growth of technical and economic experts and an unchanged rate of legal graduates. In 1937, self-recruitment (those coming from business families) was 38%, this figure dropped to 26% by 1943.

By contrast, the rate of those hailing from state administrator-landowning families (37%) and from intellectual families (21%) had increased. Career patterns changed similarly: while in 1937, half of the multipositional elite of the private economy began their careers in the private economy and 36% began their careers in the bureaucratic-military apparatus. By 1943, the proportion of those beginning their careers in the bureaucratic-military apparatus rose to 44%.

The elite in the bureaucracy of economic management and control was always more highly educated and closed. Between 1937 and 1943, the rate of higher education graduates grew from four-fifths to over 90%, with 61% being graduates of law. Nearly half of the bureaucratic elite came from state administrator-landowner families, this proportion remaining practically unchanged during the war years. In contrast to that, the offsprings of bankers and enterprise leaders dropped from one-fifth to 10% and the rate of those from white-collar background significantly increased. More than half of the elite group in control of the economy began their careers in the bureaucratic-military apparatus in 1937 with nearly one-third of them in the private sphere and one-seventh as intellectuals. During the war economy, the rate of the first group remained unchanged, while that of the latter two were equalized slightly above one-fifth. In 1943, three-fourths of the multipositional elite controlling the economy had positions in the private economy.

In 1939, 33% of the 97 politically right-wing members of parliament making up 55% of the deputies of the governing party were administrative officials and army officers, 17 were owners of middle-size estates and 30 were intellectuals. Regarding the recruitment mechanisms of political groups, these figures prove that the political weight of these social groups was over-represented, but several analyses suggest that right-wing centralist orientation was especially strong among these social groups.[76]

Thus, during the war years, the recruitment patterns of the economic and the bureaucratic elites came considerably nearer to each other due to the forced changes in the ethnic composition and the extension of the system of personnel overlappings. As a result, in both groups, the bureaucratic pattern gained predominance. The consequence was a re-politicized ambiguous professionalization, although both groups remained extremely closed downwards regarding intergenerational mobility. The members of the traditional business elite were gradually squeezed out of power, their political-ideological activity being reduced to mere defense. After the German occupation, the Jewish members of the elite were either taken to concentration camps, forced into hiding or in fortunate cases allowed to emigrate at the price of relinquishing their property.[77]

Ideological and Manipulative Movements

The ideological framework of the war was provided by the permanent mobilization based on dictatorship, an economic order divided by occupations and planning. The elements of the ideology with a favorable bias to the rightist Christian-nationalist views were bound together by the conviction that under the given circumstances neither "liberalism based on the imaginary cooperation" of individual forces, nor the "see-sawing class struggle" of mature capitalism could ensure the appropriate working of the economy. In this sense, the official ideology was opposed to "cosmopolitan free-masonry" embodying liberal individualism and the "class-struggle and popular front of Marxism" producing the value-destroying popular man, complemented by the criticism of "the instinctive carrier of both: the Jews." In this conception, the central power could not confine itself to the controlling-correcting function directed at finding the equilibrium in the struggle between employers' associations and the trade unions. Thus, executive power had to become independent because of the war and because "fears from changing directions or just speculating about it anticipate the destruction of long-term planning and purposeful implementation."[78]

The necessity of a strong and stable central power justified by the wartime conditions was not questioned by the business elite on the defensive. On the contrary, it was raised on the eve of the war in political circles close to the business elite that a dictatorship by the regent should take control over the chaotic situation in autumn 1938. This idea was proposed to the regent at an audience by the Small Holder Party Leader, Tibor Eckhardt, who had previously shared it with István Bethlen and Ferenc Chorin. Talking to Prime Minister Imrédy, Bethlen remarked that in his place, "he would have long declared martial law."[79] After the personnel changes in the wake of the anti-Jewish laws, the war press of the Manufacturers' National Association also began to voice support for some elements of centralization, planning, autarchy and the values of entrepreneurship.[80]

One of the most frequently encountered moments of the Hungarian right-wing economic ideology of this time was the corporate model. According to one interpretation, the corporative model "retains the possibility of private property, entrepreneurial initiative and to some extent competition, but it tries to regulate the economic life by rallying the producers into various organizations and exerting its regulatory influence through these bodies."[81] The Italian fascist corporate model was characterized by a hierarchic structure constructed from a combination of occupational and regional divisions. This hierarchy did not imply the modification of the actual mode of economic management, but functioned as a new regulatory mechanism of the economic sphere by ignoring the parties and interest-groups. Thus, the stability of the system depended on submission to the goals of a confrontational ideology built on enemy image, rather than on a disposition for consensus. In his plan for a constitutional reform, Prime Minister Pál Teleki proposed legislative authority combining corporative, regional and party-political structures. He suggested that voters should have weighted voting rights according to their social status. Consequently, the members of the various corporative chambers and high-school graduates would be entitled to more votes.[82]

Besides the corporative economic conception integrated into the state, there was an ideal self-governing corporative construction as well. In this scheme, the district organs of corporations would be pooled in national centers for each occupation which would be coordinated by the house of corporative representation with the participation of special production committees. According to the proposition of the National Occupational Organization of Hungarian Workers, the corporative hierarchy would be independent of the state though the state's supervisory right would be retained; it would not be dictatorial though its subunits would be set up by forced association; and it would be free from politics as no politician could be involved in the leadership.[83] Those features, according to the proposal not exempt from contradictions, would differentiate it from the Italian model which was dictatorial and politicized, the German model which was dictatorial and did not create corporative associations and from the Austrian and Portuguese models, which were fully subordinated to the state.

Though the idea of corporations and the corporative state became one of the central elements of Hungarian rightist economic ideologies, it was never translated into practice. That was evident by the sharp criticism expressed in the right-wing press charging that instead of a frontal clash and final showdown with political and economic liberalism, the government had led Hungary back to the liberal-capitalistic path within the borders established after the Trianon Peace Treaty of 1920. The liberal form of government that "hang on us loosely like cast-off clothes in which we never felt comfortable and which perverted our national character" as they wrote, was not superseded by an up-to-date Hungarian national state that "would have been the most effective tool for recapturing the territories robbed from us."[84] In this regard, the Hungarian economic policy was defensive and translated only that much of a controlled economy into practice that was required by the military's demands and foreign policy orientation. It was central to this defensive attitude that in the first years of the war, the economic policy was working under the institutional conditions of parliamentarism.

The propaganda coming from the extreme right-wing claimed that excessive parliamentarism present in "thoughtless criticism" was not compatible with the new economic policy because of the war situation.[85] The war economy required the temporary control of the economy, the restriction of parliamentary forms, the independence of executive power and the extension of the united bureaucratic-political control everywhere. In rightist economic ideologies, however, this series of measures was interlaced with the corporative concept, aggressive nationalism and racialism. Though reference to the state of war was the ultimate argument in the ideological arsenal of the political right, they did not regard the emerging structural forms as transitional at all. They declared that "people tend to call the new economic order a war economy, but just as the practical achievements of the national economic policy were attained during World War I, so are the economic results being achieved during World War II and will become public property after the war all over Europe."[86]

Throughout the war economy period, the political right was dissatisfied, since the measures of a controlled economy were not followed by a radical change of the administrative structure and the initiatives to create a corporative scheme were aborted.[87] Until the German occupation in March 1944, the Hungarian economy was practically managed within a controlled liberal structure. How could a model work which tried to maintain the formally independent interest groups under the conditions of a dictatorship? The criticism by the political right blaming the failure to introduce the corporative form to resolve difficulties was unjustified. Though the formal structure of the institutional system of interest protection remained unchanged, there were such shifts of proportion and functional modifications within the unchanged structure which allowed the operation of the controlled economy. The general framework for these changes was provided by those economic policy orders which reorganized and regulated the economic processes. The function of the chambers was considerably modified.

Prime Minister Béla Imrédy announced in the Lower House as early as May 1938 that he wished to improve the institution of the chambers as it was the very institution that "must be permeated with the Hungarian spirit."[88] As he judged, only slight alterations were needed in the chamber of agriculture, while in the chamber of commerce and industry the small-scale industry, the crafts, mass production and trades had to be separated. The proposals suggested that each chamber be subdivided into three councils: one including the leaders of enterprises, another comprised of white-collar workers in enterprises and the other, consisting of blue-collar workers. In 1940, the autonomy of the chambers was suspended and the general assembly was replaced by expert panels. That meant converting the chambers from advisory and interest-protecting organs into administrative public offices.

After the fascist coup in October 1944, the party-appointed general secretary of the chambers issued a circular regulating the cooperation of the chambers and corporations asserting that the corporations then on the rise had to be integrated in the work of the chambers.[89] Besides the chambers sandwiched between the interest-protecting organs and the state sphere now endowed with the function of transmitting directions, there was some modification within the organs of interest-protection themselves leaving their formal structure untouched. A large number of rightist watchdog committees were added to the traditional safeguarding institutions (e.g. the Baross Manufacturers Group and the Association of Christian Manufacturing Enterprises). These groups applied those elements of the rightist-etatist ideology that pointed to militarism and racial-religious discrimination.

Finally, a certain degree of adaptation took place within the traditional various interest-groups as well. This process of adaptation was characterized by the inner conflict between the drive for integration and the need for interest-manifestation. This drive at integration was initiated to gain the right's participation in various exports, advisory and quota-defining panels of the control apparatus. Interest-protection was to counteract state intervention, principally military interference, in price fixing, taxation and foreign trade. In addition, it was to respond to the activity of the interest protecting bodies of workers and employees and to crush pay-raise demands and strikes. As a significant concomitant to adaptation, there were personnel changes within the chambers and interest-protecting agencies, which alone modified the actual workings of economic management. Ministerial commissioners were appointed to lead the chambers and most members of the advisory panels came from the Baross Manufacturers Group. Due to the interpenetrating of interests, a lot of chief government councilors and ministerial commissioners could be found on the boards of interest-protecting organs. In addition, during the changing of the guard these agencies became filled with people who accepted not only the transitory manner of economic management but its lasting politico-economic effects as well for their own immediate benefit.

By creating the institutions of the war economy, not only the weight of regulating production through orders but also that of social demagogy increased. The latter found its outlet, besides the press organs of varying standards in different manipulated movements. In order to centrally organize the channels of manipulation, a department of social policy was set up in the prime minister's office in June 1938. Just like in the case of some organs of economic policy, the formal institutional character and the actual function was separated in the department of social policy too: formally its domain was social policy but actually it dealt with propaganda as well. Besides biased information on the idea of revisionism, the popularization of the emergency measures was a key task of the department.[90] Similar goals called to life the Leisure Time Institute and the attempt to establish the "Association of Model Villages."[91] Having given up its transcendental elements and mobilizing character, the economic policy itself was down to regulative tasks. Typical even in its extremity, they issued the "ten commandments of a war factory" to regulate war production.[92]

Concluding Remarks

This author's point of departure was the interaction of the system of economic institutions, the economic ideology and the power relations. At the turn of the century, state intervention in industrialization served the development of the market system while the role of the interventionist economic ideology was also strengthened. At about the same time, the outlines of the triple division of the ruling elite was also becoming discernible: next to the elite fragments of landowners-aristocrats and capitalists-*haute bourgeoisie*, a separate group of the elite emerged of bureaucrats and military officers, comprised of the middle nobility forced into offices and representatives of the middle classes. The pressures of World War I brought about the institutions of a controlled economy. These institutions, however, were eliminated shortly after the war because they failed to work properly. In the 1920s, state intervention was again supportive and the coalition of the representatives of large estate and big capital squeezed the extremist groups of the bureaucratic elite from the higher reaches of power. The unfolding depression interrupted the reorganization of the state-supported liberal market. The bureaucratic-military elite became activated again and strengthened their positions; the ideology of a controlled and planned economy became dominant and irredentist ideas calling for the restoration of the pre-World War I borders seemed to attract considerable international backing.

The radical reorganization of the institutional system began in 1938 with the proclamation of the armaments program. Price control, as well as the centralized institutional system and an arsenal of raw-material and labor management was developed during this time. By the end of the period, trade unions were abolished. Forced industrialization converted the structure of production into industrial-agrarian form, whereas the social structure of the economy retained its traditional agrarian character. Diverging from the logical construct of its operation, the redistributive hierarchy displayed several dysfunctional signs. War economy and its precedent, the controlled economy no longer involved transactive market relations, but it was not yet a control system that would eliminate private property. Conflicts between interest groups representing private capital and the controlling apparatus and conflicts in the mechanisms of production and distribution, grave disproportions in the sectorial structure, rapid inflation and the significant drops in real wages and the lasting shortage of raw materials and consumer goods were all characteristic of the war economy. That is why the narrow ruling elite could only replace the consensus of interests by dictatorial means. Power shifted gradually into the hands of the bureaucratic-military elite and from there, to the political right wing. Because they were Jewish, a considerable fraction of the big capitalists were excluded from the ruling elite. The Hungarian ruling elite drifted into the war in hope of a territorial revision. The mistaken political decisions of the Hungarian elite and their persistence on the side of the losers cost the nation at least 420,000 lives. By the end of the war, 40% of the national wealth was destroyed.

While the economic mechanism of World War I was the result of emergency measures, the war economy for World War II emerged even before the conflict as a consequence of revisionism and political designs to set up a permanent controlled economy which was designed to function even after the war. Despite the fact, that after the war, the recruitment of the business elite, the system of political institutions and the economic ideology were changed radically, the persistence of the war economy could be discerned in the economic structure and the system of economic institutions.

Notes

1. Iván T. Berend and Miklós Szuhay, *A tőkés gazdaság története Magyarországon 1848-1944* [A History of Capitalist Economy in Hungary] (Budapest, 1973), 94-103; Iván T. Berend and György Ránki, *Magyarország gyáripara 1900-1914* [Hungary's Manufacturing Industry 1900-1914] (Budapest, 1955); Miklós Szabó, "Uj vonások a századfordulói magyar konzervativ politikai gondolkodásban," [New Traits in the Conservative Political Thought in Hungary at the Turn of the Century], *Századok,* (1974), 3-66.

2. József Szterényi and Jenő Ladányi, *A magyar ipar a világháborúban* [Hungary's Industry in the World War] (Budapest, 1934); Mihály Futó, "Gyáripari termelésünk irányitása a két világháborúban," [The Control of Industrial Production in Hungary During the Two World Wars], *Magyar Közgazdasági Szemle,* (1943); Peter Pastor, "The Home Front in Hungary, 1914-1918," in Béla Király and Nándor F. Dreisziger, eds., *East Central European Society in World War I* (New York, 1985), 124-134.

3. György Péteri, *Effects of World War I: War Communism in Hungary* (New York, 1984).

4. Relying on the researches of Ferenc Jánossy, Mihály Vajda elaborated the problem in his study titled, "A fasiszta diktatura funkciója," [The Function of a Fascist Dictatorship], *Magyar Filozófiai Szemle*, (1970), 525-574. See also: Vera Pécsi, "Az állam gazdasági szerepének néhány vonása a II világháború elött" [Some Features of the Economic Role of the State prior to World War II], Doctoral dissertation, Karl Marx University of Economics, (Budapest, 1975).

5. Sipos Péter, *Imrédy Béla és a Magyar Mepgújulás Pártja* [Béla Imrédy and the Party of Renewal] (Budapest, 1970).

6. László Márkus, *A Károlyi Gyula-kormány bel- és külpolitikája* [The Foreign and Home Policies of Gyula Károlyi's Government] (Budapest, 1968).

7. See the minutes of the first crown council held during the Gömbös cabinet. *Miklós Horthy titkos iratai* [The Secret Papers of Miklós Horthy] (Budapest, 1963), 131-135.

8. Documents of the Ministry of Finance, Hungarian National Archives, K/168/12/63.

9. Béla Marton elaborated a scheme upon German and Bulgarian models which would have had all the male population of the country render compulsory labor to the state. Under his scheme the National Labor Squad could have been a regionally divided hierarchic organization directly controlled by the prime minister. In this way, Marton hoped not only to solve the current problems of the economic crisis, but also to create a permanent institution "which makes cheap labor available for the state and at the same time ensures the subsistence of large masses of the needy," Hungarian National Archives, K. 278/12/63.

10. Horthy, *op. cit.*, 257; See also: Mrs. Rudolf Dósa, "A Nemzeti Munkaközpont szerepe az ellenforradalmi rendszer munkáspolitikájában," [The Role of the National Labor Center in the Labor Policy of the Counter-Revolutionary Regime], *Párttörténeti Közlemények*, (1968), 135-166; Mrs. Rudolf Dósa, *A MOVE. Egy jellegzetesen magyar fasiszta szervezet 1918-1944* [The MOVE: A Typically Hungarian Fascist Organization] (Budapest, 1972).

11. The government's working program to direct crucial tasks. Béla Imrédy's Papers, Hung. Nat'l Archives K. 278/12/63.

12. Miklós Kállay commented on calling András Mecsér to the Ministry of Agriculture: "Now that the perspective of a planned economy is unfolding I deemed it necessary to have someone deal with matters related to such specific production and selling and represent the ministry....But Mecsér turned down my offer arguing that he was a producer in the first place and did not wish to give up his independence for the time being." Béla Imrédy's Papers, Hungarian National Archives, K. 278/12/62.

13. "Gerlózi (8 O'Clock News) is humbly inquiring whether it is true that 1. the call for domestic loan is going to appear; 2. His Excellency the Prime Minister is going to announce it in Győr on Saturday. Gerlózy begs to have the honor of receiving a reply by telephone to the above two questions since he wishes to write about it in today's 8 O'Clock News," (Budapest, February 25, 1938), (Note in pencil on margin: "His Exc.: Not true!"). Lajos Reményi-Schneller's documents, Hungarian National Archives, K. 280/1/2. At that time the letters were still addressed to Finance Minister Tihamér Fabinyi.

14. *Honi Ipar* [Domestic Industry], March 19, 1938, 1-2; April 30, 1938, 13-14.

15. *Magyar Ipar* [Hungarian Industry], (March-April 1938), 22.

16. Act XX/1938 on the development of defense and economy, on some welfare investment and the coverage of their costs, *Magyar Törvénytár* [Hungarian Code of Laws] (Budapest, 1939), 250-251.

17. Sándor Ausch, "A háború finanszirozása és az 1938-1944. évi infláció Magyarországon," [Financing the War and the Inflation of 1938-1944 in Hungary], *Magyar Közgazdasági Szemle*, (1955), 1194-1214.

18. "The Finance Minister allotted 500,000 pengős to Baja for school construction," *Magyar Közérdek*, [Hungarian Public Interest], Nov. 5, 1939, 2; "It is with great enthusiasm that the public of Baja present the freedom of the town to Finance Minister Dr. Lajos Reményi-Schneller," *Magyar Közérdek*, Nov. 20, 1939, 1; "Minister of Agriculture Count Mihály Teleki Has Become Freeman of Halas," *Magyar Közérdek*, Feb. 5, 1939, 2; "Construction Worth 1.5 Million in Halas," *Ibid.*

19. *Magyar Közgazdasági Szemle*, (1942), 4.

20. Iván T. Berend and György Ránki, *Magyarország gyáripara a második világháború elött és a háború idöszakában (1933-1944)* [Hungary's Manufacturing Industry Before and During World War II] (Budapest, 1958), 369-372; Sándor Ausch, *Az 1945-1946. évi infláció és stabilizáció* [Inflation and Stabilization in 1945-46] (Budapest, 1958), 41 (with corrections).

21. Béla Csikós Nagy, László Hantos, and Gyula Rézler, *Magyar gazdasági élet* [Hungarian Economic Life] (Budapest, 1944), 262-263.

22. Alexander Eckstein, *National Income and Capital Formation in Hungary* (London, 1955), 152-223.

23. *A nemzeti jövedelem hosszúsoros indexeinek felülvizsgálata 1938. és 1950-1965 évekre* [Revision of the Long-Series Indices of the National Income for the Years 1938 and 1950-65], Budapest Central Statistical Office, (1967), 32; See also: Eckstein, *op. cit.*, 192; András Bródy, "Gazdasági növekedésünk üteme 1924-töl 1965-ig," [The Growth Rate of the Hungarian Economy from 1924 to 1965], *Magyar Közgazdasági Szemle*, 1967/4, 417-431; Bekker Zsuzsa, "Néhány gondolat Magyarország gyáriparának fejlődéséről," [Some Thoughts on the Development of Hungary's Machine Industry], *Magyar Közgazdasági Szemle*, (1970), 1033-1048; Special Publication no. 20 of the Research Institute for the Hungarian Economy, (Budapest, 1942), 11.

24. Iván T. Berend and György Ránki, *Közép-kelet-Európa gazdasági fejlődése a 19-20. században* [The Economic Development of East Central Europe in the 19th-20th Centuries] (Budapest, 1976), 514; Nicolas Spulber, *The Economics of Communist Eastern Europe* (New York, 1957), 478.

25. Research Institute for the Hungarian Economy, *Bulletin* no. 4, "Magyarország nemzeti jövedelme," [Hungary's National Income], (Budapest, 1947), 6.

26. Berend and Ránki, *Magyarország gyáripara (1933-1944)* 428; Archives of the Capital of Budapest XI, 127/A.

27. Central Statistical Office, *Census of 1949*, "6. Foglalkozás-statisztikai eredmények," [Occupation Statistical Findings, no. 6], (Budapest, 1950), 13.

28. Bekker, *op. cit.*; ACB XI 115/Á Hungarian National Archives, Z. 371/75, Z. 403/4.

29. The calculations were carried out with the Cobb-Douglas function.

Its familiar form is:
T = F * L(k) * C(1-k), where T = gross surplus produce
F = productivity coefficient
L = wages
C = capital value
k = production flexibility of work
1-k = production flexibility of capital

The production flexibility of work was computed by Kálmán Kádas on the basis of wages. The value of this parameter is 0.66 in machine production and the iron and metal industries, 0.5 in paper production and 0.88 in the production of stationary goods. See: Kálmán Kádas, *Az emberi munka termelékenységének statisztikai vizsgálata a magyar gyáriparban* [A Statistical Analysis of the Productivity of Human Labor in the Manufacturing Industry] (Budapest, 1944).

We calculated with the value of 0.66.

Year	Gross Surplus	Fixed	Capital Wages
1938	1,309,617,000	2,013,780,000	346,858,000
1943	2,075,539,100	1,607,369,100	559,166,690

F(38) = 2.1
F(43) = 2.6
F(43/38) = 1.238, a growth of 24% or an annual 4.4%.

With a constant volume of capital and labor, the annual growth of work productivity was 2.4% and the growth rate of the productivity of capital amounted to 11%.

30. Ferenc Jánossy, "Gazdaságunk mai ellentmondásainak eredete és felszámolásuk útja," [The Sources of Today's Contradictions in Hungary's Economy and How to Eliminate Them], *Magyar Közgazdasági Szemle*, (1969).

31. Goldberger Papers, Hungarian National Archives, Z. 668/43/178.

32. See: Prime Minister Pál Teleki's proposition to Miklós Horthy about the growing influence of the military on the civilian government, in Horthy, *op. cit.*, 239-252.

33. Decree no. ME 6830/1938, *Közgazdasági Értesítő*, October 8, 1938, 1001; see also: Mihály Futó, "Gyáripari termelésünk irányítása a két világháborúban," [The Control of Manufacturing Production in Hungary in the Two World Wars], *Magyar Közgazdasági Szemle*, 1943/11-12, 19.

34. Decree no. ME 10670/1939. *Közgazdasági Értesítő*, December 3, 1939, 1077.

35. Decree no. ME 12113/1939. *Közgazdasági Értesítő*, September 10, 1939, 801.

36. Documents of the Department of Economic Policy of the Ministry of Foreign Affairs, Hungarian National Archives, K. 69/797/12.

37. Ministry of Industry Decree no. 55100/1939. *Közgazdasági Értesítő*, November 5, 1939, 973.

38. Decree no. 4570/1940. *Közgazdasági Értesítő*, June 30, 1940; Ministry of Industry Decree no. 24000/1940. *Közgazdasági Értesítő*, June 9, 1940, 517.

39. "...We have the honor to inform you that...we have not received the arrears of 400 metric tons of coal to this day despite the fact that we have despatched the order. But we are not given the coal we require for our daily subsistence either, although we have pressed for it most forcefully...," Goldberger Papers, Hungarian National Archives, Z. 668/43/180.

40. *Ibid.*

41. Decree no. 2340/1942; Decree no. 24800/1942; Decree no. 24900/1942 *Közgazdasági Értesítő*, April 19, 1942, 547-548.

42. Ministry of Industry Decree no. 41700/1943. *Közgazdasági Értesítő*, August 8, 1943, 1239.

43. Ministry of Industry Decree no. 14500/1943. *Közgazdasági Értesítő*, March 7, 1943, supplement, 11; Ministry of Industry Decree no. 39500/1943. *Közgazdasági Értesítő*, July 25, 1943, 1087; Ministry of Industry Decree no. 14000/1943. *Közgazdasági Értesítő*, March 7, 1943, supplement, 10; Decree no. 3790/1943, July 25, 1943, 1985; Ministry of Industry Decree

no. 17600/1943, *Közgazdasági Értesítő*, April 4, 1943, 439.

44. Letter of S. Goldberger and Sons, Ltd. dated December 1, 1944 to the Ministry of Defense, Hungarian National Archives, Z. 668/43/178. This degree of under-utilization of capacity was largely due to the conception of sectorial structure during the war. See also: Berend and Ránki, *Magyarország gyáripara a második világháború elött, 1933-1944*, 537-544.

45. Decree no. 8500/1939, *Közgazdasági Értesítő*, September 10, 1939, 813.

46. Hungarian National Archives, Z. 668/43/178. Letter of the Defense Minister to S. Goldberger & Sons, Ltd.

47. Decree no. 12112/1939, *Közgazdasági Értesítő*, October 1, 1939, 873; Decree no. 7310/1941, *Közgazdasági Értesítő*, October 19, 1941, 1437.

48. Decree no. 3000/1949, *Közgazdasági Értesítő*, May 5, 1940, 413.

49. Decree no. 201000/1941, *Közgazdasági Értesítő*, May 18, 1940, 702; Decree no. 5560/1942, *Közgazdasági Értesítő*, October 4, 1942, 1353.

50. Decree no. 2220/1938, *Magyar Ipar*, May-June 1938, 31; Hungarian National Archives, K. 513, Documents of the National Committee of 33, 36 or 42 Members, Vol. 20.

51. Hungarian National Archives, K. 280/11/1942/1.

52. Iván T. Berend, "Az állami beavatkozás háborús rendszerének főbb vonásai Magyarországon a második világháború idején," [Main Features of the War System of State Intervention in Hungary during World War II], in *Marx Károly Közgazdasági Egyetem Évkönyve* (1958), 223-247.

53. Lipót Baranyai, "Mi a teendö? Takarékosság vagy infláció," [What to Do? Economizing or Inflation], *Magyar Ipar*, May 1, 1941, 40-41.

54. "The Great Speech of Iván Szabó, Member of the Upper House for Kecskemét," *Magyar Közérdek*, May 20, 1940, 1.

55. Hungarian National Archives, Z. 669/43/180.

56. *Ibid.*

57. Documents of the Department of Economic Policy of the Ministry of Foreign Affairs, Hungarian National Archives, K. 69/797/12; See also: Evgenii S. Varga, *Ekonomicheskie Krizisi* (Moscow, 1974), 330-347.

58. Decree no. 7310/1941, *Közgazdasági Értesítő*, October 19, 1941, 1437.

59. See: Károly Szabó's and László Virágh's study in the present volume.

60. Decree no. 510/1941, *Közgazdasági Értesítő*, February 2, 1941, 165.

61. New Hungarian Central Archives (NHCA) III/40, Documents of the Peace Prepatory Department of the Ministry of Foreign Affairs.

62. Mihály Futó, *op. cit.*, 42-52; Iván T. Berend, *op. cit.*, 238-244.

63. Hungarian National Archives, Z. 668/43/180.

64. *Ibid.*

65. Decree no. 115600/1942 of the Ministry of Agriculture, *Közgazdasági Értesítő*, August 2, 1942; Decree no. 4430/1942, *Közgazdasági Értesítő*, July 26, 1942; "The labor market must be controlled in a carefully planned way through labor exchange, since when the equilibrium of supply and demand is disrupted by the specific circumstances, an uncontrolled labor market may throw up forces that act contrary to the nation's interests. As a result, in order to improve their position large numbers of workers may take on jobs they have neither experience nor qualifications to do properly." Opening address by Kálmán Kádas at the statutory meeting of the Central Committee of Labor Exchange, in *Közgazdasági Értesítő*, January 31, 1943, 166.

66. Decree no. 1350/1944, *Közgazdasági Értesítő*, April 16, 1944, 401; Ministry of Industry Decree no. 32000/1944, *Közgazdasági Értesítő*, July 23, 1944, 939.

67. Decree no. 2700//1944, *Közgazdasági Értesítő*, July 30, 1944, 977.

68. Decree no. 2970/1944, *Közgazdasági Értesítő*, September 3, 1944, 1140; Decree no. 3170/1944, *Közgazdasági Értesítő*, September 17, 1944, 1176.

69. Hungarian National Archives, K. 280/11/1942/1, Lajos Reményi-Schneller Papers, Reports to the Council of Ministers.

70. Gyula Szőke's address to the Upper House meeting of May 11, 1938 in *Journals of the Upper House of the Parliament,*

Vol. 3, (1938), 234.

71. Tibor Folkmayer and Sándor Török, "Nagybirtok az ellenforradalom korszakában," [Large Estates in the Period of the Counter-Revolution], in György Lengyel, ed., *Történeti szociológiai tanulmányok a 19-20. századi magyar társadalomról* [Studies in Historical Sociology about 19th-20th Century Hungarian Society] (Budapest, 1987), 45-69.

72. *Bethlen István emlékirata, 1944* [The Memoirs of István Bethlen, 1944] (Budapest 1988), 123-155.

73. The data of the business elite derive from an empirical survey investigating the positional composition of the leaders of the largest enterprises, banks, employers' associations, economic organizations and bodies of economic policy in the years 1926/27, 1936/37 and 1942/43. When studying the multipositional elite cumulating three or more positions, we extended the investigations to a wide circle of social indicators.

74. István Vida, "Három Chorin-levél," [Three Letters by Chorin], *Századok*, (1977), 369.

75. Some aspects of these problems are analyzed by György Lengyel, "The Ethnic Composition of the Business Elite in Hungary in the Interwar Period," (Paper presented at the Conference of Contemporary Issues of Central European Jewry, Paris, August 1985); *idem.*; "Education, Ethnicity and Career Patterns of the Hungarian Business Elite in the Interwar Period," Paper presented at the Conference on the Economic History of Hungarian Jewry in the Interwar Period, Jerusalem, January 1988; *idem.*; "The Segregation and the Housing Conditions of the Business Elite in Budapest Between the Two World Wars," Paper presented at the Budapest-New York Conference of Hungarian and American Historians, (Budapest, August 1988).

76. Péter Sipos, Miklós Stier and István Vida, "Változások a kormánypárt parlamenti képviseletének összetételében, 1931-1939," [Changes in the Composition of the Representation of the Governing Party in the Parliament], *Századok*, (1967) 602-620; György Ránki, "Az 1939-és budapesti választások," [Elections in Budapest in 1939], *Történelmi Szemle* (1976), 613-630; Miklós Lackó, *Nyilasok, nemzetiszocialisták* [Followers of the Arrow-Cross Party, Nazis] (Budapest, 1966).

77. György Lengyel, *The Hungarian Business Elite in*

Historical Perspective (New York, 1987), 51-58; Elek Karsai and Miklós Szinai, "A Weiss Manfréd vagyon német kézbe kerülése," [How the Property of Manfréd Weiss Went into German Possession], *Századok*, (1961), 680-719.

78. Béla Imrédy, "Az új Európa irányitó eszméi," [The Leading Ideas of a New Europe], *Új Magyarság*, (1940), 151-152.

79. Documents of the Salgótarján Coal Mine, Ltd. Hungarian National Archives, Z. 248/9/206.

80. Éva Kovács, "A gyáriparosok sajtója, 1900-1944," [The Press of the Manufacturers], *Társadalomkutatás*, (1989).

81. Dénes Kislégi Nagy, "A korporativ gazdaság alapelvei," [Basic Principles of a Corporative Economy], *Pannonia*, (1940).

82. Horthy, *op. cit.*, 273-284.

83. Vid Mihelics, *Hivatásrendi társadalom* [Corporative Society] (Budapest, 1940); József Bartocz, *Új jelenségek és intézkedések a gazdasági életben* [New Phenomena and Measures in the Economic Life] (Budapest, 1938); Dénes Bikkal, *Totális állam, érdekképviseleti állam, munkakamarák* [Totalitarian State, Corporate State, Chambers of Labor] (Budapest, 1941); Pál Vágó, *A magyar munkaállam* [The Hungarian Labor State] (Budapest, 1940); László Varga, *Szociális reform és hivatásrendiség* [Social Reform and the Corporation] (Budapest, 1941); Béla Kovrig, *Korfordulón* [On the Verge of a New Epoch] (Budapest, 1940); József Freesz, *Hivatásrendi gazdaság. A modern gazdasági élet megszervezése* [Corporative Economy: Organizing a Modern Economy] (Budapest, 1942).

84. Committee records of the Association of Christian Manufacturing Enterprises, January 14, 1942, ACB XI/127/d.

85. An economic memorandum preserved among the documents of Finance Minister Lajos Reményi-Schneller says: "The liberal social and economic forces, that have become accustomed to pressing the government toward compromise by their influence (or weight in the Casino), must learn...that the new Hungarian economic policy knows no compromise of principle...we are the only country where the government assumes responsibility for the controlled economy while it allows for criticism constantly disturbing the work of the

government, often being irresponsible and opposed to the principle of governance. It is a luxury of constitutional law indulged in by the parliamentarian spirit, but forbidden by the law of war," Hungarian National Archives, K. 280/11/1.

86. ACB XI/127/d.

87. "If we take a closer look at the structure of Hungarian industry so far, we must conclude that it was rooted in the previous liberal system based on free enterprise...and rested on the representation of the economic interests of each trade and profession. What alone activated these organizations was the government measures or labor demands endangering the interests of certain groups, otherwise they took pains to avoid even the appearance of interfering with the matters of the individual enterprises. It must come as a shock to realize that not only did the liberal organs of interest protection ignore the tasks of making production more rational and therefore cheaper, but they did not even realize them. One may realize, but not understand, this indifference and all the officials involved in the previous regime are guilty of this negligence." ACB XI/127/b.

88. Address of Prime Minister Béla Imrédy to Parliament on May 14, 1938, Budapest.

89. *A Budapesti Kereskedelmi és Iparkamara működése 1945-ben* [The Working of the Budapest Chambers of Commerce and Industry in 1945] (Budapest, 1946).

90. Loránt Tilkovszky, "A magyar kormányzat társadalompolitikája 1938-1942-ben," [The Social Policy of the Hungarian Government Between 1938-42], *Párttörténeti Közlemények*, (1971), 72-103.

91. László Gesztelyi Nagy, "Mezőgazdaságfejlesztő törvény eredményeinek biztosítása. Mintafalvak szövetségének megalakítása," [Ensuring the Results of the Law for the Development of Agriculture: Founding an Association of Model Villages], *Magyar Közgazdasági Szemele*, (1943).

92. József Füleky ed., *Hadiüzemi útmutató* [A Guide to War Factories] (Budapest, n.d.), quoted in Péter Hanák and Katalin Hanák, *A magyar pamutipar története* [History of the Hungarian Cotton Industry] (Budapest, 1964).

THE ECONOMY OF OCCUPIED EUROPE

György Ránki

Nazi leaders never made any secret of their plan to put Germany in a dominant position in the European economy. From time to time, Hitler indicated with brutal frankness that he felt Germany needed *Lebensraum* (Living Space), which meant that Southeastern Europe and the Ukraine in particular were to come under German economic control. The German drive for economic hegemony was never a secret. Nor was the *Lebensraum* concept an invention of the Nazi party; it had deep roots in German policy and ideology. As early as the beginning of the 20th century, the idea that Europe should be united under German economic leadership to compete with the three major economic units (the British Empire, the Russian Empire and the United States of America) was heartily embraced by a number of leading economic and political organizations in Wilhelmian Germany.[1] The idea was formally based on economic rationality. An economy of scale using the benefits of the factors of production were emphasized by the large numbers of statistics to demonstrate the complementary relationship between a developed and industrially advanced German economy and with the other Central and Southeastern European countries that were stronger in the production of agricultural goods and raw materials. Therefore a constant exchange of goods with the German economy would serve a vital function for these countries.

Friedrich Nauman's highly controversial book written during World War I on *Mitteleuropa* (Central Europe) focused on a strong tendency towards absolute German domination based on economic power.[2] In his concept of a counterbalance to the

Russian and Anglo-Saxon centers of power, the territorial shape of *Mitteleuropa* stretched northward from Italy toward the Baltic Seas and from the Adriatic to the Danube delta.

The defeat of Germany during World War I obliged her to shelve the *Mitteleuropa* plan for a time. No more than ten years had passed when the destructive effects of the Great Depression which were particularly strong in the small states of East Central Europe had returned the issue with a new name to the agenda. Federation plans from customs unions were put forward strongly by French politicians as well. In the late 1920s and early 1930s, there was no statesman in France who did not come up with some proposal related to this.[3] But after long negotiations, their plans were all but dead and buried and their failure cleared the way for the re-emergence of plans based on Germany's economy. It was no longer called *Mitteleuropa*, but rather *Grossraumwirtschaft* (Great Regional Economy).[4] Adolf Hitler, in one of his confidential conversations with the leader of the Sector for Economic Policy in the Nazi Party (who later became Minister for Economy in the first Nazi cabinet) expressed his aims quite clearly:

> Then we must form an economic community built on common interest with such countries as Poland, Austria and Hungary. Equally with the Czechs and the Balkan countries, and furthermore with Denmark and Holland and also maybe with Belgium, Luxembourg and Switzerland. This is how a middle European economic bloc would come about offering singular advantages, which would ever more strongly unite the various countries.[5]

The "economic federation of the Danubian states under German leadership" or "an extensive area for trade under the overall leadership of German industry, in full accordance with the law of natural development" was formulated by the theoreticians of *Grossraumwirtschaft*.[6] Although not all of the economic writing which began to flourish in the 1930s subscribed to the Nazi line of thinking, all of it, inevitably, served to give economic, political and ideological support to the increasingly vigorous implementation of German foreign and economic policy. Among the remarks contained in a memorandum submitted to Hitler in May 1933 was the following:

> Germany must identify the economic territory in which it is capable of becoming the ruling factor; through its spirit of enterprise and organizational ability Germany must draw a definite line across Europe from the north through the north-west to the south-east and designate the countries that are to receive economic favors through mutual economic relations.[7]

The designated countries were Norway, Denmark and the Netherlands on the one hand and the countries of Southeastern Europe on the other. Who would not be reminded of the Germans' plans in World War I? An offensive under the new circumstances, with many new means, was launched to realize what was in many respects the old plan. It was not very difficult to provide abundant statistics to prove the need for economic ties between Germany and Southeastern Europe, which could be supported by historical, ethnic and cultural arguments too. The economic ideas which finally crystallized are summed up by the expression *Ergänzungswirtschaft* (Complementary Economy).[8]

Clearly the starting point for *Ergänzungswirtschaft* was that Southeastern Europe could not be considered as a unified, independent economic region; its existence and operation could only be conceived of within a system of relations with Germany. This tie was declared to be natural, while all the other great powers were explained in German as *Raumfremd* (Alien Space) and their role was regarded as artificial. So all these factors predestined Southeastern Europe or the Danubian basin to be united with Germany (with Central Europe) within the *Grossraumwirtschaft*.

Although the concept of *Grossraumwirtschaft* was distinguished in Nazi ideology from Western capitalism, it rested economically on an extremely static interpretation of Ricardo's classical economic theory of the comparative advantages of the international division of labor. In certain expressions, one can discern Ohlin's version of the neoclassical concept of interegional trade.[9] Despite the promised mobility of production factors (i.e. capital movement), the actual possibilities and framework hardly pointed beyond a static level which maintained and exacerbated the differences in the level of development. Thus, the concept of *Grossraumwirtschaft* became embodied in actual measures of economic policy and in the emerging foreign trade offensive put forth by Germany. In Nazi ideology, the expression "trade offensive" became distorted into a phrase describing the new regulation of trade relations.

The incorporation of Austria and the Bohemian part of Czechoslovakia into the Third Reich extended the German economic and war potential even before the war had begun. The valuable raw materials found in these two countries — notably Austrian timber, oil, iron-ore and magnesium and Czech coal was essential to Germany's economic industrial capacity and war materials production. In addition, the iron and steel industries, machine factories, vehicle industries and armament factories from these countries considerably increased German industrial potential. Germany's financial position was strengthened by obtaining the Austrian and Czechoslovakian share in capital investments and foreign trade in the other South European states.

In the period after the first military success in Poland, no particular economic policy was applied. The German authorities did not even take the trouble to build up a kind of systematic exploitation of the country. Based upon ad hoc decisions at one time they took 4,000 machine tools out of the country, at another a few hundred thousand workers. They carried away raw materials and they even dismantled some railway lines. Production was down in every branch of the Polish economy.[10] Later, when it became clear that Great Britain was not ready to compromise as demonstrated by their fateful triumph at *Blitzkrieg*, Germany realized that it had to face a longer war, the inclusion of occupied Europe into the German economy became a real issue. Under the given political circumstances, Hitler was not willing to allow a repeat of those unsystematic robberies which had been carried out in Poland. German business interests cried out for a plan to organize, use and control all the vast economic potential which would come directly or indirectly under German control.

On June 22, 1940, Hitler instructed the Ministry of Economy to coordinate the amalgamation of the occupied territories under German leadership. With geographical borders stretching from as far as the Danube, the Main and the Rhine, this seemed to recall the *Mitteleuropa* plan of World War I, even though the ideological reasoning was slightly different this time. Germany's vocation in Europe, the creation of European unity, was stressed. The Europeans were supposed to acknowledge that they belonged neither to the West nor to the East; they had to overcome the extreme capitalism of the West and the sterile Marxism of the East in a new synthesis to be economically successful.[11] The first flush of victory strengthened the resolution to realize *Grossraumwirtschaft*. Even those who had been a little dubious about Hitler's plan of conquest and about his methods and had been urging moderation, agreed that the program for Europe's economic rearrangement contained a narrower, yet very important core. It was an attempt to define the role of Southeastern Europe in the economy under German hegemony.[12]

A note written by the "Gesellschaft für Europäische Wirtschaftsplannung und Grossraumwirtschaft" (Association for European Economic and Great Regional Planning), as a preparation for the future, clearly formulated the idea that a "continental European Great Regional Planning under German leadership" was supposed to be established through "inclusion of the people from Gibraltar to the Urals and from the Northern Cape to the island of Cyprus." In the same article, it was revealed that this great regional economy would and should have a similar impact upon the economies of Siberia and Africa as well. Minister of the Economy Walter Funk, stressed in a speech that political, military and economic power were clearly interlinked. He claimed that he who has political power in Europe has the right to create a "new economic order serving its own needs," and all the countries had to "orient themselves accordingly."[13]

The first steps that were taken to implement Germany's economic plan included the intensification of trade among the

European countries and the control of all trade flow through Germany. The aim after the war was to achieve, "an economic hegemony of Germany over Europe and the rest of the world and provide the highest standard of living to the German people."[14]

Various measures were taken and different institutions were established to build up an organic and systematic dominance by the German economy over Europe. A special institution was created to shift from bilateral to multilateral clearing. Berlin took the privilege of deciding what goods could be traded, with whom this trade could be carried out and for what purpose this multilateral clearing might be used. "The expansion of the German Clearing System to a European Central Clearing System" was regarded as an important function in the establishment of the New Order. During the latter part of 1940 and the first month of 1941, the build-up of the German "New Order in Europe" went ahead without any difficulty. However, it became clear that if Germany wanted to face the United States and Britain successfully, she would have to gain control over the important raw materials in the Soviet Union. The die was cast, "to secure by conquest all the regions that are of particular importance to our war economy."[15] After the attack on the Soviet Union failed to achieve its military and economic targets, however, the immediate needs of the war became the dominant feature of Germany's economic policy; further plans for the reorganization of Europe within the framework of the New Order were shelved in favor of the immediate tasks of the war. Long-range plans were not abandoned, but short-range benefits were the main targets; much of the emphasis in Germany's war decisions were focused on what could be achieved through the systematic looting and exploitation of the conquered territories and the economies of the satellite countries. By and large, the economies of occupied Europe can be divided into three major zones where the function, role and result was to achieve German hegemony through the total collapse of economic life in Europe. The three zones were:

a. Occupied Western Europe
b. The satellite countries of Southeastern Europe

c. The conquered territories of the Soviet Union, Poland and Czechoslovakia.

A different type of war economy was developed by Germany's allies in Southeastern Europe which included: Hungary, Romania, Bulgaria and Slovakia. In those countries, the elements of formal political independence and of a domestic policy were allowed to survive, though only under the influence of German pressure. German troops were stationed in Slovakia from the creation of that state by Germany, in Romania from the autumn of 1940 and in Bulgaria from the spring of 1941. But these troops did not interfere directly in daily politics; the military occupation of Hungary did not take place until the spring of 1944.[16]

The German attitude toward the satellite states was articulated in the spring of 1941 in a series of articles in the semi-official *Berliner Börzenzeitung*. According to that paper, the countries of Southeastern Europe "will have to adapt themselves to their natural endowments," and that

> industrialization was incompatible with the agricultural character of these countries.... Simultaneously with political revision, the countries of Southeastern Europe will have to adapt themselves to the requirements of a continental *Grossraumwirtschaft*. Their agricultural production will be determined by the needs of the rest of the continent. Their major produce was to be grain and seed oils. The production of raw materials was to be supplemented by their local processing into semi-finished goods through the usage of local water power.[17]

The German plans for the industries of Southeastern Europe were threefold — They wanted the agricultural industries to develop through "directed cooperation," that is, exclusively and totally to serve the needs of the German market. The other existing industries were to be transformed into German concerns. And finally, all means were to be used to prevent the development of any industry incompatible with German aims.[18] Although consistent attempts to realize the first two points of the program continued until the end of the war, they met with only partial success.

At first, record agricultural production in Hungary in 1938 and a similarly outstanding harvest in Romania in 1939 concealed the true state of affairs. During the first years of the war, there was still a significant increase in the volume of agricultural produce sent from these countries to Germany. It appeared that the manpower deflected to industry and the army would be compensated by the massive imports of agricultural machinery from Germany. Within a few years, for example, thousands of tractors, combines and other agricultural machines arrived in Romania. Even with this massive influx of machinery, the level of production did not rise because this only replaced a fraction of the manpower lost. Even the desperately small quantity of artificial fertilizer used during the 1930s was no longer available during the war. Therefore expansion of the area under cultivation was out of the question. In fact, there was a slight reduction in the land cultivated. Under these circumstances, except for one or two outstanding years, production was well below the pre-war level. During the war, there was a 20-30% decline in the average yearly agricultural production of the Southeastern European countries compared to the second half of the 1930s, resulting mostly from the drops in grain production.[19]

Grain Production in Hungary, Romania and Bulgaria
(in million metric tons)[20]

	1934-1938	1940	1941	1942	1943	1944
Hungary	5.5	5.7	5.2	4.5	5.3	6.3
Romania	8.2	6.9	6.9	5.4	7.3	8.5
Bulgaria	3.4	2.9	2.7	1.6	2.8	2.8

Up until the German occupation, Hungary delivered less than 900 thousand metric tons of grain to Germany altogether which was well below the pre-war level.[21] After the war, the

Romanians claimed that 1.4 million metric tons of grain were delivered.[22] The unmistakably negative overall picture was brightened by increased output in a few special branches — principally in the production of seed-oils which was enforced by the Germans. But even here, there were more increases in the area of land under cultivation and in production in the late 1930s and during the first years of the war than in its later phases. In Bulgaria, where response to German demand was the strongest during the 1930s, sunflower-seed production reached its peak in 1937; the yield in 1942-43 was only 50% of this. In Romania, the area of land devoted to industrial and other plants grew from 7.4% to 11.5% between 1940 and 1943. There was considerable increase in the production of beans and peas, but that of oil seeds and industrial plants for the most part did not reach the 1939 level. With a 25% fall in production and an increase in domestic consumption, none of these countries could satisfy Germany's demands. In Bulgaria and Romania, the supply of livestock declined by 15-25% between 1941 and 1944. Therefore, the export of livestock to Germany had to be terminated during the second phase of the war which in turn decreased the amount of animal and milk products exported.[23]

Germany's policy of making her allies supply her with food and raw materials was, in many respects, more successful. Hungary's bauxite and Romania's oil were of most significance in this respect, but wood and non-ferrous metals from Romania and oil and manganese from Hungary were also essential elements of the German war economy. The Germans, therefore, did everything within their power to increase production in these branches, frequently making considerable investments to have a greater productive capacity to serve their purposes. During the war, Hungary's bauxite production more or less doubled, 90% of it (900,000 metric tons) went straight to Germany. Hungarian manganese-ore production also roughly doubled: the amount exported to Germany was 60%. As for petroleum and grain, Germany's 1939 trade agreement with Romania guaranteed plentiful supplies.

German firms established a series of companies with the aim of increasing the volume of these products to be exported. The oil contract in the spring of 1940 stipulated that Romanian oil had to be sold at pre-war prices. The contracts of December 4, 1940, guaranteed increased exports of agricultural and forestry products. In 1940-41, more than 60% of the oil produced in Romania went to Germany. Between 1940 and August 1944, 10.3 million metric tons of oil were exported to Germany, while the amount of petroleum consumed by the German army in Romania was estimated at 1 million metric tons. During the war, even Hungary started to produce oil. In 1943, at the height of production, 800,000 metric tons were produced; half of it went to Germany.[24]

After the attack on the Soviet Union, the German war machine even needed the modest industrial capacity of her satellites. In 1941, Hungary established new war industries and placed 70% of her capacity at Germany's disposal. From 1941 on, the German army placed more and more orders in Hungary. Notable among these was the production of airplanes which became part of the Messerschmitt program. Six hundred modern Messerschmitt, 109 fighter planes, 100 all-purpose planes and 1,000 airplane engines were mass produced in Hungary starting at the end of 1943. German investments developed Hungary's aluminum oxide and aluminum industries. The Danube Airplane Factory and the Danube Valley Aluminum Plant, the two largest plants built during the war were built with German assistance.[25] The industrial capacities of the other satellite countries were more modest and played a correspondingly modest role in German plans. The development of a war economy in these countries was therefore sharply one-sided. With the decline of the consumer industries, in 1943, overall industrial production was only 38% above the pre-war level in Hungary and 18% in Bulgaria.

Concurrent with the one-sided, moderate war boom, the satellite countries began to experience the dire economic consequences of the despoliation wrought by subordination to the German war machine. For they were shipping an ever-growing volume of food, raw materials and industrial goods to Germany without any recompense. In fact, the Germans made no particular efforts to conceal the debt they accumulated during the war years — as they had done concerning the clearing liabilities of the 1930s. Litter, a senior civil servant in the German Ministry of Finance openly declared Germany's new policy: "The mass of the goods shipped by Hungary must, in fact, be considered contributions to the common war effort, contributions whose value will be booked."[26] The value of these unpaid goods, especially after 1941, grew by leaps and bounds. For instance, Germany's debt to Hungary in 1941 was only 140 million marks. By 1942, it was 850 million; by 1943, 1 billion marks; while by 1944, an additional 1.5 billion marks of debts had been accumulated.

Germany's debts to Bulgaria show a similar trend. In 1941, Germany owed Bulgaria 210 million marks; in 1942, 380 million; while by the end of 1943, her debt was 680 million. The provisioning of the German troops stationed in Bulgaria throughout the entire war cost another 250 million marks. Altogether, up to September 1944, the total financial contribution of Bulgaria was in the order of 1.2 billion according to Bulgarian sources.[27] Germany's debt to Slovakia between 1939 and 1944 rose to 1 billion marks. Romania's financial support of Germany during the war amounted to 2 billion marks.

The amount owed to Hungary was proportionate to the amounts owed the other satellites and greatly contributed to the development of an inflation economy. The unpaid German orders had to be paid for by the governments of the producing countries. To do this, they had no alternative but to issue great quantities of unbacked paper currency. In Hungary, it was precisely the German debts which necessitated the issuing of 40% of the unbacked money. The exploitation by Germany became a decisive factor in the wartime inflation suffered by the satellite countries. Recently, the accounts relating to German clearing debts kept by the Deutsche Verrechnungskasse have been published.[28] According to this account, Germany accumulated 1.11 billion in clearing debts to Romania, 1 billion to Hungary, 816 million to Bulgaria and 579 million marks to Slovakia.

The statistics issued by the German authorities usually differed from the statistics published by other countries. The nature of the difference lies in the fact that German statistics usually claim a smaller import surplus, periodically even showing an export surplus, in sharp contradiction to the data concerning the clearing debts. Russian estimates put the loss for the Romanian economy as high as 8.1 billion marks just through keeping Romanian export prices relatively low vis-a-vis imported German goods. Slovakia accumulated a debt of 1 billion marks, which included the value of rail transport and German troop maintenance while German sources claim the debt to be only 600 million marks.[29] The debts to Bulgaria including the cost of maintaining the German troops stationed in that country, were likewise higher than German sources are willing to admit. Furthermore, all available German data are up until June 1944 and do not include the goods and merchandise taken away by the withdrawing German troops.

The role of the satellite Southeastern European states in the German labor supply was insignificant, because of the increased demand for labor in the economy. On the other hand, the Germans were not able to use direct pressure or other methods to round up workers; those who did volunteer took their jobs because they expected better salaries, since German wages were usually far above average wage levels in Southeastern Europe. Altogether, among all foreign workers in Germany between 1943-1944, the number from these countries was less than 3% - around 230,000.[30]

All of the West European countries were occupied by the German army very early on in the war. The impression created by the easy victories was that the war in Europe was more or less over and that German hegemony was well established. With this impression came the idea that the time for shaping the German New Order had arrived and that it could be done peacefully. The unbelievably large number of proposals from different German companies, banks and industrial enterprises, not to mention, the German economists and party bureaucrats who provided their blueprints including the various economic resources, were clearly indicative of Hitler's policy contradictions with Western Europe.[31] In contrast to Poland and the Soviet Union, German economic policy designated the resources of the occupied countries as war booty.[32] There is a noticeable two-way approach in Hitler's policy concerning

Western Europe. On the one hand, the Germans were unable to resist the challenge of looking upon the resources of these countries as economic booty. Levies for the enormous occupation costs, the confiscation of large stockpiles of raw materials, the takeover of French, Belgian or Dutch investments in Southeastern Europe all pointed in this direction.[33] On the other hand, the local business community, with the exception of the Jews, was accepted as a bargaining partner, in a new European economic community dominated by Germany.

France can be regarded as the best example of German economic policy in Western Europe. First, from an economic and political point of view, she was the most important among the subjugated countries because of the size of her economy. Second, France's economy during the war was studied more than any other. Historical studies dealing with German economic policy vis-a-vis France and with the policy of exploitation, are inclined to distinguish three periods in Franco-German economic relations during the war. As far as the time span of these periods is concerned, the first period extends from the military defeat of France to the end of 1940; the second period runs up to the subjugation of the unoccupied territories and Vichy France and the third period stretches from December 1942 to the liberation of the country. In the first period, no established economic strategy can be discerned. This was the period when war booty was taken from the other counties, when the "great wealth of the country; raw materials, all goods and products, will be made available to Germany."[34] The only discernible economic strategy was Germany's negotiations with French business circles to collaborate in the war effort.

The second period is the period of collaboration. Collaboration was on a semi-voluntary basis under the pressure of the German military presence in the country. This was the period when German industry was willing to give more and more contracts to the French, to supplement German war production and to replace the shrinking German consumer goods industry. This was the policy under which the French were required to contribute their labor and the production of necessary raw materials and industrial goods. During this period, the large number of unemployed French workers volunteered for jobs in Germany. Finally, the last stage began when Vichy France was taken over by the German army and desperate efforts were made to mobilize all the economic resources of France and the other European countries for German war needs. This period of "total war" was also one of sharp contradictions. One the one hand, French industry and the French economy were more necessary than ever in order to achieve the maximum level of assistance for the German economy. On the other hand, the clear signs of the decline of German power made French business leaders less cooperative. The arrangement between Albert Speer, the German Minister of Armaments and War Production and Jean Bichelonne, Minister of Industry in the Vichy government to use French resources to deliver consumer goods to Germany failed for two reasons. First, the Germans pushed for more and more armaments and heavy industrial goods from France and second because fewer French workers were prepared to volunteer for work to Germany, making it necessary to use "press gang" methods.

Since the French economy had always been heavily dependent on foreign raw materials, the Germans could not put the French economy into full gear. Since France was importing one-third of her coal and Germany was unable to increase her production, the shortage of coal put an automatic limit to the collaboration of French industry. In spite of the growing German demand and increasing contracts, French industrial production was constantly declining for this reason. According to Alfred Sauvy, the French GNP developed in the following way during the war:

French Gross National Product during World War II[35]

	GNP in billion francs	Percentage
1938	328	100
1939	351	107
1940	290	88
1941	230	70

	GNP in billion francs	Percentage
1942	205	62
1943	195	54
1944	165	50

The Germans used 50% of France's timber production, 29% of her coal, 51% of her metallurgical and 75% of her aluminum production. There were a few key sectors where German interests were particularly dominant: Alsace-Lorraine was extremely rich in iron-ore and strong in metallurgical production; these spoils automatically went to Germany in their entirety.[36] The same was true of Luxembourg. From 1942, production in these areas increased systematically, but never reached the pre-war level.

The aluminum industry was another key sector. Before the war, French bauxite production was one of the largest in the world. During the war, by gaining complete access to the Hungarian, Yugoslavian and French reserves, the Germans were assured of producing enough aluminum for the airplanes they needed. After the occupation, the Germans wanted to take advantage of the bauxite and the aluminum industries. Mines and factories in those areas were among the first where German-French industrial cooperation was established. Actually bauxite and aluminum were among the very few items where production did increase for a while.

French Bauxite and Aluminum Production and Export to Germany (in 1,000 metric tons)[37]

	Production		*Exports*	
	Bauxite	Aluminum	Bauxite	Aluminum
1938	683	45.3	84	—
1940	489	—	—	15.4
1941	586	51.5	232	34.5
1942	644	44.3	231	17.5
1943	912	46.5	489	27.3

As the war progressed, the Germans relied more and more upon the French airplane industry. France's airplane industry was comparable in size to that of Germany in the pre-war period. When France was occupied, production capacity was estimated at 800 aircraft per month. A large amount of the industry's stock of machine tools were confiscated and special concessions were offered to lure its skilled workers to Germany. As it was later put in a German document:

> In the occupied areas, (apart from the East, we have) not been able to get down to organizing for a long war. In the West, we have concentrated on short-term methods of doubtful effectiveness, on seizing stocks, on black market production and on the removal of labor to the *Reich*. There has not yet been an effort at planned intensive development of the productive assets of German dominated Europe that could raise its arms-producing potential.[38]

In spite of the fact that the French military leaders volunteered the cooperation of the French aviation industry as early as the time of the armistice negotiations, the first German order was only placed in 1941. Even this order for 2,500 machines was mainly for transport planes, since the French were not really trusted. Under the armistice agreement nearly all French airplanes were confiscated and Vichy was only allowed to retain 900. Later, a common program was elaborated which allowed the French to produce airplanes and engines for themselves as well on a ratio of two to one. However, owing to circumstances such as the shortages in manpower and coal, difficulties in producing the mechanically unfamiliar German airplanes and acts of sabotage, French deliveries were always well below German expectations. French contracts were not usually fulfilled by more than 50%. Nevertheless, airplane contracts were becoming more important.[39] Various estimates have tried to arrive at reliable figures for the value of German exploitation of France during the war. Alan Milward came up with a fairly reliable estimate. He based it upon the value of confiscated goods, the occupation costs, the revaluation of the

French franc and an artificially created balance of trade deficit in a form of clearing debts.

Surprisingly, France turned out to be Germany's most important agricultural supplier. It was well known that France was second in Europe only to the Soviet Union in her volume of grain output. The Germans were aware that French agriculture was producing more than was needed for domestic consumption. However, they were so full of expectations that the countries of Southeastern Europe and the conquered areas of the Soviet Union would provide abundant agricultural supplies that they regarded France as secondary in this respect. The average wheat production went up to 8 million metric tons between 1934-38, with exports and imports balancing each other. During the years of occupation, wheat production varied between 5.7 million to 6.5 million metric tons — 22.2 million metric tons altogether. From this quantity, more than 800,000 metric tons went as exports to Germany and another 2 million were taken by the German army stationed in France. It is estimated that domestic per capita consumption in France must have declined by 30 to 40% during the war.[40] Significant French food contributions to Germany included 9 million hectoliters of wine, 2.3 million metric tons of fodder grain and 735,000 metric tons of meat. Since agricultural production was 20% below the pre-war level between 1941 and 1943 and around 50% in 1944, the magnitude of what was delivered to or confiscated by Germany caused enormous difficulties for the French population.[41]

Occupation Costs and Other Payments from France[42]

	French Occupation Cost in Million Francs	As a % of GNP at War Exchange Rate	Total Payments incl. Clearing Debts (million Francs)	As a % of German National Income
1940	80,000	2.8	81,600	2.8
1941	121,500	3.9	144,300	4.6
1942	109,000	3.9	156,700	4.8
1943	194,000	5.7	273,600	8.0
1944	126,900	3.1	206,306	5.9

Total French Payments as a Percent of National Income and GDP in 1939

	Percent of French National Income	Percent of GDP
1940	10.9	9.3
1941	19.3	16.5
1942	20.9	17.7
1943	36.6	31.3
1944	27.1	23.6

Other French estimates put the value of material goods taken by the German occupation at 83 billion for the material losses and 275 billion for the financial losses. The overall French contribution was equal to 5% of the German GNP in 1941 and 1942 and 9% in 1943. The available estimates put the French contribution as high as 42% of all foreign tributes.[43] All in all, the French contribution during the war was equal to the French national income in a typical pre-war year. We wish to underline that the small size of the French contribution was only due to the confiscation and occupational costs imposed by Germany. German debts in 1944 reached 8.4 billion marks.[44] Altogether, the most cautious estimates put the financial contribution of France to the German war economy at 862 million francs or around 42-43 billion German marks; this was equal to 5.4% of the German GNP in 1941, 8.3% in 1942, 8.2% in 1943 and 7.4% in 1944.[45]

Norway is the other country where a comprehensive picture has been provided.[46] After the occupation of Norway, Germany demanded cash and raw material contributions to the war, immediate mobilization of resources and reorientation of her foreign trade with Germany. Industries like metallic ores and metallurgy that would help the German war effort were encouraged; other industries were simply regarded as subsidiary branches of German industries. Due to Norway's large coast line, geographic location and strategic role, many more German troops were stationed there as an occupation army. That is the reason why Norway's per capita occupation costs were much higher than anywhere else.

One of the major economic plans concerning Norway was to use her electrical energy resources to build up a strong aluminum industry.[47] Norway produced around 30,000 metric tons of aluminum before the war. Under a new agreement the country was supposed to increase production to 120,000 metric tons and later, up to 1944, to 244,000 metric tons. To accomplish this, the German project needed enormous amounts of investment and tremendous amount of organization, since it was based on the assumption that bauxite would be shipped into Norway from France and Hungary.[48] However, from 1943, all these large investment intensive projects were either partially or entirely abandoned for the short-term needs, using industrial capacity for war contracts and producing consumer goods for Germany.[49] Even Norwegian aluminum production fell below the pre-war level since the necessary bauxite was not available.

Norway was the only country in Western Europe from which Germany was unable to extract significant monetary contributions because the country was so dependent upon foreign food and coal imports. Real wages fell by 33% and consumption was limited to keep the economy running. To avoid eventual military and political turmoil, the German authorities delivered large quantities of coal and food to the country. With the exception of 1944, Norway consistently had an import surplus in her trade with Germany which meant that no clearing debt was credited. Norway paid more than 8 billion krones as occupation costs during the war years which was equal to 5 billion marks. Other sources, however, put the Norwegian occupation costs at 12 billion krones, which includes German requisitions and which deducts the value of the Norwegian import surplus with Germany during the war. This amount was equal to one-third of the average national income during the war, with the trend rising from 25 to 40% between 1941 and 1943.[50]

Unfortunately, we do not have a comprehensive picture of the war economy for the other occupied Western countries except for a book published in Brussels describing the wartime economy of Belgium in 1945.[51] Recently, a controversial study estimated the German occupation at 73.1 billion Belgian francs.[52] Of that amount, 5.89 billion marks in real value requisitions assessed at 5 billion marks were not included in this amount.[53] The Belgian industry became a very important war contractor to the German army. After a few months of requisitions and confiscations, Belgian industrialists were approached with the offer of lucrative contracts binding them to the New German Order.

Alan Milward calls our attention to the fact that during World War I, Belgium was not required to contribute to the German war effort; this, however, was not acceptable to Nazi Germany.[54] Belgium had a great many raw materials which were essential for German war industries. She was extremely rich in black coal, steel and the engineering industry. From 1941, Belgian industry received more and more war contracts from Germany. At the beginning of the occupation, Belgium's steel industry was one of the most significant in Europe. In 1941 and 1942, according to different estimates between 30 and 50% of Belgian industry worked for the German army. But production only reached about 65% of pre-war output because the necessary fuel, raw materials and capital were not available.[55] Even coal production was 20% below the pre-war level.

After 1943, Germany made a serious effort in Belgium to use industry in a more effective way to build up its agricultural contribution to Germany's wartime needs. But the contradictions here were too strong. Plans to get as many workers as possible to Germany were incompatible with plans to simultaneously increase Belgian war production. In some areas like transport, railways and ship-building almost 100% of Belgium's rolling stock went to Germany. In other areas of heavy industry, between 50 and 70% of the Belgian factories worked for Germany. In December 1940, the *Deutsche Verrechnungskasse* in Berlin was created to act as the central clearing house for multilateral trade between Germany and the occupied countries.[56] The *Verrechnungskasse's* major function was to account for the increased debts. The debts to Belgium alone had reached more than 5 billion German marks when the

Germany's Clearing Debts, Assimilated Accounts, and Amounts Outstanding (in million marks)[60]

	France	Holland	Belgium	Denmark	Hungary	Bulgaria	Slovakia
December 1940	200	160	250	390	---	100	90
December 1941	800	1,410	930	820	180	440	170
December 1942	2,450	2,490	2,420	1,240	540	700	330
December 1943	5,400	4,270	4,280	2,280	980	1,100	450
March 1944	6,300	5,030	4.670	2,610	---	---	---
June 1944	7,500	5,590	5,130	2,990	---	---	500
September 1944	8,000	5,790	5,370	3,360	---	1,200	---

	Sweden	Switzerland	Romania	Bohemia/Moravia	Totals
December 1940	-60	50	-20	600	1,770
December 1941	80	250	280	1,100	6,460
December 1942	70	500	500	1,600	12,840
December 1943	50	600	500	3,200	23,110
March 1944	40	600	---	3,400	22,650
June 1944	10	600	900	3,700	26,920
September 1944	---	600	900	4,600	29,820

Allies started to liberate the country from the Germany occupation.[57]

Unlike many of the other occupied countries during the war, Holland and Denmark did not have significant heavy industries which could be used for armaments, but their industrial function was still by no means insignificant. In two areas — ship-building and electro-technical equipment — they made significant contributions to German production. Besides France, the Netherlands and Denmark were Germany's major suppliers of agricultural goods (The Netherlands supplied meat, fat and potatoes and Denmark supplied meat, fat and butter). Most of this produce was delivered as a compulsory contribution to the German war economy or as unpaid credit in foreign trade. Denmark and Holland covered between 25 and 33% of German agricultural imports during the war.[58] Both the Dutch and Danish industries obtained contracts, but the shortage of fuel and raw materials made them less workable. During the war, for instance, Danish textile output fell by 50%. The occupational costs of the country were 2.9 billion marks and the clearing debts of Germany on September 3, 1944, were 340 million. In the Netherlands, the occupation costs were 10 billion marks and the clearing debts were around 6 billion marks.[59]

These debts included a significant part of German agricultural imports, various industrial goods and armaments production of 1943.[61] As far as occupation costs and clearing debts are concerned, occupied Western Europe and the allies of South East Europe were the main contributors sources to the German revenues which covered its war expenses. Of the estimated 55.6 billion occupation costs, 53 billion were covered by the West European countries. According to the records of the Bank of International Settlement, the occupation costs plus defense contributions paid to Germany in September 1944 were 84 billion. The Bank for International Settlement calculated the occupation costs and clearing debts totaling 124 billion marks, which equaled about 25% of all German war expenses.[62]

Different estimates are available concerning the role of the financial exploitation of the occupied territories in German war expenses. Among others, even the German authorities tried to evaluate the financial gains from the occupation. Part of this estimate has been published. In early 1986, the calculations carried out in 1944 by the *Forschungsstelle der Wehrwirtschaft* to evaluate the financial gains from the occupation were published.[63] This estimate contains very reliable calculations on the financial contribution of all occupied territories except Italy up to the first quarter of 1944. The document, however, does not calculate all the losses the various economies suffered through the German occupation since only a part of these losses directly contributed to the German war economy. The German calculation puts the financial contribution of occupied Europe at 85-90 billion marks. In spite of the methodology used, this calculation still suffers from a number of deficiencies. First, it only goes up to March 1944. We can assume that this increases the actual contribution by at least 10%. Second, this does not include the money and goods taken by the German army personnel and the German government. Even with all these reservations, it's worth taking a look at these calculations.

The Financial Contribution of the Occupied Territories to Germany until the end of March 1944 (million marks)[64]

	Until September 1943	Until April 1944
France	32,290	35,060
Netherlands	10,300	12,030
Belgium	7,770	9,300
General Government	2,965	5,015
Norway	4,250	4,900
Occupied Eastern Territories	3,500	4,500
Denmark	1,760	2,530
Protectorate	4,100	2,310
Yugoslavia	480	630
Greece	110	500
Total	**68,525**	**77,775**
Additional Estimates	6-11,000	7-12,000
Total Production	**76-85,000**	**85-90,000**

It is true that formally the occupation costs include 2.1 billion marks from Poland (General Government) and 1.1 billion marks from the occupied Soviet territories as defense contributions, but we have no doubt that this must have been a tiny sum in comparison with what was taken from Poland as plunder; yet we must bear in mind the instructions concerning Poland:

> In the General Government...all raw materials, scrap, machinery and so forth, which can be used in the German war economy must be removed from the territory. Enterprises which are not absolutely necessary at a low level for the basic existence of the inhabitants must be transferred to Germany.[65]

In the instructions given by Reich Marshal Hermann Göring to Minister of Economics Walter Funk on August 17, 1940, the major aim of German economic policy was "...[to] increase the food supplies and other products that are important for the war effort to the highest level. This should be done to strengthen the war economy in the areas controlled by Germany."[66]

Nazi racial obsession against the Slavic peoples resulted in a far less effective systematic exploitation of East European resources than might have been expected, because of the reckless plundering, killing and destruction carried out by German troops in the first period of the war. Because of this, the Eastern European countries did not supply the food they were expected to produce in spite of the fact that the consumption of the local populations was far less than half of the pre-war level. Polish agricultural production declined by one-third during the war while production by the conquered Soviet territory was even lower. In the occupied Soviet territories, more than 9.1 million metric tons of grain were confiscated by the German troops and only 13% of this was delivered to Germany.[67]

Food Seized from the Occupied Soviet Territories by Germany (thousand metric tons)[68]

Products	1941-1942	1943	1st Qtr of 1944	Total	Transported
Grain	3,999	4,653	641	9,293	1,301
Meat	336	169	25	561	78
Fat	288	286	16	620	320
Butter	-108	-64	-4	-207	-21
Potatoes	1,768	1,408	105	3,282	---
Fodder	883	1,332	293	2,508	---
Sugar	149	231	22	401	62
Eggs	575	498	6	1,079	133
Fish	25	41	1	68	1
Vegetables	95	99	16	210	32
Fruit	219	268	16	503	10

Only a small part of the confiscated food actually reached Germany; the rest was needed to feed the occupation army and the Ukrainian police forces hired by the Germans.[69] In Polish territories, until 1943, 3.3 million metric tons of wheat, 3.9 million metric tons of potatoes and 400,000 metric tons of sugar were confiscated.[70] In the Soviet[71] and the Polish occupied territories, agricultural production was far below pre-war output; in Poland, it was about a third below pre-war output. This confiscation meant that the local population had barely enough for subsistence. German agricultural imports from Eastern Europe in 1942-1943 were 17% of domestic grain, 23% of fat, 25% of meat and 18% of sugar consumption. It is not clear whether these figures represent war booty, individual plundering, destruction or a real contribution to the German war expenses by Poland and the Soviet territories.

In Yugoslavia and Greece, there are many questions about the reliability of the war contribution figures. During this time, Yugoslavia delivered significant amounts of various ores (such as copper, zinc, lead, iron) to Germany. In 1942, it delivered

3,000-4,000 metric tons per month; in agriculture 320,000 metric tons of wheat and 600,000 metric tons of iron. In addition, a large number of German troops were stationed in Yugoslavia during the war.[72]

The Germans were not able to plunder Greece as much as they would have liked since Greece's economy collapsed with the German-Italian occupation. In the winter of 1941 to 1942, when agricultural production was not even half the pre-war level, there was a famine which caused 360,000 deaths among the population.[73] Other factors which contributed to the famine included: feeding the German troops, the division of the country into different occupation zones and the collapse of the transport system. The Germans finally felt obliged to comply with the demand of the Red Cross to allow Anglo-American food parcels to be distributed among the population to avoid further starvation. Some industrial enterprises worked in Greece for the Germans, but probably not more than on the local level. The famine, the harvest failures and the occupation costs contributed to the collapse of Greek finances and caused the biggest inflation in the financial history of the world.[74]

In a speech given on July 11, 1944, Albert Speer claimed that "25 to 30% of the German war production had been furnished by the occupied Eastern territories and Italy."[75] Germany was unable to obtain as much from the conquered East European territories as it had expected because their destructive policy made organized production increasingly impossible. But there were drawbacks to Hitler's attitude toward Russia which prompted him to say: "The essential thing is to carve up this gigantic cake so that we may firstly rule over it, secondly govern it and thirdly exploit it."[76] If we attempt to compare German war expenses with the contribution of the occupied countries, then the 25% mentioned by Speer seems to be a very conservative estimate. If we take the German budget expenditure between 1940 and 1944 as 450 billion marks, then the 124 billion is close to 28%. Therefore, the contribution and exploitation of the conquered and satellite countries can be estimated between one quarter and one-third of all German expenditure during the war which falls in the range expressed by Speer.

During these years, even the neutral countries of Europe were utilized by the German war economy. Some of them had a key role in the German economy. Swedish iron ore and ball bearing deliveries played a decisive role in the German war effort. This ore which had a very high iron content saved Germany a lot of manpower and fuel.[77] After the defeat of France, Switzerland was willing to extend clearing credit to Germany. Within the framework of this credit the Swiss factories were engaged in various war contracts with Germany. The highly developed Swiss engineering industry was involved in producing various machine tools and armaments. By 1943, the Germans were 600 million marks in debt to the Swiss.[78] As German pressure was eased, the Swiss became reluctant to extend further credit. Spain and Turkey's major contribution to the German war industry was in the delivery of wolfram and chromium.[79] Hitler felt that Germany had a marked advantage, since much more of her budget was being devoted to war preparations and since German industry was more fully converted to armaments production than that of any other country.

The German concept of *Wehrwirtschaft* (War Economy) was seemingly an up-to-date version of how to carry out warfare in a period when the economy was decisively the outcome than at any time before. The first two years seemingly proved that this approach was correct. By using the *Wehrwirtschaft* to overcome some of the built-in bottlenecks and strains in the German economy and to face a longer war against countries which were better supplied with resources, but less organized. In spite of all the preparations it became clear that the economic needs of World War II surpassed anything that had been anticipated. Technological developments accelerated in a way which outdated all preparations. The weapons which were supplied were regarded as obsolete after two years of war. The crucial question, however, was whether Germany's temporary advantage would be adequate or whether time and circumstances would allow the Allies to catch up. Once the war had begun, all the other countries were able to find answers to the problem of transforming their economies to meet wartime needs. The size, scope and success of those answers were dependent upon a number of factors: whether the country involved was well provided with resources which could be utilized for modern war, whether the political and institutional systems were suitable for mobilizing these resources and whether the necessary means and levers would be found to carry out the job successfully.

All of the belligerents, in spite of the fact that they faced more or less the same issues, tackled these problems in different ways. Their success or failure was ultimately tested on the fields of battle, where armies — of a size and with armaments such as had never been seen before — confronted each other. But a clear insight into the facts of how the world actually went about its business at this time demonstrates the relationship between politics and economics, the links between potentialities and their use, between environment and people, between economic and human factors, between plans and reality, between hopes and disillusionment. We have tried to look at how the various economies were transformed in terms of their links to trade, the similarities in the parallel processes and the distinguishing features as well.

In the literature about the World War II, a great deal of effort has been devoted to the political history, the military events and the phenomenon of resistance and partisan warfare. Considerably less attention has been given to the economic aspects of the war despite the crucial role it played. Alan Milward said it best when he referred to

> the seemingly countless works on military history in which armies and navies come and go, commanded by greater or lesser figures deciding momentous historicalissues and nothing is said of the real productive forces which alone give such events meaning or indeed make them possible...[80]

The turbulent economic events of the war give us warning, as well as evidence: a warning to understand the economic constraints imposed on war economics by nature's endowment and evidence of how human beings work. Though, as we have seen, one must accept the concept that "War stimulates, sometimes produces an invention that may be also serviceable in peace."[81]

Because of the enormous investment carried out by the Soviet Union during the war, it was able to establish a strong new industrial base behind the Urals. This gave a new starting point for Soviet economic development in general and for Soviet Asia in particular. In a number of countries, particularly in the United States, in place of disinvestment and reduction of national wealth, the war demands provided a stimulus to economic development. As part of the war effort, scientific research, technical inventions and innovations were accelerated thrusting it into modern economic development.[82] Diligence and intelligence were able to overcome the difficulties and contribute to the eventual victory. There is evidence that in modern war intelligence does not express itself only on the battlefield, but in quiet studios or laboratories far removed from the front, where the growth of science plays a crucial role in the process of winning the war; in the workshops and factories where management, organization, skill and heavy manual work actually prepare the tools without which the job will never be finished. Therefore, the study of the economic history of World War II has a continued relevance. The more we know about its achievement and limitations, the better equipped we are to deal with similar questions. The warning of C. Wright Mills - unfortunately - carries a large amount of truth: "The immediate cause of World War III is the military preparation for it."[83]

Notes

1. Wolfgang Schumann and Ludwig Nestler, eds., *Dokumente zu den Europe- und Weltherrschaftsplänen des deutschen Imperialismus von der Jahrhundertwende bis Mai 1945* (Berlin, 1975).

2. Freidrich Nauman, *Mitteleuropa* (Berlin, 1915), 20, 153.

3. György Ránki, *Economy and Foreign Policy: The Struggle of the Great Powers for Hegemony in the Danube Valley, 1919-1939* (New York, 1983), 4-5.

4. Andrei Mitrovic, "Ergänzungswirtschaft: The Theory of Integrated Economic Area," in *Yugoslavia and the Third Reich* (Belgrade,1979).

5. Henry A. Turner, ed., *Hitler aus nächster Nähe. Aufzeichnungen eines Vertrauten. 1929-1932* (Stuttgart, 1978), 282.

6. Mitrovic, *op. cit.*

7. Ránki, *op. cit.*

8. Mitrovic, *op. cit.*

9. Bertil Ohlin, *Interregional and International Trade* (Cambridge, 1967).

10. Czestraw Luczak, "Die Wirtschaftspolitik des Dritten Reiches im besetzten Polen," *Studia Historie Oeconomicae*, (1982); Wactaw Dlugoborski, "Die Besetzungssysteme der Achsenmächte. Versuch einer komparativen Analyse," *Studia Historie Oeconomicae*, (1979), 87-123.

11. Wolfgang Schumann, ed., *Griff nach Südosteuropa, Neue Dokumente über die Politik des deutschen Imperialismus und Militarismus gegenüber Südosteuropa im Zweiten Weltkrieg* (Berlin, 1973), 96.

12. Dietrich Eichholz and Wolfgang Schumann, eds., *Anatomie des Krieges. Neue Dokumente über die Rolle des deutschen Monopolkapitals bei der Vorbereitung und Durchführung des Zweiten Weltkrieges* (Berlin, 1969), 261.

13. Jean Freymond,*Le IIIe Reich et la réorganisation économique de l'Europe, 1940-1942: Origines et Projects* (Leiden, 1974), 223.

14. Freymond, *Ibid.*, 245-246 and see further on the *Grossraumwirtschaft*, E. A. Radice, *The German Economic Programme in Eastern Europe 1939-1944* (Oxford, 1972).

15. As quoted in Rolf Dieter Müller, *Das Scheitern der wirtschaftlichen Blitzkriegsstrategien. Das deutsche Reich und der Zweeite Weltkrieg* (Stuttgart, 1982) Vol. 4, 950.

16. Hans-Erich Volkmann, "N. S. Aussenhandel in 'geschlossenen' Kriegswirtschaftsraum (1939-1941)," in Freidrich Forstmeier and Hans-Erich Volkmann, eds., *Kriegswirtschaft und Rüstung am Vorabend des Zweiten Weltkrieges*, 129.

17. Iván T. Berend and György Ránki, *Economic Development in East-Central Europe in the 19th and 20th Centuries* (New York, 1974), 324-325.

18. Berend and Ránki, *Ibid.*, 325.

19. Slavcho Zagorov, Jenő Végh, and Alexander D. Bilimovich, *The Agricultural Economy of the Danubian Countries 1935-1945* (Stanford, 1955), 127.

20. E. A. Radice, "Agriculture and Food," in M. Kaser, *The Economic History of Eastern Europe* Vol. 2, (Oxford, 1986).

21. Iván T. Berend and György Ránki, *Hungary: A Century of Economic Development* (New York, 1974), 178.

22. Radice's chapter in Kaser, *op. cit.*

23. Zagorov, Végh and Bilimovich, *Ibid.*, 127.

24. N. N. Constantinescu, "L'éxploitation et le pillage de l'économie roumaine par l'Allemagne Hitlérienne dans la période 1939-1944," *Revue Roumaine d'Histoire*, (1964), 93-114.

25. Berend and Ránki, *Hungary,* 167-184; Loránd Dombrády, *A magyar gazdaság és a hadfelszerelés 1938-1944* [The Hungarian Economy and the Armament] (Budapest, 1981), 66-88.

26. Iván T. Berend and György Ránki, *Hungarian Economy in the Twentieth Century* (New York, 1985), 166.

27. D. Koen, *The Pillage and Destruction of the Bulgarian Economy by German Imperialism During World War II* (Sofia, 1966).

28. Holm Sundhaussen, *Wirtschaftsgeschichte Kroatiens im nationalsozialistischen Grossraum, 1941-1945* (Stuttgart, 1983), 375.

29. H. Kaiser, *Die Eingliederung der Slowakei in die nationalsozialistische Kriegswirtschaft. Das Jahr 1945 in der Tschechoslowakei* (München, 1971); Bank of International Settlements "Report 14," (Basel, 1944) and "Report 15," (Basel, 1945), 1151.

30. Published by Sundhaussen, *op. cit.*, 375; Dietrich Eichholtz, *Geschichte der deutschen Kriegswirtschaft, 1939-1945* (Berlin, 1985), Vol. 2, 512.

31. Eichholz and Schumann, *op. cit.*

32. C. Luczak, "Grundlegende Probleme der Landwirtschaft und Erhnährung in Ost- und Südosteuropa während des

zweiten Weltkrieges," *Studia Historie Oeconomicae*, (1982), 279-297. As for the question of the German economic policy toward South Eastern Europe, see: E. A. Radice, "Economic Developments in Eastern Europe under German Hegemony," in Kaser, *op. cit.*

33. In France, they found, among other items, 89,000 metric tons of iron, 295,000 metric tons of rolled iron, 72,000 metric tons of copper, 36,000 metric tons of zinc and a large quantity of other alloys. H. Winkel, "Die Ausbeutung des besetzten Frankreich," in Freidrich Forstmeier and Hans-Erich Volkmann, *Kriegswirtschaft und Rüstung, 1939-1945* (Düsseldorf, 1977).

34. Cited by Winkel, *ibid.*, 326. Winkel's article was largely based on the explanation in Milward's book, the best on the history of the French economy under German occupation, see: Alan S. Milward, *The New Order and the French Economy* (Oxford, 1970).

35. Alfred Sauvy, *La vie économique des Français de 1939 à 1945* (Paris 1978), 100.

36. Pierre Gérard, "Le Protectorat industriel. Allemand en Meurthe-et-Moselle," *Revue Histoire de la Deuxième Guerre Mondiale*, (1977), 9-28.

37. Milward, *op. cit.*, 328

38. Quoted by John Gillingham, *Belgian Business in the Nazi New Order* (Ghent, 1977), 911.

39. Peter Klemm, "La production aéronatique française de 1940 à 1942," *RHDGM*, (1977), 53-74; Patrick Facon and Françoise de Ruffray, "Aperçus sur la collaboration aéronautique franco-allemande," *Revue Histoire de la Deuxième Guerre Mondiale*, (1977), 85-102; Hans-Erich Volkmann, "L'importance économique de la Lorraine pour le IIIe Reich," *Revue Histoire de la Deuxième Guerre Mondiale*, (1980), 69-93.

40. See: Karl Brandt, *Management of Agriculture and Food in the German-occupied and Other Areas of Fortress Europe: A Study in Military Government* (Stanford, 1953), 566.

41. Sauvy, *op. cit.*; M. Cepède, *Agriculture et Alimentation en France durant la IIe guerre mondiale* (Paris, 1961), 351.

42. Milward, *op. cit.*, 273.

43. Paul Grandjean Guèrres, *Fluctuations et croissance*

(Paris, 1967). Estimates which try to include net deficit of foreign trade and devaluation, put the value absorbed by Germany almost twice as high.

44. Bank of International Settlements, "Report 15," (Basel, 1945), 149.

45. See: Winkel, *op. cit.*, 361 in Milward, *op. cit.*, 273.

46. Alan Milward, *The Fascist Economy in Norway* (Oxford, 1972); F. Hodnes, *The Norwegian Economy 1920-1980* (London, 1983), 100-130.

47. Hodnes, *ibid.*, 111.

48. Milward, *The Fascist Economy*, 172-185.

49. While in most cases like in aluminum, zinc, nickel and copper wartime production was far below the pre-war records, in those two, production grew. Hodnes, *op. cit.*, 114.

50. Milward, *The Fascist Economy*, 280; Kjell Aukrust and Petter Jakob Bjerve, *Hva krigen koslet Norge* (Oslo, 1945), 29.

51. F. Bandhuin, *L'économie belge sous l'occupation 1940-1944* (Brussels, 1945).

52. Gillingham, *op. cit.*

53. Bank of International Settlements, "Report 15," (Basel, 1945), 17.

54. Alan Milward, *War, Economy and Society* (Berkeley, 1974), 130-131.

55. Bandhuin, *op. cit.*, 289; Milward, *War, Economy and Society,* 143.

56. For the debts see: Bandhuin, *ibid.*, 337; D. Eichholz, *op. cit.*, Vol. 2, 510; and Bank of International Settlements, "Report 14," (1944).

57. In the case of Belgium, see: H. van der Wee, *Monetary Policy in Belgium during and after World War II* (1985).

58. Brandt, *op. cit.*

59. Werner Warmbruch, *The Dutch under German Occupation 1940-1945* (Stanford, 1963), 81; H. Winkel, "Die wirtschaftliche Beziehungen Deutschlands zu Dänemark in den Jahren der Besetzung 1940-1945," in *Probleme der national-sozialistischen Wirtschaftspolitik* (Berlin, 1976).

60. Bank of International Settlements, "Report 14," 149; *Vierteljahrshefte für Zeitgeschichte*, (January 1986), 1 Heft.

61. Eichholz, *op. cit.*, 308.

62. Bank of International Settlements, "Report 15," 163.

63. *Vierteljahrshefte für Zeitgeschichte*, (January 1986), 1 Heft.

64. *Vierteljahrshefte für Zeitgeschichte*, (January 1986), 1 Heft., 123. During the first quarter, the value of exploitation increased by 10 billion. During the second quarter, the territories held by the Germany army had not yet been reduced significantly. Yet, from June to September most of France, a part of Belgium, Romania, Bulgaria, Finland, and part of Poland had been lost. Therefore, the 10-15% estimated growth is very conservative.

65. Arnold Toynbee and Veronica M. Toynbee, *Hitler's Europe* (New York, 1954), 617.

66. As quoted in Wacław Dlugoborski and Czełav Madajczyk, "Ausbeutungssysteme in den besetzten Gebieten Polens und der UdSSSR," *Studia Historie Oeconomicae*, (1982), 376.

67. Alexander Dallin, *German Rule in Russia 1941-1945. A Study of Occupation Policy* (London, 1957), 406.

68. D. Eichholz, "Die Ausbeutung der Landwirtschaft der Faschistisch besetzten gebiete durch die Okkupanten und die Taktik der Materiellen Korompierung in Deutchland Während des Zweiten Weltkrieges," *Studia Historie Oeconomicae*, (1982), 153-171.

69. Czestaw Luczak, "Grundlegende Probleme für Landwirtschaft und Ernährung, in Ost and Südosteuropa während des Zweiten Weltkrieges," *Studia Historie Oeconomicae*, Vol. 17, 279-297.

70. Eichholz and Schumann, *op. cit.*, 464.

71. *Deutschland im Zweiten Weltkrieg*, (Berlin, 1976), Vol. 2, 454.

72. John R. Lampe and Marvin R. Jackson, *Balkan Economic History, 1550-1950, from Imperial Borderlands to Developing Nations* (Bloomington, 1982).

73. Dimitri Kitsikis, "La famine en Grèce (1941-1942), Les consequences politiques," *Revue Histoire de la Deuxieme Guerre Mondiale*, (1969); Heinz A. Richter, *Griechenland zwischen Revolution und Konterrevolution (1936-1946)* (Frankfurt, 1973), 135.

74. Gail Makinen, "The Greek Hyperinflation and Stabilization of 1943-1946," *The Journal of Economic History*, (September 1986), 795-805.

75. Lampe and Jackson, *op. cit.*

76. Müller, *op. cit.*, Vol. 4, 938.

77. Martin Fritz, "German-Swedish Relations During World War II," *Studia Historie Oeconomicae*, Vol. 14, 15-22; Martin Fritz, "Les relations économiques germano-suedois durant la seconde guerre mondiale," *Revue Histoire de la Deuxieme Guerre Mondiale*, April 1978, 33-58.

78. Klaus Urner, "La Suisse pendant la quèrre: économie et neutralité - neutralité et politique commerciale pendant la seconde guerre mondiale," *Revue Histoire de la Deuxieme Guerre Mondiale*, (1981), Vol. 31, 35-39; Daniel Bourgeois, "La Suisse pendant la quèrre: Les relations économiques germano-suisses 1939-1945," *Revue Histoire de la Deuxieme Guerre Mondiale*, (January 1981), 49-61.

79. Klaus Jorg Ruhl, "L'alliance à distance: les relations economiques germano-éspagnoles de 1936 à 1945," *Revue Histoire de la Deuxieme Guerre Mondiale*, (1980), 69-102.

80. Milward, *War*, XII.

81. Henry R. Barbera, *Rich Nations and Poor in Peace and War* (Lexington, 1973), 8.

82. H. Van der Wee, *Der gebremste Wohlstand. Wiederaufbau, Wachstum, Strukturwandel, 1945-1980* (München, 1984), 23.

83. C. Wright Mills, *The Causes of World War Three* (London, 1958), 85.

II. ARMY, ECONOMY, SOCIETY

FINANCING THE HUNGARIAN REARMAMENT

Lóránd Dombrády

The program of Hungarian rearmament proclaimed in Győr on March 5, 1938 made it possible to equip a combat-ready army capable of supporting the revisionist aspirations. The obstacle had been removed from the way of rearmament so far bridled under political and economic compulsion. As a result of these talks, during which the maximalist needs of the Hungarian military leadership had inevitably clashed with the financial reservations of the government, a credit of 1 billion pengős was placed at the disposal of the army. In light of the fact that the country's economy had significantly improved and the pressing need to modernize the army quickly, this credit was a meager offering. The Lower House hurriedly carried the bill on rearmament in April and the Upper House approved it in May. Act XX/1938 was announced on June 2nd. It entitled the government to issue a non-recurrent property tax of 600 million and a loan of 400 million, 600 million of which was to be spent directly on armaments and 400 million on investment indirectly improving the defenses of the country. The act authorized the finance minister to contract short-term loans to be paid back from long-term loans contracted under the act and to obtain newer short-term loans equivalent to temporarily repaid short-term debts from the state funds."[1] The finance minister got a free hand to execute the program planned for five years in a considerably shorter time than was needed.

The question arises why the 1 billion pengő program of deploying the so-called "Huba I" organizational plan met with the approval of the military top brass when the 600 million directly allocated to armaments was far from the 1.5 billion actually required by the organizational plan. One reason was that the army was forced to accept that in a situation of looming crisis the government did not want to burden the capital more heavily and was afraid of resorting to cruder methods of finances afflicting the masses. As Lajos Reményi-Schneller later said, they saw that the appropriation of 600 million was only the first step in this direction and "we were clear at that time that the program would have to be extended substantially."[2] Béla Imrédy himself remarked, "All our efforts focus on one thing: that the implementation of the program be as fast as possible under the circumstances and that the orders be issued as soon as possible."[3]

The other reason why the army rested content with the low sum was that the technical and economic elaboration of the plan was in an initial phase. The discussions held in February-March 1938 did not specifically outline the structural and hence the economic aspects of the future organizational plan; therefore, they only had some ideas about the type of resources to be obtained and the manner of acquisition and were poorly informed of the cost. Since by early 1938, the "Huba I" organizational plan was expected to be completed by 1941, the available financial resources seemed to be sufficient at the given pace.

It was vital for the rearmament program that the country's industry be adapted to war production quickly and smoothly. The main question was how to adjust all the existing economic factors to this goal immediately. The guiding principle, based on the German model was to utilize the military, economic and social factors with perfect organization, placing them in the service of war preparations. This would have included the technical conditions of the change-over to war economy, the preparation of the factories and machinery for war production in peace time, the stockpiling of necessary raw materials and having a sufficient number of technical experts and laborers at the ready. Such a comprehensive plan of mobilization should have rested on carefully deliberated political, military and economic considerations. An authoritative journal of industrial production noted:

> Industrial mobilization will not be as efficient as expected, unless the industrial management keeps a

> constant check on the technical productive capacity and level of productive processes in each war factory on the one hand and on the capability of the rest of factories to turn out finished and semi-finished goods and to deliver raw materials.[4]

Such preparations, however, were beyond the means of the Hungarian military leadership. In vain had they been urging for more intensive preparations, for a government policy based on increased state intervention to pave the way for war mobilization and for the relevant measures to be taken. This was a frequent point of contention between the military and civil leadership. Preparations went on very slowly, due to the political consternation, not to mention the poor economic conditions of the country. This was not what the high command needed.[5] The industry refused to make preliminary investment without the necessary backing by the state and without actual orders based on concrete plans for the development of the army. For want of the necessary financial means the state had no chance to take the required measures earlier. Consequently, when the program of 1 billion pengős was at last proclaimed, the military leaders took great pains to see such measures taken in a hurry to increase the influence of the government and the military management over the economy thereby mobilizing the industry and shifting it to war production. The Defense Act of March 1939 only summarized and sanctioned the wide variety of measures to create the possibility and the tools for effective state control over the economic and social life which led to the emergence of the war economy.

The acceleration of events brought the realization that the development program had to be extended and accelerated. The events of summer 1938 convinced the political and military leaders that the immediate set-up of an action-ready army brooked no delay. The outbreak of the war and the mounting tensions with Romania over Transylvania made it imperative to finish the program more quickly and extensively. This, in turn, required several times as much effort by the country as planned requiring the immediate expansion of industrial capacities, the boosting of raw material imports and the considerable increase of the credits for the investment program.

The need to increase capacities, however, met with mistrust in the middle and large-scale industries. The expansions that could not be financed by these industries without state aid created concern for management as new orders were not secured. On November 4, 1938, Manfréd Weiss' Factory sent a letter of concern to the Ministry of Industrial Affairs:

> Over the past weeks the Ministry of Defense has wished to accelerate the production of war materials to such an extraordinary extent that the manufacture of the quantities in question at the required pace needed the considerable extension of the workshops and facilities. After the termination of the present war preparations, probably in the near future, these costly investments would become redundant since the production at the regular pace of the products normally commissioned by the Ministry of Defense could be easily done with the existing machinery and the deadlines of orders related to the emergency situation never exceeded one year.[6]

Though the anxiety of the factory seemed exaggerated at the time, there is no doubt that the exhaustion of financial resources foreshadowed the decline.

Industrial investment showed considerable increase in 1939 due to the extension of the "Huba I" program in March 1939 and to commissions under the "Huba II" vehicle program aimed at modernizing the army. Twenty four new factories were founded and 411 workshops were extended into factories. In the new program, 6.6 million pengős was invested in new factories and extensions, but the existing factories invested a far more substantial sum of 315.5 million.[7] The investment of the Manfréd Weiss factory for military purposes was 6,197,000 pengős in 1938 and 16,166,000 pengős in 1939. Due to delay in placing the orders and external circumstances of production extensions still exceeded demand. Lajos Reményi-Schneller informed the Council of Ministers that he felt the additions to the cannon factory of the Hungarian Wagon Works under the program of forced extensions were in excess of realistic need. As the required types of guns diminished, the big commissions promised by the high command failed threatening the factory with bankruptcy.[8]

Prime Minister Pál Teleki and his government were gravely concerned about finding ways to keep up the favorable business cycle in the future. During the summer 1939, industrial production was up by 22% from the previous year and employment reached a record 769,000.[9] As its effect spread, the economic boom began to be felt in the light and consumer industries and even in agriculture. In the summer of 1939, the Institute for Economic Research assessed the future economic growth in the following way:

> The course of the business cycle will depend on whether the state keeps at the present level its spending on armaments and investments or not. This is possible from the technical viewpoint of the present technical capacity of industry whereas its further increase would encounter difficulties, for several branches are already working at full capacity and there is some shortage of skilled personnel. Naturally, the upkeep of the present level of state investment is not merely a question of the productive capacity of the industry, but also a financial problem.[10]

The leaders of industry, Teleki and many government members saw that the upswing of production would stop after the completion of the war orders, producing idle capacities and a decline in the business cycle. The question was how to keep the people at work and supply industry with state commissions not directly connected to war production. Already on May 7, 1939, Teleki touched upon this problem in Szeged in a speech on the need to re-arm the army. After the imminent termination of the rearmament program there was the danger of unemployment. The prime minister tried to reassure the public when he announced, "Preparatory work is going on in this regard and we shall know how to do the reorganization...." It would be possible "to turn out products that need many working hands."[11]

A columnist for *Honi Ipar* (Domestic Industry) also raised his voice against the increasing industrial capacity in his analysis in the summer of 1939:

> Some 40-50% of the public commissions at a value of 1 billion have already been completed. If the pace of upswing set by the state slows down, there will be decline in industrial production. Under these circumstances further investment would prove erroneous.[12]

At the same time, the military leadership and the political right entertained the goal of further increasing war production and adopting the policy of territorial increase beyond the Transylvanian revision. The escalation of war preparations encouraged these efforts.

While the development was going it, it was impossible to ignore the views about the "New Order" in Europe openly advocated by Germany which targeted a reduction of Hungarian industry and then integrating it into the German economy. In a memorandum sent to Joachim von Ribbentrop before the German-Hungarian economic negotiations in 1939, Embassy Counsellor Kurt Heinburg suggested that further intensification of ties be conditional upon "Hungary's capability to increase her agricultural production and her willingness to reduce her industry as required." According to this, "the agricultural produce needed by Germany would be increased" and "Hungary would stop with the considerably advanced industrialization, while in branches in which the independent Hungarian industry would hardly be viable, production must be gradually stopped so that Hungary's capacity to absorb German industrial products would increase."[13] Thus, the repeated talks ended with a complete fiasco and the military leaders had to content themselves with the purchase of outdated German weapons and vehicles. It became more difficult to acquire the spare parts, machine tools, semi-finished products and vital raw materials ordered from Germany which were indispensable for the production of Hungarian vehicles and weapons in Hungarian factories.

The acquisition of raw materials for the war industry and the accumulation of reserves were not insurmountable problems for Hungary's foreign trade until the end of 1940. Things changed for the worse from June 1940 when Italy entered the war. Overseas commerce was confined to Spanish and Portuguese harbors. To circumvent their trade difficulties, the Hungarian government strove to maintain its relations with the British who backed up the Hungarian economic contacts and helped transport overseas shipments despite the marine blockade in the hope of a political alliance. The only stipulation in this trade agreement was that raw materials of military importance should not be made available to the Germans. Teleki made a pledge to this effect, but upon learning about it, the Germans let him know that "they had the right for political and commercial reasons to expect that all possible export surplus on the continent would be offered to us first."[14] This policy statement practically blocked the channels of raw material imports.

As a result of the breakdown in the Hungarian-British Trade Agreement, the exports of Hungarian foreign trade dropped from 603.7 million in 1939 to 503.6 million in 1940. At the same time, the total of imports grew from 498.9 million to 597.7 million.[15] Imports exceeded exports, which caused a negative trade balance. The foreign trade deficit was due to the exceptionally poor harvest and to increasing raw material and manufactured goods imports. The various imported materials had to be paid for in hard currency, which largely exhausted the country's reserves. The most important raw material imports from overseas fell short of the imported quantity the previous year. Imports increased from the neighboring Balkan states, the Soviet Union, United States, Sweden and some South American states. Imports from Germany and Italy also increased slightly, but not in basic raw materials. Hungary's exports chiefly increased to the neighboring Balkan countries and neutral states where Hungarian businesses tried to place a modest amount of manufactured products as well, but the majority of exports were still delivered to Germany and Italy. Owing to the bad harvest in 1940, exports to Germany fell somewhat below the previous year's level. In 1939, 50.3% of total exports went to Germany, against 49.4% in 1940. In this year, the imports from Germany slightly exceeded German exports, but this did not change the heavy volume of German debt to Hungary. Hungarian industry was encouraged by the commercial and trade agreement concluded with the Soviet Union in September 1940 which included raw material imports and consumer goods exports. They set the value of mutual trade at 3.7 million dollars.[16] But the contract which was scheduled to take effect in January 1941 never materialized because of Hungary's participation in the war against the Soviet Union.

Raw materials were sufficient for the production of current orders, but insufficient for the stockpiling of necessary reserves for further development of the army. Reserves were hindered by the extension of the marine blockade from summer 1940, which led to the freezing of overseas transports. The problems of raw material management could not be solved by economizing or finding substitutes. The further development of the army's armored, motorized and flying troops met with difficulties that were hardly surmountable. Not only the raw material supply posed grave problems for industry. The problems of under-utilization of the increased industrial capacity began emerging in summer 1940. Until this point, war production had been meeting the requirements at the expected pace, with temporary setbacks by the difficulties of raw material supply.

National Industrial Production 1939-40 for the War by Industry Scale[17]

	Small-Scale Industry	Large-Scale Industry	Total
1939	4.4%	6.2%	5.7%
1940	3.2%	11.2%	9.1%

Despite the ominous signs, the industrial branches increased production, with the exception of the textile industry. Most conspicuous was the production growth of the iron and metal industry and machine production. Machine production increased from 19% in 1939 to 43% in 1940 due to the upswing of tank and motor vehicle production. In 1939, the branch had a share of 145 million, in 1940, 347.3 million totaling 492.3 million in two years out of the total war production of 787 million pengős in this period.[18] It should be noted, however, that the actual value of manufactured goods delivered by the industry to the army was higher because of the sums retained until the final settlement.

Though signs of decline began to multiply from mid-1940, 20 new factories and 194 factory extensions were built. Compared to 315.6 million pengős in 1939, a mere 161.3 million was spent on industrial investment.[19] The rentability of industrial production further deteriorated. The costs of production also increased which caused the slump in employment. The Hungarian industry employed 845,000 people in June and let 17,000 go in July. Due to price rises and the decline of employment real wages decreased which had a direct effect on living standards.

As expected, the acceleration of the rearmament program soon exceeded the original appropriation of 1 billion pengős. The 487.7 million pengős planned to be used until the end of 1940 did not even cover half of the necessary costs. Availing itself of the provisions in the Defense Act, the government drew credits from the National Bank and other banking institutions to satisfy the army's repeated demands to cover the military spending. The costs of the army's equipment were chiefly covered by the ever increasing investment credits. The growing costs of maintenance, operation and mobilization, as well as a considerable part of replacing the equipment used up on the front were paid from the credits allocated to the Ministry of Defense by the state budget and from mobilization credits.

The increase and acceleration of investments and the concomitant great demand for money resources took the Ministry of Finance by surprise as they were still working on the original programming of the credit operation. However, to satisfy the demands of the army to some extent, they immediately began issuing credits. By late October, they had transferred 162.8 million pengős to the costs of "Huba I." That meant far exceeding the 120 million pengős originally planned until the end of 1938. The events connected to the re-annexation of Upper Hungary gave a new impetus to armament, prompting an increased demand for funds by the Ministry of Defense. Since the extension of "Huba I" was necessary with new commissions to be issued, it became obvious that the credit of 600 million would not cover the costs. Using its powers bestowed upon it by the Defense Act, the government allocated new credits of 136.2 million, code-named "Jenő," to the military in September 1938.[20]

Soon the Ministry of Defense asked for a supplementary credit of 86.3 million pengős for the development, reorganization and replacement of used materials in connection with the re-annexation of Upper Hungary. On January 14, 1939, the Council of Ministers granted the required sum as a supplementary credit. Later it was decided that the money would be used as investment credit to subsidize the increasing expenditures in the "Huba" program. That increased the total of investment credit to 822.4 million pengős.[21] The high command deemed it necessary to expand "Huba I" by introducing the "Huba I/A" organizational plan on March 15, 1939 which increased the demand of the program to 837 million pengős. In the summer of 1939, new demand arose for credits. Bartha warned Teleki that the volume of ammunition produced from the credits so far was too small and only covered the starting requirement. Another investment loan was necessary for boosting active and reserve gun production. In September 1939, the government consented to an investment credit of 200 million pengős for the acquisition of guns.[22] Previously, in August 1939, the army had been granted an urgent credit of 107 million pengős for the increase of the effective force.[23]

As the issuance of credits increased, the Ministry of Finance put ever larger sums at the disposal of the army with increasing frequency from summer 1939. By the end of the year, 773 million pengős had been part of the "Huba" credits and 480 million had been paid in advance for finished goods. Payments of 80 million pengős had been effected out of the nearly completely tied 200 million pengős loaned for ammunitions.

With that the spending of investment credits came near to the original 600 million pengős.[24] The equipment and maintenance costs of the army was now like a bottomless pit. The top brass solicited the government for more credits. Without extending the program of armored and motor vehicles, the urgent development of the air force the combat-readiness and efficiency of the army could not be ensured and this in turn questioned the value of investments done so far. The failures caused by an ill-prepared army would also be blamed on the government. At the meeting of the Supreme Defense Council on December 19, 1939, the proposition about the further expansion of the "Huba" organizational plan jointly tabled by the chief-of-staff and the defense minister was thrashed out and approved. They asked for and were granted, another credit of 430 million pengős for the execution of another organizational plan code-named "Huba II". The new loan was planned to be used for the improvement of the air force, acquisition of tanks and for the building of the antitank and anti-aircraft defenses.

At the Council of Ministers on August 2, 1940, the defense minister was granted another credit of 196.8 million for additional war materials. He told the other ministers that "the analysis of war experiences show that more material would have to be acquired for the development of certain branches." The required sum was actually 300 million pengős, but "in view of the financial difficulties he revised the requirements and took only the most important materials into account."[25] Considering the difficulties, he asked for 116.5 million pengős of the required sum to be put at his disposal by the end of the year.

The high command was reluctant to agree to the compromise. This was the first time that the government refused to accede to the military's request. Though implicitly, they blamed it on the usual captiousness of the "civil" line that the reduction effected a loss of 1,500 trucks. Thus, a significant portion of the corps were not ready to march and they had to forget about armored vehicles in the same way. This was not a consequence of the reduction, but on the failure to realize the planned acquisition of armored vehicles from Germany. The only way then to acquire tanks was to produce them in Hungary, to which end the military asked for 74.8 million pengős in August 1940 which could not be declined. They were granted the "Turan" credit, the third investment loan within a year. These three investments credits were treated later collectively as the "Huba II" credit.[26]

War expenditures during 1940 saw additional financial outlays other than investment credit. To cover the costs of mobilization against Romania and of a possible Transylvanian operation, the army was loaned 310 million pengős for the raising of the effective force, immediately supplemented by an extra budgetary credit of 59.5 million pengős to make it 370 million pengős altogether.[27] In October 1940, credit was made available in the form of an investment, appropriating 26.5 million pengős for the equipment of the 9th Army Corps to be mobilized in Transylvania. This sum was complemented by another 58.5 million pengős in April 1941. The new loan was used as part of the "Huba II" credit.[28]

In 1940, expenses suddenly rose again. The Ministry of Finance had to resort to the treasury more frequently and generously. The war, the long mobilization and eventually the march into Transylvania further increased the expenditures already high due the frequent investment loans. By the end of 1940, the army's re-armament plan proclaimed in Győr had terminated and the extended version, "Huba I/A," had also been completed. With the peaceful resolution of the Transylvanian question, the forced rate of armament became unnecessary. After the expenses exceeding manifold the Ministry of Finance hoped to gain time to recoup from is monetary depletion. They believed that if they were to grant the "Huba II" credit for further modernization of the army to the end of 1942, they could reduce the state's indebtedness slowing down the inflationary process.

Utilization of Credit in 1940

	Total Credits (million pengős)	Credits Used (million pengős)[29]
Budgetary Credit	1,048.6	936.8
Credit to Increase the Effective Force	693.2	492.9

	Total Credits (million pengős)	Credits Used (million pengős)[29]
Investment Credit	1,780.9	1,059.3
Total	3,522.7	2,489.0

Military Spending and the National Income 1938-1940

Year	National Income	Military Spending	Percent for Military
1938-1939	5,192	791	15.2
1939-1940 (18 months)	9.311	1,689	18.2

The plan of 1 billion pengős projected the contracting of loans worth 400 million pengős. After the issuing of the first installment in July 1938, the second installment of 150 million pengős followed, with the third in January 1940 amounting to 141 million pengős. Under the pretext of exchange rate changes the state had 416 million pengős subscribed to instead of 400 million pengős. As this was still insufficient, the state raised different amounts of extraordinary loans with the banks. These were contracted against deficiency bills with an interest rate of 4% which the National Bank was willing to discount or advance against collateral security. This is how they tried to conceal that the bank of issue was meeting the need of the state through issuing bills. As a result, there was a currency expansion from 863.4 million pengős in 1938 to 1.3866 billion pengős in late 1940.[30]

Loans Contracted From 1938-40[31]

Name of Loan	Date of Issue	Amount of Pengős
Investment Loan of 1 billion	August 1938	125 million pengős
	May 1939	150 million pengős
	January 1940	141 million pengős
Sub-total		**416 million pengős**

Name of Loan	Date of Issue	Amount of Pengős
Advance Loan	July 1939	50 million pengős
	May 1940	150 million pengős
Sub-total		**200 million pengős**
Current Account Loan	April 1939	90 million pengős
Extraordinary Loan	August 1939	100 million pengős
	July 1940	180 million pengős
	September 1940	95 million pengős
Sub-total		**465 million pengős**
Total of Loans Contracted		**1.081 billion pengős**
Annual Distribution		1938 - 125 million pengős
		1939 - 390 million pengős
		1940 - 566 million pengős

With the issuance of these loans, the state's debt increased by leaps and bounds. At the close of the 1938-1939 fiscal year, the state's debt was 2.1316 billion pengős, rising by 1.2072 billion pengős to 3.3388 billion pengős by the end of 1940.[32] In spite of all this, the 1.081 billion pengős loan was not enough to cover the military costs even together with the 582 million pengős received from budgetary subsidies until the end of 1940. The missing millions had to be raised from taxes. As a result of tax rises in the fiscal year 1939-1940, the state had an increase of 689.142 billion pengős in tax revenues over the previous year's amount.

The government hoped that by re-annexing a part of Transylvania peacefully, it would get a chance to settle some of its re-armament debt. Concerns were increased when Northern Transylvania expressed the desire to remain economically integrated with Hungary. No acquisition of new territories could be expected in the near future. The imminence of entering the war, the increased commitment to the Germans and consequently, the jeopardizing of relations with the British were the most serious problems facing Teleki and the finance capitalists sharing his position. Under these circumstances, the government did not plan to put considerable amounts of investment credit at the army's disposal. This move enraged the army officers who thought the prime minister was aborting the war effort. Further German intentions of conquest were not doubted by the high command. In the fall of 1940, the high command expected that the Nazi war machine would turn against the Soviet Union. Hitler might not yet have been considering Hungary's participation in a military offensive against the Soviet Union, but the Hungarian military leaders thought about the possibility of Hungarian troops joining the conflict. It was their hope that by maximally supporting the Germans, they could join forces to further their territorial claims. These goals required the further development of the army.

Teleki's government had to make concessions. By joining the Axis and consenting to the transportation of German troops to Romania they managed to appease the high command and the political right, but this constituted a strengthened war commitment. The failure of Teleki's politics meant the success of Chief of Staff Henrik Werth's endeavors. The government could no longer refuse the development of the army. The mobilization of industry would mean maintaining orders for war materials and state commissions that would keep the workshops and machinery in operation. These facilities would have to be prepared to shift to war production, should there be an acceleration in the war effort.

The top brass emphatically described the need for army development. The experiences of the previous war had proven that the level of armament they had reached was below the requirements. Consequently, the originally planned development would have to be extended to a higher level. When detailing their demands, the high command proposed to the government that the deadline of orders to be delivered until the end of 1942 ("Huba II" credit) be shortened by a year. That would ensure productive capacity and the level of employment in iron and machine production. Immediate contacts should be made with Germany, offering them free industrial capacities that would earn their goodwill and readiness to support Hungary's war material and armaments production. Despite its intentions, the government's economic policy kept shifting gradually to a war economy which was favored by the military. As a concession to the military leadership and the political right, the government appointed Lajos Reményi-Schneller as a prominent leader of the Hungarian economy.

The next phase of development would be the "Huba III" organizational plan to be processed by March 1, 1942. Preparations had to be made as soon as possible since "Huba III" laid the foundation for the development of armored troops and the air force which were highly material intensive.[33] With Prime Minister Teleki's suicide and the ascendancy of Werth's military leadership brought about Hungary's entrance into the war. The declaration of war on Yugoslavia and Hungary's decision to join the ongoing German offensive against the Soviet Union seemed to realize the plans of the military leaders. The increased military expenditures in 1941 and the 18.2% share of war production of the national produce clearly show the economic impact of Hungary's entry into the war.

After the failure of the *blitzkrieg* against the Soviet Union and the dismissal of Werth, a new line of military policy gained prominence. The General Staff Chief Colonel-General Ferenc Szombathelyi set the goal of preserving the existing forces, in compliance with the government's political ideas. This goal was timely when the Second Hungarian Army and two-thirds of the total armaments had been lost at the front. In 1943, the Hungarian government tried but failed to pull out of the war with the help of the British. The Hungarian leaders rejected the opposition to the Germans as the precondition of a truce and refused to cooperate with the Soviets. In this political impasse, the Hungarian government and military leaders tried to make efforts beyond the country's means to develop the army, to replace its losses and improve its efficiency. This required the growth of Hungarian war production to such an extent that between 1942-43, it could not yield the expected results.

In addition to increasing the productive capacity of each workshop, the Ministry of Defense tried to involve all small and medium-sized factories in war production. The list of war factories made in the mobilization year of 1942-1943 included 1,370 war factories. For 1942 and 1943 it is impossible to establish the war industry's share of the total industrial production. However, the value of total industrial production was 7.4324 billion pengős in 1942 and 10.1705 billion pengős in 1943.[34] The growth of production value affected all the industrial branches involved in war production except for timber and building industry, where production dropped over the two years. The percentage growth of production value at current prices gives the following figures:

Production Growth (1941-1943)[35]

Year	Production Value (million pengős)	Percentage of Increase
1941	5,607.1	---
1942	7,432.3	32.5
1943	10,170.5	36.8

Based on the available data in stands to reason that there was a conscious delay by the treasury in making defense payments to industry. War materials completed and delivered one year were paid much later, if at all. At the same time, the price rises were not incorporated in war industrial payments, since the Ministry of Defense tried to yield as little as possible to industry demands. Fortunate for the government, the delay in executing the previous orders there was no need for a significant monetary advance in the first quarter of 1944. Another favorable sign was that the factories were content with a small interest charge on the initial sum to avoid lengthy bargaining. All in all, 80% of total industrial production for the army between 1942-43 was covered by military expenditures affected from early 1942 to the end of March 1944.

It was easier to asses the investment credits and the "Partial Mobilization" loans whose percentage used for war materials can be established with relative accuracy from the lists of items and payments. It was more difficult to count with the value of such items not included in the defense credits as the value of wage labor for Germany as well as the machines and spare parts produced and delivered under the joint aircraft production program. These were subsidized by the state so they weren't included in the Ministry of Defense credits.

Industrial War Expenditures During 1942 and 1943 (in million pengős)

Payments	1942	1943*	Total
On Investments	429	1,169	1,598
On Partial Mobilization Credits	300	820	1,120
On German Wage Labor	200	400	600
German Share of Joint Aircraft Production	---	70	70
On Armaments from the Ministry of Defense's Budget	150	170	320
Totals	**1,079**	**2,629**	**3,708**

* Including transfers of 509 million pengős until April 1944.

The payments made by the Ministry of Defense to the industry only approximates the value produced by the war industry. In 1942, it was 14.5% of total industrial output, rising to 25.8% in 1943. The figure for 1943 seems excessive compared to the year before, since the production value shown for 1942 does not include the output of the last quarter. Thus, the share of the war industrial potential in the entire industrial production was larger due to the delayed payments than is expressed by the registered production value. This share reached 21% in 1942, up from 18.2% in 1941. In 1943, during the peak year of war production, value was around 30%. The boom of war industry from 1941 was caused first of all by orders for armored and motor vehicles, aircraft and cannons, with considerable orders for infantry weapons. This could only be carried out through the expansion of existing productive capacity and that in turn required new investments.

The state was not short of money having borrowed from the Hungarian National Bank and other financial institutions. In turn, the largest factories including the Manfréd Weiss Győr Wagon Factory, MÁVAG, Ganz, and Láng were granted 31.3 million and 62 million pengős government loans for the increase of their capacities to produce motor vehicles and aircraft. In consultation with the factories, the ministries of defense and industry drew up plans for factory expansion and set quotas for the production of aircraft, motor vehicles and guns within a specified time frame. In 1942, 100 million pengős of central credit was made available for this purpose, raised to 236 million pengős in 1943. This does not include the extensions made by the factories from loans they had raised themselves especially in late 1940, e. g. the Danube Aircraft Factory founded for joint Hungarian-German aircraft production by Manfréd Weiss and the Hungarian Credit Bank with a capital stock of 600 million pengős.

As a result of the central credits flowing into industry significant extensions were made. The substantial growth is also attested by the rise in the average annual labor force and the number of workdays and working hours.[36]

Labor Statistics (1941-1943)

Year	Average Labor Force	Number of Workdays	Work Hours
1941	405,126	116,531.022	973,692.840
1942	454,635	130,443.787	1,128,277.131
1943	666,077	133,883.654	1,182,135.527

The growth of production can also be monitored by the rise in the efficiency of power machines.[37]

Power Machine Production and Efficiency (1941-43)

Year	Power Machines	Efficiency of Power Machines	Total Horse Power
1941	1,192,703	803,176.8	1,995,979.8
1942	1,195,875	868,115.5	2,063,991.5
1943	1,532,000	1,042,000.0	2,574,000.0

This boom reflected in the rise of war industrial production, but the quantity of produced goods did not meet the Ministry of Defense's time and volume expectations.

Machine Imports (in billion pengős)[38]

	1941	1942	1943	1944
Imports	91.7	113.3	141.8	101.6

The utilization of credit and the acquisition of various machinery became increasingly difficult. The following table shows the distribution of machinery imports among the groups of products most important for the war industry (per 100 kilogram weight):[39]

Machine Imports According to Products

	1941	1942	1943	1944
Metallurgical Machines	12,359	11,654	14,596	7,828
Instruments	2,751	2,922	2,860	1,717
Bearings	5,947	7,286	6,534	1,175
Steam and Combustion Engines	4,820	6,863	8,421	7,620
Electric Motors	11,117	10,340	13,180	12,137
Automobiles and Parts	27,405	18,461	20,782	12,666

The hopes of the military leadership for a production growth based on expansions did not come true. The factories, however, were not to blame. Their expansion plans were in accord with the orders received from the army and with those the army had anticipated to issue. They had ordered the necessary machinery and materials. The implementation, however, fell far below the expectations. The German and even the Swedish and Swiss partners were reluctant to accept the bulk of the orders and the ones they accepted were delivered at a delay of several months or not at all. There were products that no foreign contract could be found for. Germany, which was interested in a part of the orders, delivered most inaccurately. Struggling against increasing difficulties, the Germans could not have satisfied the Hungarian demands even if they had wanted to. Their shipments were principally meant to support the joint aircraft production, with decreasing effectiveness.

A significant hindrance to production growth was the labor shortage. Skilled workers and semi-skilled machine operators were in demand, but the draining effect of agriculture produced constant shortage among unskilled workers as well. The production of tanks, vehicles and aircraft suffered tremendous shortages of skilled labor so that only 75% of machine tools and other equipment could be utilized in the second shift and only 40% in the third shift. Simply put, the plan to increase Hungary's industrial capacity was unrealistic. Consequently, expectations for the quantitative and qualitative improvement of military equipment did not materialize.

Supplying the war industry with increasing amounts of raw materials proved a great burden to the Hungarian government from 1942. The stockpiled reserves were depleted and their replacements were not available in many areas. Raw material imports became increasingly uncertain because of Hungary's dependence on German exports. Germany would not exchange Hungary's natural resources of bauxite, oil, manganese, foodstuffs for materials in short supply since Germany lacked a sufficient supply as well. At the same time, Germany exploited Hungarian resources with threats and blackmail.[40]

Given the economic situation, the minister of industry could only recommend increased production to which he said, "new resources have to be explored and synthetic and substitute materials produced." In the period of 1941-44, the government tried to satisfy the demands of the army, by exploiting the financial resources of the country through increased credits and taxes to the verge of total economic bankruptcy. As a result, the budgetary, mobilization and investment credits soared. The difficulties of industry, however, did not allow for the necessary improvement of production and the desired development in the military so the funds could not be used effectively. Thus, only 56.5% of the credits granted to the army were utilized. It stands to reason that the army was never short of credits. The credits could not be put to use effectively.

Despite the partial advances in industrial development, the Hungarian military leadership failed to accomplish its plans for rearmament. The Hungarian leadership assumed fundamental expectations that were beyond its reach and the country's economic potential.

Summary of Credits from January 1938 to November 1, 1944 (in million pengős):[41]

Budgetary Credits

	Available Credits	Used Credits
1938-1939	316.0	258.5
1939-1940	732.6	678.3
1941	641.8	541.2
1942	794.5	748.6
1943	1,136.2	1,047.1
1944	2,033.6	1,134.0
Total	**5,654.9**	**4,408.7**

Credits to Increase the Effective Force

	Available Credits	Used Credits
Autumn 1938	102.7	102.7
Spring 1939	43.3	43.3
Summer 1939	107.0	107.0
Spring 1940	59.5	59.5
Summer 1940	310.7	205.1
Total	**623.2**	**517.7**

Credits for Partial Mobilization

	Available Credits	Used Credits
1941	454.9	147.0
1942	1,728.1	738.3
1943	2,397.0	1,502.2
1944	2,470.2	1,394.8
Total	**7,051**	**3,782.3**

Investment Credits

	Available Credits	Used Credits
Huba I	822.4	814.5
Huba II	700.0	650.5
Transylvania I	58.5	58.5
Transylvania II	26.4	26.4
Munitions	200.0	197.7
Huba III	1,549.6	1,525.0
Huba II Supply	1,617.7	464.5
Szabolcs	2,890.8	90.0
Total	7,865.4	3,827.3
Overcharge Subsidies	990.0	
Total	**8,855.4**	**3,827.3**
Grand Total	**22,184.5**	**12,536.0**

Notes

1. *Magyar Törvénytár* [Hungarian Code of Laws] (Budapest, 1939), 250-251.
2. *Képviselőházi* Napló [Parliamentary Records], October 22, 1940, Session 144.
3. *Függetlenség*, March 23, 1938.
4. *Honi Ipar*, 1942/7, 7.
5. Archives of the Institute of Military History, Eln. Vkf.1. 1938/2238.
6. Hungarian National Archives, Manfréd Weiss Papers, Z. 402/96.
7. *Magyar Statisztikai Szemle*, 1941/9, 621.
8. Hungarian National Archives, Council of Ministers Records, October 20, 1943.
9. Magyar Gazdaságkutató Intézet [Institute for Hungarian Economic Research], 1939/43, 18.
10. *Ibid.*, 1939/2, 19.
11. *Függetlenség*, May 9, 1939.
12. *Honi Ipar*, 1939/15, 16.
13. György Ránki, *et al.*, ed., *A Wilhelmstrasse és Magyarország* [Wilhelmstrasse and Hungary] (Budapest, 1968), 338.
14. *Ibid.*, 483.
15. Béla Katona, *Magyarország közgazdasága 1940* [The Economy of Hungary] (Budapest, 1941), 490.
16. *Ibid.*, 504.
17. Archives of War History, HM Eln. 6.k. 1942/14853.
18. *Ibid.*
19. *Magyar Statisztikai Szemle*, 1941/9, 620.
20. Archives of War History, HM Eln. III. Csfség. 1938/968/Bbk.
21. Archives of War History, HM Eln. 6.k. 1941/77714.
22. Hungarian National Archives, Council of Ministers records, November 30, 1943.
23. *Ibid.*
24. Archives of War History, HM Eln. 6.k. 1939/1449/Bbk.
25. Hungarian National Archives, Council of Ministers Records, August 2, 1940.
26. Archives of War History, HM Eln. 6.k. 1940/46263.

27. Archives of War History, HM Eln. 6.k. 1941/46486.
28. Archives of War History, HM Eln. 6.k. 1941/2284.
29. On the basis of the monthly bulletins by the finance minister as well as the relevant documents of the III. Csfség, 6.k. and other departments of the Ministry of Defense.
30. *Magyar Statisztikai Zsebkönyv* [Pocketbook of Hungarian Statistics] (Budapest, 1941).
31. Hungarian National Archives, Council of Ministers Records for 1939-40.
32. Hungarian National Archives, Council of Ministers Records, February 7, 1941.
33. Archives of War History, HM Eln. III. Csfség. 1941/604.
34. On the basis of data in the Hungarian Statistical Yearbooks 1941-43, *Magyar Statisztikai Szemle 1942-43* and material from the Financial-Material Department of the Ministry of Defense.
35. *Ibid.*
36. *Ibid.*
37. *Ibid.*
38. András Nagy, *Magyarország külkereskedelme a második világháborúban* [Hungary's Foreign Trade in World War II] (Budapest, 1961), 205.
39. *Ibid.*, 204.
40. *Magyar Statisztikai Zsebkönyv* [Pocketbook of Hungarian Statistics] (Budapest, 1948).
41. The statistics were based on the monthly reports of the finance minister to the council of ministers as well as on the documents of III. Csfség. and 6.k. of the Ministry of Defense.

THE COMPOSITION OF THE HIGHER MILITARY ELITE

Sándor Szakály

The history of Hungary during the period between 1919 and 1944 has been attracting increasing attention. In particular, there is marked interest in the events of World War II and in Hungary's participation in the war. Though several important questions have been answered by the authors of books discussing Hungary's performance in the war, there are still many essential issues left unresolved. The role of the military elite during this period is one such issue.[1] In most cases, we rest content with simplified statements claiming that the majority of the generals and the staff officers were of German (Swabian) origin who betrayed their country, with the exception of a few patriotic Hungarians.[2]

To this day, there has been only one work, Lajos Mikics' *Politika, uriság és becsület Horthy tisztikarában* [Politics, Breed and Honor in Horthy's Staff of Officers] (Budapest 1981), which addresses the social composition and motivation of the officers of Horthy's army. This paper will outline the social, political and military portrait of the colonel-generals at the apex of military leadership.[3] It will also explore the social base, roots and character of the Horthy regime. The findings presented are the result of archival research spanning the period between November 2, 1938 (the day of the first Vienna Award) and April 4, 1945 (Hungary's Liberation Day).[4] The 35 people involved in the survey constituted the Hungarian army elite during World War II.

The criteria for this sampling were officers with the rank of colonel-general or greater that exhibited military or political activity. Three people — Gábor Faraghó, Jenő Ruszkay and

Döme Sztójay were not included in the sample.[5] More than twenty aspects have been examined, subsumed under four major categories. The aspects selected for investigation are sufficient to present a realistic picture of the top military brass. One aspect not included in this study is an analysis of nationality. This aspect was excluded because all 35 people declared that their nationality and mother tongue was Hungarian. Facts fail to verify the view based on the names which claimed that a general or officer bearing an apparently German name was "Swabian" or "ethnic German" and consequently pro-German, while those with Hungarian or Slavic names were pro-Hungarian.[6] This position is particularly untenable since the researchers did not extend their investigations to the mother's or grandparents' names.

The traditional German orientation of the Dual Monarchy, the Austro-Hungarian-German alliance in World War I, the German support for Hungary's revisionism, the quick successes of the Germans in World War II and affiliations with the national socialist ideas had a significant impact on many of the generals and officers who served at that time and were reinforced by pro-German sentiments in most of the generals and officers. This does not contradict the fact that there might have been some officers and generals who were of Swabian origin. Hungarian nationality of a person, however, is not determined by lineage and the sound of his name, but by his actions. The famous 20th century Hungarian writer, Gyula Illyés wrote,

> To me a Hungarian is one who cannot tolerate obscurity, either in prison or in thought. A Hungarian is one who likes reason, who gives vent to his passions only when the word has failed to get justice accepted. All peoples are communities. A good Hungarian is a humane and good member of the Hungarian community.[7]

After this brief introduction, let us take a look at the data, realizing that all the aspects of investigation were not given the same weight. For instance, I ascribe less importance to religion than to birth place or father's occupation. The honorific title, "vitéz," and the title of nobility were purposely indicated after the appropriate names. In most cases, the acquisition of the title vitéz given to World War I veterans who showed valor in battle entailed the Magyarization of the family name. Other variables include place and date of birth and religion.

Members of the Military Elite Analyzed In This Study

Name	Place of Birth	Date of Birth	Religion
József Bajnóczy, vitéz	Szinérváralja (Seini)	02/27/1888	Calvinist
Károly Bartha, vitéz squire	Budapest	06/18/1884	Roman Catholic
Alajos Béldy, vitéz	Budapest	07/08/1889	Roman Catholic
Károly Beregfy	Cservenka (Crvenka)	02/12/1888	Lutheran
Lajos Csatay, squire	Arad	08/01/1886	Lutheran
Zoltán Decleva	Alsószemeréd (Dolné Semerovce)	07/30/1887	Roman Catholic
Gusztáv Denk, vitéz squire	Nagyszeben (Sibiu)	03/18/1882	Roman Catholic
Ferenc Farkas, vitéz squire	Kismarton (Eisenstadt)	05/27/1892	Roman Catholic
Ferenc Feketehalmy-Czeydner, vitéz	Piski (Simeria Veche)	11/22/1890	Lutheran
Elemér Gorondy-Novák	Budapest	02/23/1885	Greek Catholic
Sándor Győrffy-Bengyel	Budapest	02/15/1886	Roman Catholic
Gusztáv Hennyey, vitéz	Kolozsvár (Cluj)	09/25/1888	Lutheran
József Heszlényi	Igló (Spišská Nove Ves)	07/24/1890	Roman Catholic
István Hindy, vitéz squire	Budapest	06/28/1890	Roman Catholic
Gusztáv Jány, vitéz	Rajka	10/21/1883	Lutheran
Emil Justy, vitéz squire	Dvenkova	03/14/1890	Roman Catholic
Lajos Keresztes-Fischer, vitéz	Pécs	01/18/1884	Roman Catholic
Géza Lakatos, vitéz squire	Budapest	04/30/1890	Roman Catholic
Dezső László, vitéz	Lovászpatona	07/23/1893	Lutheran
András Littay, vitéz	Szabadka (Subotica)	08/15/1884	Roman Catholic
Sándor Magyarosy, vitéz	Óbecse (Stari Bečej)	10/13/1891	Roman Catholic
Jenő Major, vitéz	Baksa	08/06/1891	Roman Catholic
Béla Miklós, vitéz lófő	Budapest	07/11/1891	Calvinist
István Náday, vitéz	Nagymihály	06/20/1888	Roman Catholic
Vilmos Nagy, vitéz lófő	Parajd (Praid)	05/30/1884	Calvinist
Jenő Rátz, vitéz	Nagybecskerek (Veliki Bečkerek)	09/20/1882	Roman Catholic

Name	Place of Birth	Date of Birth	Religion
Imre Ruszkiczay-Rüdiger	Vaşcău	11/20/1889	Roman Catholic
Szilárd Schindler	Körmöcbánya (Kremnica)	07/24/1887	Lutheran
István Schweitzer	Németszentpéter (Sînpetru German)	12/25/1887	Roman Catholic
Hugó Sónyi, vitéz	Wölkersdorf	03/02/1883	Roman Catholic
Ferenc Szombathelyi, vitéz	Győr	05/17/1887	Roman Catholic
Kálmán Ternegg	Tát	09/14/1887	Roman Catholic
Lajos Veress (Dálnoki)	Sepsiszentgyörgy (Sfîntu Gheorghe)	10/04/1889	Calvinist
János Vörös, vitéz squire	Csabrendek	03/23/1891	Roman Catholic
Henrik Werth	Rezsőháza (Knićanin)	12/26/1881	Roman Catholic

The previous list reveals that of the 23 of the 35 subjects in the sample or 65.71% had the title "vitéz" and 18 (51.43%) changed their names. 16 of these (45.71%) received new names while 2 (5.71%) had permission to change the spelling of their names. In the next chart, the colonel-generals are analyzed by their year of birth, how many were born in the same year, the year they were appointed colonel-general and if they were appointed by Ferenc Szálasi during his short-lived fascist dictatorship (October 1944-March 1945).

Colonel-Generals According to Year of Birth and Year of Appointment

Year of Birth	Number Commissioned	Year Appointed to Elite Position	Note
1881	1	1 in 1938	—
1882	2	2 in 1938	—
1883	2	1 in 1938	—
		1 in 1941	—
1884	4	1 in 1936	—
		3 in 1940	—
1885	1	1 in 1941	—

Year of Birth	Number Commissioned	Year Appointed to Elite Position	Note
1886	2	1 in 1941	—
		1 in 1943	—
1887	5	1 in 1941	—
		3 in 1943	—
		1 in 1944	appointed by Szálasi
1888	4	2 in 1942	—
		2 in 1944	—
1889	3	1 in 1943	—
		2 in 1944	—
1890	6	2 in 1943	—
		3 in 1944	—
		1 in 1945	appointed by Szálasi
1891	3	3 in 1944	2 appointed by Szálasi
1892	1	1 in 1944	appointed by Szálasi
1893	1	1 in 1944	appointed by Szálasi

The table shows that the birth dates of the 35 people fall within thirteen years. Over fifty percent of the subjects were born between 1884-1890. The explanation is simple. Most of the generals born in earlier years were retired whereas the younger generals had not yet reached the age and years of service required for promotion. Those born between 1881 and 1884, with the exception of Gusztáv Jány, were colonel-generals by 1940. The following chart provides a breakdown of the sample according to religious affiliation with a comparison to the national percentages.

Religious Affiliation of the Military Elite and the Hungarian Population

Religion	No.	Percent in Military Elite	National Percentage Rates in 1910	in 1941
Roman Catholic	23	65.7	49.3	52.8
Lutheran	7	20.0	7.1	5.5
Calvinist	4	11.4	14.3	19.7
Uniate	1	2.9	9.7	11.9

This comparison shows that the number of Roman Catholics and Lutherans is much higher than the respective national rates. It would stand to reason that Horthy's Calvinist affiliation did not significantly affect his elite officer selection. Although 3.5% of the population was Uniate in 1941, there was only one Uniate representative among these officers. Even though 6.2% of the population was Jewish there were no Jewish officers of higher ranks, since the anti-Jewish laws were in effect during this time. By 1942, most of the Jewish officers and those who had Jewish relatives had retired from the Honvéd army. It should be noted that the majority of the army's Jewish officers and generals had converted to Christianity earlier. General Márton Zöld of Sióagárd was an exception. He maintained his Jewish identity.

The family background, indicated by the father's occupation, was decisive for our sample's future course of life:

Father's Occupation of the Colonel-Generals

Engineer 4	Army Officer 2	Restaurateur 2
Shoemaker 2	Retail Merchant 2	Court Clerk 1
Railways Supervisor 2	Physician 1	Estate Bailiff 1
Municipal Prosecutor 2	Blacksmith 1	Bank Clerk 1
Corporate Lawyer 2	Small Holder 1	Vine Grower 1
County Treasurer 1	Museum Director 1	School Teacher 1
Primary School Teacher 2	Town Clerk 1	Mine Official 1
Steamship Line Agent 1	No Data 3	

This breakdown demonstrates the Hungarian Honvéd army elite involved in World War II included members of the *petit bourgeoisie*, the intelligentsia and clerical families at the lower fringes of the middle strata.[8] There is no representation of the ruling agricultural (landowning) aristocracy, the families of industrial and financial magnates, nor from the working class. Only one of the colonel-generals had a peasant upbringing.[9] The data reveals that 3 families owned property and 25 families did not.

The income of fathers around the turn of the century was around 1,500-4,500 crowns a year. For most families, this income was apparently too little to have the children educated in secondary schools and in institutions of higher learning. That would explain why the *petit bourgeoisie* and middle strata attended military schools since these schools were financed by foundations or by the state. At the beginning of the century the annual tuition fee at the Honvéd Academy of Sopron was 400 crowns. Since the average annual income of *petit bourgeoisie* and lower middle-class intellectual families with 3-5 children was 2,500-3,000 crowns, without financial assistance, they could not have afforded that education. We will now analyze the size of families. Exact data is available in 26 cases:

Children in the Colonel-Generals' Family

Number of Children in the Family	Number of Family Cases
2 children	6 cases
3 children	4 cases
4 children	7 cases
5 children	3 cases
6 children	2 cases
8 children	3 cases
9 children	1 case

Five elite officers in the sample (14.29%) were fatherless when they studied in military school. These five families were dependent on the deceased father's meager pensions and the goodwill of the guardians for subsistence and education subsidies. The data suggests that emphasis was placed on securing an application at a military school where students only required 24-36 crowns annually for "pocket money."

It is also revealing to know what were the professions of the sisters and brothers of the officers in our sample. In 18 cases, the sibling's profession was provided: 8 were army officers, 3 were primary school teachers, 1 was a lawyer, 5 were college students (3 of the 5 were law students) and 1 was a pharmaceutical auditor. From 1902 to 1910, several sisters and brothers of the elite officers were still in secondary school. The husbands of sisters were usually teachers, lawyers, clerks, county officials.

The following table shows the distribution of the 35 people by place of birth, taking into consideration that sovereignty over these places changed after World War I:

Birthplace of the Colonel-Generals

Place of Birth	Number of Officers
In pre-World War I Hungary	33
In pre-World War I Austria	2
In post-Trianon Hungary	14
In post-Trianon Romania	9
In post-Trianon Yugoslavia	5
In post-Trianon Czechoslovakia	4
In post-Trianon Austria	1

It is clear from the table that only 40% of the highest military leaders were born in territory which remained part of Hungary, 54.29% coming from the areas which were ceded to Hungary's neighbors in the Trianon Peace Treaty of 1920. This rate applies to the staff of officers and generals. This is part of the reason why the army supported and even urged for, a revisionist policy. Had the birth place of parents or grandparents been included in the investigation, the balance would even more heavily tilt in favor of the areas that were not annexed.

An important career determination factor in our sample was their schooling. There is little information available on students who enrolled in general (civilian) schools, whereas the data for students attending military schools were more complete. Since only the first four years of the eight-year secondary school had to be completed to gain admission into the cadet schools, it is enough to note that only 9 of the 35 finished secondary school (25.71%), the other 26 (74.29%) decided to enlist in the army between the ages of 10-14.

Military Schools Attended by the Military Elite

Type of School	Number
Hungarian Honvéd Cadet School	4
Imperial and Cadet School	7
Hungarian (Ludovika) Military Academy	13
Imperial and Military Academy	11
Total	**35**

General Staff College or equivalent	Number
General Staff College (Wien) Before 1915	13
Staff Academy (Budapest) After 1920	17
Higher Training Course for Gunnery Officers and Staff Engineers (Wien) Before 1915	3
Did not attend staff training	2
Total	**35**

Before analyzing the military career of the Hungarian elite, it would seem that a grasp of foreign languages could prove very useful in later military service. The findings are extraordinarily useful in this regard. We have exact information in 29 cases, most of it showing the degree of language competence as well.

Language Skills of the Military Elite

Language	Degree of Knowledge				
	Perfect	Fair	Poor	No Proficiency	Total
German	34	1	---	---	35
French	8	7	6	3	24
English	3	3	2	2	10
Italian	1	3	1	3	8
Romanian	1	1	5	---	7
Serbian	---	1	4	---	5
Croatian	---	---	---	---	3
Russian	---	---	---	1	3
Slovakian	---	---	---	---	3
Czech	---	---	---	2	2
Polish	---	---	---	---	1

Language Knowledge Summary

Languages Known	Number of Officers
6 Languages	1
5 Languages	4
4 Languages	9
3 Languages	7
2 Languages	8
1 Language	6

Since in six cases only the graduation from the military school alluded to the knowledge of a certain language, it cannot be precluded that these six people also knew other foreign languages besides German. It is noteworthy to see how little they knew the languages of the neighboring peoples. In the Austro-Hungarian army the official language was German while in the Hungarian Honvéd army the language of command was Hungarian and Croatian. Thus, the knowledge of these languages made communication possible throughout the dual monarchy. In the 1920s, there was some modification in the army's language requirements. Young staff officers had to learn the language of one of the neighboring countries belonging to the Little Entente, so the army's need for the Romanian, Czech, Slovakian and Serbo-Croatian languages would be satisfied.

The breakdown of the sample by branch of service shows that 21 (80%) of the colonel-generals came from the infantry, 8 (22.86%) from the artillery, 4 (11.43%) from the cavalry and 2 (5.71%) from engineering.[10] As can be seen, the largest number of colonel-generals came from the infantry while the elite cavalry (Hussars) only had four promoted to the rank of colonel-general. These rates approximately coincide with the percentage breakdowns within the monarchy's army and later in the Hungarian territorial Honvéd army.

Another important military aspect is how many rendered "staff service" and how many were staff officers before being promoted to the rank of general. The figures are as follows: 33 (94.29%) were officers on the general staff and 2 (5.71%) were combat officers. Except in the period of the Hungarian fascist rule, the highest military rank could not be reached without staff training and service.[11] Without general staff training the highest ranking officer was the general, or exceptionally the lieutenant-general. Of the officers from the pre-1918 Hungarian Honvéd army and the Austro-Hungarian armed forces who continued their army career during the Horthy era, 10 of the officers (28.57%) served only in the joint army and another 10 served in both.

A highly important and intriguing aspect is the participation of the colonel-generals of World War II in the armies of the post-1918 revolutionary and counter-revolutionary movements.

Elite Officers Who Served in the Red Army of the Hungarian Soviet Republic (March 21-August 1, 1919)

18 of the colonel-generals (51.4%) took part:

József Bajnóczy	Károly Bartha	Alajos Béldy
Károly Beregfy	Lajos Csatay	Gusztáv Jány
Gusztáv Hennyey	Géza Lakatos	András Littay
Béla Miklós	István Náday	Vilmos Nagy
Elemér Gorondy-Novák	Hugó Sónyi	János Vörös
Ferenc Szombathelyi	Sándor Győrffy-Bengyel	Henrik Werth

4 of the colonel-generals did not serve in the Red Army:[12]

Imre Ruszkiczay-Rüdiger	Lajos Keresztes-Fischer
Gusztáv Denk	Zoltán Decleva

In Horthy's National Army, three officers were involved from its inception (June 6, 1919) in Szeged to the fall of the Hungarian Soviet Republic:

Zoltán Decleva
Gusztáv Denk
Lajos Keresztes-Fischer

19 officers (54.3%) did not serve in Horthy's National Army from its beginning to the end:[13]

József Bajnóczy	Károly Bartha	Alajos Béldy
Károly Beregfy	Lajos Csatay	András Littay
Hugó Sónyi	István Náday	Béla Miklós
Henrik Werth	Sándor Győrffy-Bengyel	János Vörös
Vilmos Nagy	Ferenc Szombathelyi	Géza Lakatos
Gusztáv Hennyey	Imre Ruszkiczay-Rüdiger	Gusztáv Jány
	Elemér Gorondy-Novák	

There is no data available on the following 13 military elite officers (37.1%) to indicate in which army they served between March 21 and August 1, 1919.[14]

Ferenc Farkas	Lajos Veress	József Heszlényi
István Hindy	Emil Justy	Dezső László
Sándor Magyarosy	Jenő Major	Jenő Rátz
Szilárd Schindler	István Schweitzer	Kálmán Ternegg

Ferenc Feketehalmy-Czeydner

Although these facts are thought-provoking, it is not conclusive that the revolutionary zeal of these staff and field officers led them to the Red Army. Rather, we should consider that:

1. Both the military and the political leadership of the country pledged to defend the integrity of the country. These young officers embraced this view since their majority originated from areas later annexed to Romania, Yugoslavia and Czechoslovakia.

2. There was a possibility of a meteoric rise in the ranks since the Liberal Government pensioned off the generals and most of the colonels by January 1, 1919. Thus, the young officers were promoted to ranks, that under customary circumstances, could have reached in a longer period of time.[15]

3. Personal problems of subsistence: When the officers who had served in the Red Army were later questioned by the counter-revolutionary screening committees, this was the reason given by most of the officers. Incidentally, this explanation was almost always accepted.

   There were, however, officers like Sándor Bengyel (later Győrffy-Bengyel) who had been a member of the Communist Party and did not wish to serve in the National Army.

4. The success of Aurél Stromfeld, commander of the Red Army, in attracting former officers of the defunct Austro-Hungarian monarchy.

Looking at the 18:3 ratio of the officers in the Red Army and those in the National army, one is astonished to find the great disparity. A detailed analysis of the National Army and its drafts would reveal that most of those "starting from Szeged" were not professional officers, but reservists. Yet, the profile of an army is molded by the professional officers and not the reserves.

It would seem that the counter-revolutionary Hungarians overlooked the communist service of the officers, allowing them to continue pursuing their military careers. This does not mean that officers with a communist past did not pose minor problems for them and the military and political leaders who wanted to set up a unified general staff for the army. Within a short time, the Honvéd army had its homogeneous staff incorporating officers with varied political backgrounds. Since this survey concerns those generals of the army who reached the highest rank, its of interest to see how many of them filled major military posts.

Major Posts of the Military Elite

6 (17.14%)	defense major, commander-in-chief of the Honvéd army and aide-de-camp to the Honvéd army's chief of staff
4 (11.23%)	chief of the regent's military office
20 (57.14%)	lecturer at Ludovika Academy and General Staff College
23 (65.71%)	head of department at Ministry of Defense and the General Staff
22 (62.86%)	head of group at Ministry of Defense and General Staff
24 (68.57%)	commander of brigade of all arms and division
16 (45.71%)	commander of army
10 (28.57%)	commander of Ludovika Academy and General Staff College
6 (17.14%)	chief of general staff of Honvéd army
5 (14.29%)	defense minister

From 1922-1928 and 1935-1944, the post of the chief of the regent's military office was filled by one of the 35 colonel-generals. The same applies to the post of the commander of the General Staff College in 1927-1943 and that of the Ludovika Military Academy in 1931-1941. Similar was the case in the operational staff between 1923 and 1941. The number is especially high among the brigade commanders of all arms and divisions and among lecturers of the Ludovika Academy and the General Staff College. Those who taught at these two institutions reached the rank of general, but to receive a position, the applicant had to be fully educated and trained in military affairs.

Having reviewed the question of certain military posts, we will consider the age of promotion in our sample.

Age and Year of Promotion of the Military Elite

Promoted Age	General	Lieut-General	Col-General	Promoted Year	General	Lieut-General	Col-General
44	1	--	--	1926	1	--	--
45	1	--	--	1927	1	--	--
46	2	--	--	1928	1	--	--
47	--	--	--	1929	--	--	--
48	4	--	--	1930	2	--	--
49	10	--	--	1931	--	1	--
50	9	2	--	1932	--	--	--
51	5	7	1	1933	--	--	--
52	2	12	1	1934	5	1	--
53	1	9	5	1935	1	1	--
54	--	3	12	1936	1	2	1
55	--	1	5	1937	5	5	--
56	--	1	7	1938	4	1	4
57	--	--	3	1939	5	3	--
58	--	--	1	1940	7	3	4
				1941	2	8	5
				1942	1	4	3
				1943	--	5	4
				1944	--	1	13
				1945	--	--	1

It is clear from the table that the greatest chance to reach the rank of general was between the ages of 49 and 50. At 44-45 very few officers were commissioned as generals, while those who had not risen to the rank of general by the age of 52-53 rarely reached the rank of lieutenant-general. To have the best chance to become colonel-general between 1938 and 1945, officers had to obtain the rank of general at the age of 53.

The rank of lieutenant-general was most frequently reached by officers who were between 51 and 53 years of age. Interestingly enough, the rank of colonel-general was arrived at by most officers at the age of 54 who were all promoted during World War II. The table also shows that the majority of promotions to the rank of lieutenant-general and colonel-general occurred during the war. Conspicuously high is the 13 colonel-generals commissioned in 1944 - 8 of which were promoted by Szálasi to this rank in November 1944.

The following chart analyzes the question of retirement ending the elite officer's military career.

Age and Retirement Year of the Military Elite

Retired Age	No.	Note	Retired Year	No.	Note
52	1	Feketehalmy-Czeydner forced to retire for Ujvidék Massacre	1936	1	Werth was reactivated as lieut-general in Sept. 1938
53	1	Magyarosy as lieut-general. Re-activated the same age	1938	1	—
55	2	Werth as lieut-general Activated at 57	1940	2	—
56	6		1941	2	—

Retired Age	No.	Note	Retired Year	No.	Note
57	4		1942	4	Feketehalmy-Czeydner as lieutenant-general for Ujvidék events. Reactivated after October 15-16, 1944.
58	2		1943	5	—
59	2		1944	4	Magyarosy as lieutenant-general. Reactivated after October 15-16, 1944.
60	2	Jány, Werth	1945	1	—

Most retirements occurred between the ages of 56 and 57. The two colonel-generals with longest service time — at least by age — were Gusztáv Jány and Henrik Werth.

Hungarian historiography regards October 15-16, 1944 as the last chance for Hungary to withdraw from the war.[16] Joining the anti-fascist alliance would have significantly modified Hungary's future. The uncoordinated and failed attempt brought about Hungarian fascist terror which caused the country's destruction. It is therefore worth noting the members of the military elite that were in influential positions on October 15-16, 1944.

Posts of the Military Elite on October 15-16, 1944

3 (8.75%) were performing political functions:

Lajos Csatay - Defense Minister   Géza Lakatos - Prime Minister

Gusztav Hennyey - Foreign Minister

Six (17.14%) were in active military status:

Alajos Béldy	- Commander of the national guard, head of a main group in Ministry of Defense
Károly Beregfy	- Commissioned to reorganize the Ministry of Defense
Béla Miklós	- Commander of the First Hungarian Army
Imre Ruszkiczay-Rüdiger	- Deputy Defense Minister
Lajos Veress	- Commander of the Second Hungarian Army
János Vörös	- Chief of the General Staff of the Honvéd army

The six active lieutenant-generals were:

Farkas	Heszlényi	Justy
László	Major	Ternegg

The only active brigadier general was István Hindy. Győrffy-Bengyel and Schindler were no longer alive.

Sixteen of the Military Elite were retired:

Szombathelyi	Bartha	Decleva	Denk
Feketehalmy-Czeydner	Jány	Littay	Rátz
Keresztes-Fischer	Magyarosy	Nagy	Sónyi
Gorondy-Novák	Schweitzer	Bajnóczy	Werth

Of all the colonel-generals involved in the October 15-16, 1944 events only Károly Beregfy offered his service to Szálasi's fascist government. Béla Miklós and János Vörös were captives of the Red Army and Alajos Béldy, Lajos Csatay, Gusztáv Hennyey, Géza Lakatos, Imre Ruszkiczay-Rüdiger, Lajos Veress were either in German or in Hungarian-fascist captivity.

Out of the 35 colonel-generals promoted between 1938 and 1945, 10 gave military service under Szálasi and Jenő Rátz took on political function to become the chairman of the fascist Upper House. 24 people (68.57%) did not undertake either a military or a political role and three of them (8.75%) were no longer alive in late November 1944. 26 (74.29%) of the 35 colonel-generals were promoted by Horthy and 9 (25.71%) — Farkas, Feketehalmy-Czeydner, Hindy, Herszlényi, Justy, László, Magyarosy, Major, Ternegg — by Szálasi. Of the 10 colonel-generals serving under Szálasi only one was commissioned by Horthy. Under Szálasi, 24 (68.57%) of the 35 colonel-generals refused to accept a political or military role and 8 of the 9 colonel-generals of October 15-16 and 24 of the 26 colonel-generals were promoted by Horthy. After the coup of the fascist Arrow Cross Party, 10 of the colonel-generals (28.57%) suffered demonstrable imprisonment of varying length by Germans or their Hungarian puppets: Bajnóczy, Béldy, Csatay, Hennyey, Keresztes-Fischer, Lakatos, Nagy, Ruszkiczay-Rüdiger, Szombathelyi and Veress.

We can assume based on the data that 8 out of the 9 colonel-generals who were active participants of the military and political leadership accepted the proposal to withdraw from the war. The list of those who served under Szálasi shows that they were immediately promoted in return for their services rendered to the fascist government. Several of them — Hindy, Feketehalmy-Czeydner, Magyarosy, Ternegg — would never have reached the rank of colonel-general, if Szálasi had not seized power.

To sum up, it can be stated that the colonel-generals originated from the *petit bourgeoisie* and from the lower-middle class intelligentsia. The choice of a military career by the 35 officers in the sample was strongly influenced by the prospect of a free education and the promise of improving their social and financial position. They insisted on maintaining the social system since a change in the *status quo* would have undermined their social standing. A clear distinction must be made between societal approval and recognition of the army officers on the one hand and their integration into high society on the other hand. Irrespective of social background, the narrow stratum of the officers in the military command generally proved loyal to Regent Miklós Horthy. Their education and training in the apolitical armies of the monarchy and Hungary at the onset of the 20th century meant total submission to orders and absolute respect of authority. This also implies that they were trained to wait for orders, even in crucial moments. This was aptly illustrated on October 15-16, 1944 when they were unable to take the initiative in Budapest without instructions. They resigned passively to their fate.

After World War II, the majority of the colonel-generals who refused to serve under Szálasi and retired, remained in Hungary, while almost all of those who played a role under Szálasi fled abroad. Some were returned to Hungary by the Allies to face war crimes trials. The Hungarian People's Tribunal sentenced six colonel-generals to death for war crimes: Beregfy, Béldy, Hindy, Jány, László, Werth. Four of these officers—Beregfy, Hindy, Jány, László—were executed. Béldy's sentence was commuted to life imprisonment (he died in the prison hospital in 1946) and Werth was taken to the Soviet Union as a prisoner of war where he died in 1953. Two colonel-generals, Feketehalmy-Czeydner and Szombathelyi, were sentenced to death and executed in 1946 by the Yugoslav People's Tribunal. Rátz was convicted to forced labor for life Bajnóczy was sentenced to a prison term of ten years; Ruszkiczay-Rüdiger served three years in prison. The ten active colonel-generals serving after October 15-16, 1944 were dismissed by the Honvéd army and were demoted.

Two of the colonel-generals of the counter-revolutionary period fulfilled significant political functions in the Provisional National Government - Béla Miklós was prime minister and János Vörös was the minister of defense. During the Stalinist terror from 1949 to 1953, most were imprisoned on trumped up charges. For example, János Vörös was sentenced to prison for being an American spy. The colonel-generals examined in this paper did not or could not adapt to the new socio-political system which brought about their professional and social demise.

Notes

1. The role of the army and the elite in the earlier years was studied by: István Pataki, "Az ellenforradalom hadserege 1919-1921," [The Army of the Counter-Revolution], (Budapest, 1973); Gyula Vargyai, "A fegyveres erö helye és funkciói az államszervezetben a harmincas években," [The Place and Function of the Military Forces in the State Organization in the Thirties], in Ferenc Pölöskei and György Ránki, eds., *A Magyarország polgári államrendszerek* [Bourgeois State Administrative Systems in Hungary], (Budapest, 1981).

2. This view is still true today, especially in the press; see the writings published for the 100th anniversary of Lieutenant-General János Kiss' birth (*Magyar Nemzet*, *Rakéta*, etc.). A similar position is taken by István Nemeskürthy in his book, *Requiem egy hadseregért* [Requiem for An Army], (Budapest, 1978). These ideas are also adopted by Mihály Korom in his biography of Miklós Béla Dálnoki which can be found in *Társadalmi Szemle*, (1982), no. 11.

3. The title "colonel-general" was introduced into the "Hungarian Royal Army" in summer 1941. Earlier, the generals of infantry, cavalry and artillery corresponded to this degree of rank. At the same time, the designation of the rank of general was replaced by the name brigadier general. I use the term colonel-general consistently from 1938 on while I retained the designation general despite the alteration because most of the people included in the survey became generals before 1941.

4. The list of the major archival sources includes: Archives of the Institute of Military History (Budapest) - 31st department (of officers' personnel matters) in the Ministry of Defense, 1919; 8th department (of officers' personnel matters) in the Ministry of Defense, 1920-1945; Presidential Department, Ministry of Defense, "Certificates of Lineage" 1940-1943; documents of Ludovika Academy; documents of the Honvéd Cadet School at Pécs; documents of the Honvéd Cadet School at Nagyvárad; documents of the Military Academy; documents of officers' personnel matters - for those born in 1891 or before. Dániel Kálmán, "A magyar királyi Honvédség a második világháborúban," [The Hungarian Royal Army in World War II],

manuscript. Archives of the Institute of Military History, Collected Studies 2721 and 1779. Central Archives of Ministry of Defense (Budapest). Documents of officers' personnel matters for those born after 1891.

5. There is no authentic data available on the promotion of Faragho as colonel-general. According to some verbal communication, Horthy had promoted him verbally before the armistice delegation left. Sztójay became colonel-general in inactive status after a long political career in November 1944 when he no longer had a say in the military or political decision-making. Similar was the case of Jenő Ruszkay, although he played some political role after October 15-16, 1944.

6. See: n. 2.

7. Gyula Illyés, *Ki a magyar?* [Who is Hungarian?], (Budapest, 1982), 42.

8. The categories could even have been further broadened since all people who had a certificate of finishing secondary school belonged to the intellectuals in the contemporary sense. In this interpretation, 20 people would be "Intellectuals."

9. This statement holds true not only of the 35 people in the sample but the entire military elite. Between 1919 and 1945, 1,000 people were involved in the upper strata of military leadership. As few as 2-3% of came from families in the "upper ten" percent.

10. I took into consideration the original branch of service ignoring later changes.

11. The highest possible rank in the Hungarian army was field marshal, but no one reached it between 1918 and 1945.

12. In Italian captivity at the period under study.

13. See: n. 14.

14. This does not preclude the possibility of their serving either in the Red Army or the National Army.

15. Most of them served in the post of chief-of-staff of a division or army corps, commander of a division or brigadier general in the Red Army. The majority were lieutenants and majors.

16. Detailed analyses of the events of October 15-16, 1944 can be found in Ágnes Rozsnyói, *A Szálasi-puccs* [Szálasi's *Coup*] (Budapest, 1977); Éva Teleki, *A nyilas uralom*

Magyarországon [The Rule of the Arrow Cross Party in Hungary] (Budapest, 1971); Károly Vigh, *Ugrás a sötétbe* [Plunge Into the Dark] (Budapest, 1979).

CONTROLLING THE AGRICULTURE AND THE PRODUCERS

Károly Szabó and László Virágh

Preparations for a possible European war, the changed external economic conditions with the outbreak of the war and finally, Hungary's entry into the war set new agricultural requirements to be met by the Hungarian economy. New demands were placed on agriculture which was now responsible for satisfying the consumption needs of the army and the civilian population. Similar to other countries, the subordination of the economy to war aims led to strong central regulation and restriction of the market.

State intervention was not new in Hungary, but it assumed a new meaning during the war. In the wake of World War I, there was extensive state intervention in the production and circulation of agricultural produce. During the 1930s, as a result of the Great Depression, government measures were aimed at protecting domestic production and fostering the sale of surplus in foreign markets. As part of these policies, the prices of the main agricultural goods (cereals, animal products) were centrally subsidized and related tax abatements were introduced. The planting of some produce (sugar, beets, paprika) was officially regulated. There was also a development of a state-controlled system of buying through purchasing cooperatives. It must be stressed that these state interventions were initiated by the economic policy-makers to insure the continuity of domestic production in agriculture with little structural modification.

From the mid 1930s, another etatist approach began to take shape: this one centered on the forced structural alteration of agricultural production. the theory behind the practice was "controlled agricultural production." Controlled agriculture differed from the previous state intervention on several significant points. First, its aim was not the protection, but the transformation of the prevailing structure of agricultural production. Second, it called for direct intervention in production instead of regulating financial resources and sales. Accordingly, this concept assigned a different role to the financial resources, state pricing and purchasing. Instead of protecting the agricultural producers, it sought new ways to make them adjust agricultural production to the objectives of the central authorities. Though underlying their conception was the idea of restructuring the agriculture upon the German model, Béla Imrédy and his followers undoubtedly foreshadowed a new type of state-controlled economic system.[1]

In light of later developments, it's important to stress that the state's controlling activity was closely connected with the ambitions of the politically strong agrarian lobby. In Hungary, the ministry in charge of agricultural affairs and the two largest organizations for the protection of agricultural interests were intricately intertwined and reinforced by personal ties. As a result, the economic policy-makers had to win the support of the agrarian lobby. By the end of the 1930s, central price control and a state cooperative system emerged.

Initial Government Measures

The novel economic tasks facing the Hungarian government, having just recovered from the grave economic crisis of the 1930s derived from the needs of economic reorganization and development of the enlarged territory and from the altered wartime foreign economies. Agricultural production reserves were reduced in Hungary to provide food to Upper Hungary, Sub-carpathia and later Northern Transylvania. Domestic consumption was also increased by the enlarged army in the expanded territory. Another factor increasing domestic consumption was the economic upswing following the proclamation of the Győr program.

At the same time, the character of agrarian exports to Germany, the main buyer of Hungarian agricultural products underwent a change from the late 1930s. Due to the dwindling agricultural reserves, the Hungarian government was less and less interested in exporting to Germany, while the demands of the German government kept increasing. Consequently, one of the most delicate issues of the Hungarian-German economic relations was the size and composition of Hungarian agricultural exports. A constant dilemma of the Hungarian government centered around the adjustment of agricultural exports to internal needs.

Agricultural surplus disappeared from one month to the next. In the first half of 1940, growing tension rose in domestic supply although the harvest yields of the previous years had been good. While for years one of the strongest concerns of the government had been the selling of agricultural surplus, from 1939, the focus was on the scarcity of domestic produce. At a glance, one could conclude that the solution should have been to increase agricultural production and introduce the central management of stocks. In 1940, however, when market tensions emerged, the government did not have a program to quickly boost agricultural production. The government had no control over the administrative apparatus that would have enforced these measures. The existing forms of price regulation and the state's purchasing mechanism were ill suited to solve the arising problems, which prompted the search for new alternatives. The Defense Act of 1939 allowed the state to modify the regulation of agricultural prices, extended the circle of centrally regulated agricultural goods and permitted limits on the circulation and distribution of agricultural products. Sections of this act mentioned that:

> Anyone can be obligated to deliver that part of his fodder and seed-grain which is not indispensable for his own subsistence....As for the basic products, everyone must submit the quantity that is in excess of the fixed limits of his own domestic or economic needs...the ministry has the authority to regulate and control the production, circulation and use of any raw material, agricultural produce and manufactured goods and predetermine the manner

> of their production, their prices, and consumption....In all these respects, the ministry may issue orders diverging from the existing acts.

Instead of moderating the agrarian market, the extension of central price regulation resulted in an escalation of tensions. It cut back deliveries to the market and threatened to reduce production because of the low fixed prices. In response to this, an ordinance was issued before the harvest of 1940 stipulating that the remainder of wheat and corn from the previous year be offered for central collection. This was the first concrete order for compulsory delivery. The Futura Corporation was entrusted with purchasing the grain for the government. Violators of the defense act were subject to speedy prosecution and strict penalties. The aim of these measures was to force the producers to sell their products to eliminate the signs of shortages through central purchasing and distribution.

Without the administrative registration of yields, the government could not force producers to sell their excess stocks to the state purchasers. This "indifference" was further enhanced by the low prices the state paid which was far below the black market prices. The production for inner consumption of the small and medium-scale land holders rose considerably. Proof of this is the 26% rise of cattle and 50% rise of pork stocks from 1939 to 1942.[2]

The official system of buying up agricultural products developed by summer 1940 incurred the discontent of the producers because the fixed purchasing prices were considered offensively low by the agrarian interest groups. Strong opposition by the a agrarian lobbies, the real danger of a drop in production and the persistence of difficulties in public food supply forced the government to find new ways of solving the problem. For some time after the appointment of Béla Jurcsek as state commissioner for agricultural production and trade, the government seemed to have found an outlet for the tensions of public food supply through the revival of the "controlled agriculture" concept. Without having enough time to work out his plans as commissioner, Jurcsek had to quit a few months later.[3] With the failure of "controlled agriculture," the government made an attempt at reconciliation with the agrarian interest groups and tried to find a solution, by seeking the institutional conditions for a central management of agricultural trade.

The Introduction of Central Control in the Trade of Agricultural Products

With a view to implementing the government concepts, the noted statistician Dezső Laky was appointed minister without portfolio in charge of public food supply in December 1940. At the same time, steps were taken to merge all the government agencies controlling the circulation of agricultural goods and public food supplies as the National Office for Public Supply (OKH). In this interim stage, the staff of three government organs and the department responsible for public food supply in the Ministry of Agriculture constituted the apparatus of the new office. The Royal Hungarian Office of Commerce was in control of the trade and distribution of all consumer goods except food. It had offices in each county with a total personnel of 699. The Royal Hungarian Office for Public Food Supply was the central apparatus in charge of food, trade and had a staff of 215. Prices were controlled by the National Commission for Price Control which had 234 employees.[4] Though the composition of the institution clearly reveals that it was not designed to carry out new and operative tasks, many regarded the National Office for Public Supply as the government's organ to manage the agriculture. In reality, the powers of the National Office for Public Supply were restricted to the control of agricultural trade and public food supply, while the central management of agriculture remained with the Ministry of Agriculture. Nonetheless, the establishment of National Office for Public Supply can be regarded as the first step toward creating the administrative organs in a central hierarchy of economic control.

The endeavors of Laky and his colleagues centered around a plan for public food supply based on controlled food trade. To this end, Lajos Illyefalvi, a well-known statistician, was appointed national commissioner of price control. The production of goods falling under the restrictions were registered by the local authorities while their distribution was the responsibility of the central organs like the National Office for Public Supply. By officially registering the yields and stockpiles, they hoped to limit the success of the black market while satisfying the government's needs as well.

It became an important goal to win the support of the agrarian interest groups. In January 1941, they tried to reconcile their ideas with the agrarian groups to avoid the embarrassing situations of the previous months. The agrarian interest groups did not hesitate to warn the government to give serious consideration to their proposals. They stressed that "it must be borne in mind that agriculture is not an administrative activity and it hardly tolerates forced interventions as it always has harmful 'side effects'." The shortage in cereals was blamed on the government and the producers demanded a price rise of 10 pengős (over 40%). For fear of further central measures, the landowners cut back the sowing area of winter crops by 30%.[5] In its report for 1940, the National Chamber for Agriculture reiterated the landowners' terms: they would refuse to obey the mandated deliveries unless the fixed prices covered the costs of production and left far larger reserves for estate consumption than before. Paradoxical as it may seem, the agricultural groups also urged for yield registration to validate their lower than average production.

While the negotiations were held, the government further constrained the food reserves stored in households and agricultural estates for their own consumption, followed by an order that estates over 50 cadastral yokes (29 hectares) should deliver information on 23 crops, the size of the sowing area and the livestock to get a better understanding of Hungary's agricultural production capabilities. Estates larger than 50 cadastral yokes were required to sell to central dealers or mills authorized by the state to purchase for the state. At the same time, the government guaranteed that the fodder requirements of stock breeders be satisfied.

By refusing to submit the required information, the producers stymied the implementation of the consolidated plans of National Office for Public Supply. In response, the government called in troops during the spring of 1941 to make up for losses in public supply. Task forces sought out the reserves and requisitioned the peasants to sell to them.[6] Purchases by military squads were not unfamiliar as part of the army's provisions (mostly fodder and legumes) were acquired by these troops. But it was new that the army was enforcing the economic regulations to ensure domestic food supplies and German exports.

In other respects, however, the government was more lenient. For example, the government ignored the anti-Semitic restrictions by allowing 180 provincial Jewish grain merchants to buy cereals with the condition that they sell a certain amount of bread grain to the state agencies.[7] A further loosening of state collection came when the government offered to pay more to peasants who were willing to sell more to the state. In theory, the producers could not have had salable reserves unless they had failed to fulfill their duties of compulsory delivery and registration. Such contradictory government measures, as a result of the emergency situation were not infrequent. Given this situation, the peasantry assumed a wait-and-see attitude which made it even harder for the government to issue new decrees.

The plans for the next crop year included central control over the sowing area and cereal production yields for estates over 20 cadastral yokes (11.6 hectares). They also planned to perfect the monopoly of grain trade by setting up a supreme cooperative out of the larger cooperatives and the Futura Corporation to purchase for the state. A committee was sent to Germany to study food trade and food supply to incorporate their central collection of food stocks. Laky still felt the best way to improve the system was by increasing state control by registering production results and stocks. to accomplish this, grain threshing was officially checked. An ordinance was issued requiring owners to register their threshing machines and to inform the Office of Public Food Supply of the threshing place, date and yield accumulated. The local authorities kept grain sheets that recorded the producers' needs. In this way, the official records kept track of the grain stocks from the moment of production. The estates then had to turn in what was in excess of their own needs for food and production. Threshing was controlled by the minister of public food supply and enforced by the army, the gendarmerie and the customs police. Checking the circulation of cereals incurred a large expense. The issuing of about 3 million grain sheets, the traveling costs and pay for the inspection task forces amounted to 3 million pengős, which could have purchased 3,000 wagon-loads of grain.[8] In addition, immense costs and losses of storage were burdened on the central budget.

The Failure of Trade Controls on Agricultural Produce — The Military Takes Control of the National Office for Public Supply

While the government was making great efforts to monopolize and centralize agricultural trade, a sizable black market emerged when the prices of foodstuffs increased and pessimistic speculation caused shortages of certain foodstuffs. Public supply didn't even improve in spring 1941 when Hungary annexed the Bácska (Backa) region which had excellent arable land because under the international agreements, 60% of the excess produce was due to Germany and 40% to Italy. After the rationing of sugar and fat, coupons for bread and flour were introduced in and around Budapest. Central rationing was extended to more and more staples in the provincial towns as well.

In September 1941, Colonel-General Sándor Győrffy-Bengyel, formerly the deputy minister of defense, replaced Laky as the minister of public food supply. Former military officer, István Lossonczy, was appointed to head the National Office for Public Supply and in early October, Brigadier General Lajos Rozváczy, a commissary, was appointed as the civilian head of the National Commission for Price Control. As expected, the military appointees set out to organize the crumbling public food supply with a strong hand. To crush the sale of food on the black market, they set up an "economy police" to conduct produce market raids and mass arrests. Sándor Győrffy-Bengyel called on the population in a radio address to help their fight against profiteering by urging the people to report on the black market profiteers. During the one-month campaign, 600 detectives were employed and 400 merchants were brought to court. Press reports on the activities of "fake detectives" suggested the worsening of food supply and the heightening of tensions. The deadline for delivery expired at the end of October, but the government extended it by a month to November and slightly raised the prices of products. In the meantime the government had worked out plans to enforce the requisitioning of food with the help of military troops. It proposed the deployment of 11,000 troops and 290 trucks, the costs amounting to 2.45 million pengős.

Two weeks before the troops were deployed, Sándor Győrffy-Bengyel warned the producers to deliver their surplus and a few days later the Council of Ministers sent out the task forces. The inspection, actually not differing much from open requisitioning, was to have been done by 965 military squads. In early 1942, the control was extended over Northern Transylvania and the Southern Region as well. Thus, military supervision affected 3 million homesteads.[9] At the same time, an order was issued to deliver a compulsory lard levy, which meant that 3 kilograms of lard after the first pig slaughtered and 6 kilograms of lard after each subsequent slaughtered pig had to be submitted to the central authorities. Using the pattern of grain sheets, pig sheets were introduced to register the number of fattened pigs in every homestead.

The goal of these measures was to restrict consumption among the rural population, but it compounded the problem when the Germans used the system to exploit Hungary's resources more efficiently. When German Foreign Minister Joachim von Ribbentrop and Hungarian Prime Minister László Bárdossy met in December, Ribbentrop asked for the surplus while in the actual negotiations a "certain percentage of domestic production" was demanded based on Hungary's newly-introduced system of agricultural registration.[10] In January 1942, a system of bread rations based on Budapest's per capita amount was introduced across the country. the daily bread rations were introduced at 0.24 kilograms, which were soon reduced to 0.20 kilograms and then to 0.16 kilograms. This ration was far lower than in any of the surrounding countries.

In June 1942, Sándor Győrffy-Bengyel died unexpectedly. In October, Prime Minister Miklós Kállay appointed Lajos Szász in control of the public food supply matters and Béla Jurcsek, the former government commissioner for agricultural production was appointed as head of the National Office for Public Supply. These personnel changes involved a transformation in outlook as well. After the failure of trade controls and military intervention, the organization of public food supply gained a more prominent position in the government. In the first months under the new leadership, the food administration regulated the sale and use of the agricultural products with more control and extended the delivery of goods by including all major staples. At the same time, Jurcsek and his staff were busy working out the new bases for compulsory delivery starting with the reshuffling of the management of public food supply. The central apparatus in the National Office for Public Supply was fused and regional branches of the National Office for Public Supply were set up in every county as the Hungarian Royal Inspectorate of Public Food Supply. The heads of the county administration, the sub-prefects, were appointed government commissioners for public food supply. The threshing of grain harvested in 1942 had to be reported to the county inspectorates, who despatched threshing inspectors to verify the yields. The food administration was again dissatisfied with the volume of bread-grain and barley delivered until mid-November. According to the National Office for Public Supply calculations, there was a difference between the legally retainable and the actually retained amounts of bread-grain which came to nearly 8% of the national agricultural product.

Jurcsek's Point System

The leaders of the National Office for Public Supply appointed in summer 1942 inherited a variety of problems associated with the public food supply. The central reserves kept falling behind the scheduled amounts resulting in the per capita ration decreases. Compared to 1939, the sown area of major field crops was shrinking with the exception of industrial crops. Military and police interventions further intensified the tensions and insecurity of the producers.

Changes in Sowing Area Between 1938 and 1944
(in thousand hectares)

Year	Wheat	Rye	Corn	Sugar Beet	Sunflower	Potato
1938	1,621	632	1,175	44	6.7	291
1939	1,650	627	1,186	43	7.5	278
1940	1,488	577	1,206	55	15.1	278
1941	1,346	538	1,142	48	13.6	274
1942	1,436	544	1,112	46	47.8	264
1943	1,571	555	1,064	55	83.5	266
1944	1,539	541	1,049	59	109.2	266

Source: National Statistical Office, Agricultural Database I, (Budapest, 1978), 104-120.

The restricted trade of agricultural products and the ever increasing compulsory quotas were profoundly affecting the entire agricultural production by 1942. While the central food administration took firmer steps to collect the planned volume of crops by extending its supervision over the yields and trade which affected a shrinking circle of agricultural production and trade. It further aggravated the process of collecting the centrally needed stocks by the National Office for Public Supply. Especially tense was the collection of corn in autumn 1942 when the local administrative leaders interceded to reduce the levies.

Given this situation, the new leaders of the National Office for Public Supply looked for solutions in two directions. On the one hand, they changed the procedure of imposing compulsory levies on crops and on the other, they sped up the organization of the National Office for Public Supply and its provincial institutions. The decree on the revised system of delivery was released in November 1942. As the minister of public food supply stressed in his proposal to the Council of Ministers, "the experiences gained so far have convincingly proved...that it is impossible to create harmony between the volume of publicly needed stocks and the agricultural production merely by price-policy measures. For this reason, it seems expedient to introduce a type of regulation that prescribes in advance the extent to which each producer must participate in covering the public needs."[11] Instead of defining a certain amount of reserves to be collected from the whole of agricultural producers, the government broke down its demands to individual estates. Another novelty was that it wished to achieve this goal not only by taking price-policy and trade measures, but also by indirectly interfering with production. The quotas to be imposed on each homestead was determined in the spring on the basis of the size of the arable area, which in theory, forced the peasants to produce instead of leaving the fields fallow.

Thus, the Jurcsek scheme reversed the sequence: now each producer had to hand in a fixed quota and then he could dispose over the remaining crops as he pleased, while earlier he had to deliver the amount in excess. The difference is that the Jurcsek system laid claim to a certain volume of crops irrespective of the harvest yields and not to a prefixed percentage of agricultural production or to the portion above the per capita ration. The size of the levy was defined on the basis of the quality of the estate's plowing area: after each gold crown of the value of the plowing area 50 units of wheat had to be submitted (1 unit of wheat was equal to 1 kg of bread-grain): 10 units had to be in bread-grain, 10 units in livestock or fats and the rest in crops freely chosen by the peasants.[12]

The National Office for Public Supply tried to solve two problems with this ordinance. Firstly, it sought to increase the volume of marketed goods by fixing the overall size of collected stocks. They calculated that the country's compulsory delivery would amount to 36% of the average agricultural production of 10 years whereas only a third of the production reached the market in the pre-war years.[13] On the other hand, it wished to have a predetermined calculable volume of bread-grain and meat/fats, the two most important staples.

In the spring, the local authorities registered the main particulars of the estates to calculate the liabilities of each producer. Each peasant received an estate book listing the data of his estate, his quota to be delivered and the right to grind his per capita ration for multure. The fulfilled duties were also confirmed in this booklet. The execution of duties was also entered into the estate sheets. Estate sheets for holdings smaller than 100 cadastral yokes were kept with the local authorities, while the estate sheets for larger holdings were kept with the county food inspectorate. The fine imposed on people failing to turn in their quota through their own fault ranged from 3 to 8 times the price of crops in arrears. The amounts sold to the authorities in excess of the prescribed volume were rewarded by one-third of the fixed price. The collection of crops was carried out by 10 centers of trade, each specializing in a type of produce and all were directly responsible to the National Office for Public Supply, replacing the purchasing cooperatives. From this time, the crops and products falling under compulsory delivery could only be circulated with the permission of the minister of public food supply or the National Office for Public Supply.

Jurcsek's radio announcement in October 1942 deeply shocked the peasantry, when he declared that their duty of delivery preceded the needs of their households and estates. That was the overriding principle of the scheme, but the producers were given the assurance of allowing substitutions in the per capita ration of bread-grain and seed-grain. Jurcsek added that the system of compulsory delivery would also be the basis for the post-war management of the agriculture. A month later, Lajos Szász, the minister of public food supply, tried to calm the discontent caused by those statements assuring the nation that the system was only temporary.

Agricultural Producers Adjust to the War Economy

As the period itself is relatively short and the system of delivery was also constantly changing, one can only indicate some tendencies of the system that had an impact on agricultural producers and production. When analyzing the war economy in agriculture, we look at the years between 1941 and 1944 for the various government interventions in agriculture. Prior to 1941, the government's agricultural policy interventions did not significantly differ from the previous period's remedies. After 1944, however, the war's devastation made the idea of an economic policy irrelevant.

In the studied period, between 1941 and 1944, Hungary's agricultural makeup was characterized by the duality of the large estates and small estates in regard to ownership and the manner of production. This duality meant two different modes of production and economic relations. The large agricultural enterprises were driven by a capitalist economy; they produced for the market and engaged in domestic and international trade. The principal aim of a small-holding was the subsistence of the family running it; market production played a secondary role. The relations of small-holdings with regional trade was centered around regional fairs. Small-holders running their estates in the spirit of entrepreneurship were characterized by specialization in one or two labor intensive crops and a smaller tilling area.

Before the war, Germany relied on Hungarian produce for Germany's agricultural needs. But during the war, Hungarian exports of bread-grain, corn and live pigs to Germany decreased while the exports of pork, fat and bacon were halted. Since the agreements provided for the export of a stipulated rate of Hungarian surplus, the German authorities questioned the validity of the Hungarian production figures and stopped refunding the customs duties on grain.

Grain Exports from the Post-Trianon Territories to the Re-Annexed Areas and Abroad (in thousand metric tons)

	1938	1939	1940	1941	1942	1943	1944
Wheat	436	1008	392	148	24	144	55
Corn	120	47	3	40	88	59	23
Oil-Seed	15	13	2	2	13	43	4

Source: Péter Gunst, "Agriculture and Food in Hungary During World War II," *Agrártörténeti Szemle*, (1982), 1-2.

To satisfy domestic demands without reducing the agrarian exports, Hungary would have been forced to order real requisitioning as early as 1941. Besides the export liabilities, the fluctuation of production yields determined the size of the compulsory quotas.

Harvest Yields between 1938-44 (in 1,000 metric tons)

Year	Wheat	Rye	Corn	Sugar Beet	Sunflower	Potato
1938	2,688.3	804.6	2,662.0	949.4	7.4	2,140.6
1939	2,688.6	761.5	2,185.3	918.1	8.4	2,025.7
1940	1,818.8	596.5	2,378.8	1,173.7	13.7	2,371.5
1941	1,885.5	560.0	1,806.1	906.0	8.7	2,119.6
1942	1,703.2	513.9	1,443.9	738.1	47.8	1,803.8
1943	2,278.4	669.2	1,246.2	725.8	71.2	1,821.2
1944	2,318.9	646.0	2,300.0	1,135.8	140.9	2,640.0

Source: National Statistical Office, Agricultural Database I, (Budapest, 1978), 104-114.

The unfavorable yields of 1941-1942, the ever-worsening prices, the institutionalization of compulsory delivery and the army's intervention turned the large and small producers against the Hungarian government. They both responded to the first orders for compulsory delivery and trade restrictions in differently, but with the same mindset: The large estates threatened to cut back production and the smaller landholders began to withdraw from trade. The large estates were more concerned about compulsory delivery, while the smaller estates dynamically increased their livestock to tide over the unfavorable times. This entailed a drop in the volume of marketed goods and the decline of the peasant division of labor. The local trade restrictions, originally devised to prevent sales out of the county, also restricted the normal exchange of goods between the producers. With the continuation of restrictions, the producers reduced the sowing area of those crops that were most liable to delivery to avoid surplus production. Another reaction of the producers was to postpone the date of delivery as long as possible and to squeeze out higher prices. Inadvertently, the government reinforced this behavior by encouraging additional and later deliveries with various premiums.

At this time, the raising of the delivery quotas strengthened the position of the smaller landholders because their prices on their products were not strictly fixed. The regulation of agricultural prices had a stronger impact on the producers of traditional crops (cereals), while the official food supply shortages actually boosted the circulation in some supplementary foodstuffs (legumes, onions). The gap between the buying prices and the dynamically growing production costs kept widening. It was not until 1943 that the buying prices were raised again to adjust the price rates to those in 1938. This forced the producers to restrict production and trade or to sell limited quantities to the black market. The large enterprises managed to compensate their loss of income by increasing the sown area of industrial plants (sunflowers) whose prices increased with the needs of the war. Practically the whole upswing in the production of industrial crops occurred on the large estates, although some larger peasant holders also availed themselves of this opportunity.

As the signs of disorganization in production and distribution were recognized by the agricultural interest groups and the government organs, the introduction and acceptance of the new Jurcsek system passed without incident. This was due to several factors. First, the scheme included a price rise to account for rising production costs; second, with the prices raised, the system of compulsory delivery became a calculable factor for the producers. Compared to the selling difficulties of the 1930s and the artificially low agricultural prices of the following years, this seemed like the realization of the producers' efforts. The acceptance of the new system coupled with favorable natural conditions between 1943-1944, increased the drive for production and strengthened the hands of those who designed the scheme.[14]

The quotas fixed in the Jurcsek system were broken down to individual producers. Estates with the general or average production system could, in principle, fulfill their liabilities in case of average yields. The situation of large and medium-size estates was defined by their cultivation yield which was recorded by the food inspectorate to keep the authorities aware of their business activities. As a result, the officially fixed price affected these estates more than the obligation to deliver and the trade restrictions. For this reason, their endeavors concentrated on having the delivery prices calculated in the prices of the manufactured goods they used in production. Therefore, agricultural production was seriously affected by the growing shortage of manufactured goods and machinery. It was for this reason that the producers proposed that they should be allowed to buy manufactured goods with their delivery credits. Small holders were worst hit by orders like the lard levy which affected the goods typically produced for personal use. This obligation and the precedence of delivery duties over household and estate needs incurred the greatest resistance among them. Producers with small enterprises saw the bread-grain ration as the greatest danger. This problem was handled by multiple substitution which allowed loopholes in the system for the small holdings. If the Jurcsek scheme was to be effective, it had to concentrate on large enterprises.

The Implementation of the Jurcsek Scheme and the Developments of 1944-1945

After the initial tensions, the controlled system proved far more successful than the collections of the previous years. The decline of agricultural production was halted and the sown area for cereals increased. The total required delivery amounted to 6.5 billion units of wheat after several reductions were fulfilled by the producers to 98% of what was expected. The producers turned in 157% of their bread-grain obligation, 111% of the meat and lard obligation and 75% of the freely chosen crops. As expected, the performance of holdings smaller than 100 cadastral yokes were not as successful as the larger estates.[15]

The success of collection led in July 1944 to the considerable alleviation of sanctions against producers that didn't perform as expected. When the arrears were less than 200 units of wheat or did not exceed 20% of the compulsory quota, the procedure of penalization was not enforced. When the failure was larger, only those who owed more than 5,000 units of wheat were fined. The fine was calculated on the basis of the fixed price.

The structure of compulsory quotas for 1944-1945 was determined in a different way than the first year of the Jurcsek scheme. The levy after one gold crown of the plowing field value was reduced by 20% to 40 units of wheat. At the same time, a levy of meat was imposed on meadows and pastures, although the delivery of surpluses was not required. The delivery of bread-grain remained at 10 units of wheat; quotas of freely chosen crops dropped to 13 units of wheat as 10 units of wheat had to be delivered in fats and 7 units in meat. During this time, the collection of quotas was determined by the momentary war situation. In the eastern part of the country, the authorities tried to collect and transport bread-grain as quickly as possible. By mid-October, the major areas of crop land and public warehouses were occupied by the Soviet and Romanian troops. Half the bread-grain remained in the occupied areas.[16]

The control of public food supply became completely disorganized by the end of 1944. In late November and early December, the apparatus of the National Office for Public Supply was transferred to the western part of the country. The fascist Szálasi went to great lengths to account for the collection of quotas in the western counties and ordered extra ratios to be delivered. Instead of money, they issued promissory notes for these deliveries. In the beginning of 1945, government edicts were issued which were completely absurd and irrational. The increased quotas of oats and corn did not leave enough reserves for sowing. Szálasi explained that:

> When issuing the order, the supreme leadership of the nation is looking at the situation from the aspect of the general nationalist and socialist requirements and makes its decisions in the knowledge of information that is not available to the lower

> executive organs. When the supreme leadership orders the delivery of an extremely large volume of certain crop, it may have decided that no seed-grain shall remain because in the forthcoming period this crop may not be cultivated.[17]

The Jurcsek Scheme as the Herald of the Planned Economy

Having arrived at this point, the question arises whether the management of agriculture under the Jurcsek system was a more effective form of the earlier ones or was it a new state-run economic order for the future. The Jurcsek scheme differed from the earlier methods on several points and displayed features which could be utilized after the war. As we have seen, the Jurcsek system focused on the government supervision and direct control of agricultural production. In some way, government supervisory activities placed the emphasis on "the right to control crops and products used as food from the producers to the consumers." For this goal the government demanded an efficient economy which required self-sacrifice from the producers and consumers "in the spirit of justice, equity and social understanding." On the other hand, the Jurcsek scheme demanded the fulfillment of fixed quotas of production and delivery. This significantly altered the content of cooperation: the task of the agricultural producers became the execution of central orders, which in turn changed the manner of agricultural production. Even though this period was still based on private ownership, by centrally defining the production and quotas of crops, the producers were deprived of independent economic decisions which now became illegal.

The question arises whether it was an inevitable process leading from war economy to controlled agriculture. On the one hand, the central administrative organs were faced with repeated fiascoes with the deterioration of the public supply leading to the escalation of central measures and interventions. On the other hand, the Jurcsek concept assigned a different role to the central agencies and the producers than its predecessors. It ascribed real economic roles and tasks to the state authorities restricting the economic autonomy of producers. Logically, this would have called for increased economic activity and the rise in production restrictions, but that would not have been enough for the fundamental transformation that took place in summer 1943. It required a new economic outlook put into effect by the Jurcsek system. This ideology was based on a qualitatively new economic system in which the state must always control and not be controlled by market fluctuations. Therefore, the transition from the war economy to controlled agriculture was because the advocates of a controlled economy were put into power. The government expected that the rehabilitation of these ideas which were condemned in the early 1940s would make the war economy more effective without a new economic system. The dividing lines between traditional and new concepts of economic manipulation were very vague. For instance, the tools of control ensured by the Agricultural Development Act of 1943 which were supported by the traditional interest groups could have been used by the authorities to introduce a controlled economy.

The watershed between the various conceptions was the future image of the management of agriculture after the war. The adherents of traditional economic management fought for the abolition of all war restrictions, whereas Béla Jurcsek's ideas were that: "All the agencies that were entrusted with directing sales to assure public food supply should continue and production should be directed in the future through these centers so that the producers will always meet their expectations. With the outbreak of war, this era came to a close."[18]

The system of compulsory delivery rested on an economic ideology which said that the agricultural producers should produce and the administrative apparatus would manage. The producers were expected to bring about a certain volume of produce which the bureaucracy would then distribute as it saw fit. As the creation of the central bureaucracy was time-consuming, the Jurcsek system had to cooperate with the local administration. It was not in the interest of the local authorities to risk their independence from the central government at that time by clashing with the producers' deliveries. This politically justified "countervailing-interest" was reinforced by the fact that the central levies sometimes threatened the food supply of the local population as well.

The new system tried to solve this problem by transplanting its institutions into the counties and taking direct control of large estates. In addition, the government tried to "discipline" the local village administrators by promising them penalties and rewards for compliance with the registration of yields since the local administrators provided the information indispensable for the system to work. Under these conditions, the wartime management of agriculture met the requirements, without any grave difficulties except for the last year. But even during this short period one could discern the tendencies that would have come to the surface over a longer period of time. This seems to be confirmed by the results of post-war agricultural management.

The system of compulsory delivery, particularly Jurcsek's point system, made the structure of agricultural production very rigid as it urged for the imitation of a centrally designed production structure. The delivery system gave priority to the supply of domestic needs, inevitably leading to a production structure that produced an introverted, self-sufficient production system on a national level. This tendency is clearly reflected by the decline in agricultural exports in the given period. Compulsory delivery and the price and trade regulations helped to draw earnings from agriculture without causing rapid decline in production which, in turn became the economic policy of the post-1945 times. Due to Soviet domination, however, the peacetime equivalent of a war economy was a more rigid planned economy.

Notes

1. Imrédy's address to the Upper House Meeting of the Parliament on May 18, 1934, *Journals of the Upper House of the Parliament*, Vol. 3, (1938), 360.

2. Central Statistical Office, *Állattenyésztés I* [Livestock Breeding I], (Budapest, 1978).

3. Some years later, Jurcsek recalled his former endeavors in the following way: "That was the time when I started working

out the plans that would have insured public food supply through a suitably adjusted, controlled production. Unfortunately, I failed to realize these plans at that time...." *Közellátási Szemle*, October 1, 1942. 1.

4. Documents of the Ministry of Public Food Supply, Hungarian National Archives, Proposals by the Minister of Public Food Supply, K. 253/496/1941.

5. Hungarian National Archives, Presidential papers of the National Food Office, K. 250/1737/1941.

6. During this action, the Futura Corporation purchased 2,905 wagons of wheat until the end of April, of which 428 wagons had been "reconnoitered" by the military troops. They also bought 690 wagons of rye, 673 wagons of feeder grain, nearly 4000 wagons of corn and 270 wagons of flour. These figures were from Laky's report to the Council of Ministers on April 28, 1941, Hungarian National Archives, K. 253/2115/1941.

7. The figures for 1941 show that 1,500 Christian corn dealers had license to buy up. This order also reveals that the controlled trade of agricultural products had other than economic aims as well — it also wished to exclude the Jews from purchasing crops. Crops could only be bought by merchants appointed by the authorities.

8. Hungarian National Archives, Proposal to the Council of Ministers on July 29, 1941, K. 253.

9. Hungarian National Archives, Note of October 16, 1941, or document no. 102, K. 253/640/1940; Similar figures can be found in the final accounts of Futura Corporation for 1944-47.

10. Iván T. Berend and Miklós Szuhay, *A tőkés gazdaság története Magyarországon 1848-1944* [A History of the Capitalist Economy in Hungary] (Budapest, 1972), 262-263.

11. Hungarian National Archives, Proposal on October 13, 1942, K. 253.

12. A wide range of substitutions was possible in the system of computing with wheat units, which lent considerable flexibility to the scheme. However, it required the issuing of many orders; 70 decrees were released to cover the entire system of compulsory delivery.

13. Research Institute of the Hungarian Economy, "Situational Report," no. 52, (Budapest, 1943), 82.

14. A contemporary survey calls attention to the importance of weather conditions which claims that a national average of 81% of the compulsory delivery of 1943-44 was produced in 1942 despite the poor yields, *Köztelek*, June 13, 1943.

15. *Köztelek*, August 27, 1944.

16. Hungarian National Archives, Statements of the Grain Trade Center, K. 254/September 30, 1944 and October 8, 1944.

17. Éva Teleki, *A nyilas uralom Magyarországon* [The Rule of the Arrow-Cross Party in Hungary] (Budapest, 1971), 279.

18. *Mezőgazdasági Közlöny*, July 7, 1944.

THE COMPOSITION AND POSITION OF THE WORKING CLASS DURING THE WAR*

Iván T. Berend

Changes in the Composition of the Working Class

During World War II the working class underwent significant changes which were logical consequences of the war development in the manufacturing industries. The large production growth caused by the war boom entailed a rapid increase in the number of workers and a significant change in the composition of the working class as well.

Average Number of Workers/Year Within Hungary's 1938 Borders

Year	Number	%
1938	288,512	100.0
1939	327,069	113.3
1940	348,894	120.1
1941	354,046	122.7
1942	374,299	129.7
1943	391,838	135.8

These figures do not include the number of workers employed in mining and metallurgy. For this segment of labor, the data was only available from 1938 to 1943. The number of miners and metalworkers in these areas rose by 42% from 41,536 to 59,194. This means that in the manufacturing industry and mining the total labor force rose by 36.6% from 330,048 in 1938

* To make this volume more complete, the editor added this chapter written over 30 years ago.

to 451,032 in 1943. This growth in labor far exceeded that of the previous decades. Between 1929 and 1938, the number of workers rose by one-fifth. Not only the rate of growth, but also the rise in absolute number was considerably larger. In the decade preceding 1938, the labor force increased by 60,000 workers while between 1938 and 1943 the increase was over 120,000. The labor force was twice as large in the manufacturing industries within five years as in the whole preceding decade. This rise in the labor force is solely attributed to the increase in the need for labor in heavy industry for the development of the war effort.

The Industry Shift in the Number of Workers Within Hungary's Revised Borders from 1938 to 1943

Industry	1938	Percent	1943	Percent
Mining	41,536	12.5	59,194	13.1
Steel & Metal	50,765	15.4	62,639	13.9
Machinery	40,383	12.2	112,771	24.8
Electric Power	6,987	2.1	7,979	1.8
Stone, Clay, Glass	29,773	9.3	31,547	6.9
Wood	12,728	3.8	15,620	3.5
Leather	10,265	3.1	9,628	2.1
Textile	63,918	19.3	55,953	12.4
Clothing	10,178	3.1	10,954	2.5
Paper	5,560	1.7	7,491	1.7
Food	34,047	10.3	41,726	9.3
Chemical	16,338	4.9	25,457	5.6
Printing	7,570	2.3	10,073	2.2
Total	**330,048**	**100.0**	**451,032**	**100.0**

As can be seen, the growth in labor exceeded the average only in mining, chemical industry and machinery production. As a result of the war boom, over half of the working class was employed in mining, steel and metallurgical industries, machinery production and chemical industry. Actually, however, there were far more workers involved in the Hungarian war production. Just as in actual production the territorial expansion was a considerable factor, so the increase in labor through the enlargement of the territory also played a role with regard to the economy's war capacity.

Average Number of Workers in Hungary (1938-1943)

Year	Number of Workers	Percent
1938	288,512	100.0
1939	341,636	118.4
1940	366,515	127.0
1941	405,126	140.4
1942	444,573	154.1
1943	466,077	161.5

Considering the number of miners as well, which rose from 41,536 to 71,611 including the re-annexed areas, the total number of factory laborers rose from 330,048 to 542,688. Therefore, in 1943, over 210,000 more factory workers were available for the war economy than in 1938 which was an increase of 61%.

When studying the composition of the labor force, one must examine the sources of wartime increase in numbers. In the second half of the 1930s, unemployment was considerably larger between 1935-36, well over 100,000 were out of work. However, unemployment rapidly decreased between 1937-38 and by 1938, it was down to 55,000. In the massive wartime boom, the bulk of the unemployed was taken in by the manufacturing and the small-scale industries. The rise of 60,000 in the industrial labor force between 1938 and 1940 was largely due to the positions filled by the unemployed. What's more, the available unemployed masses were not enough to meet the demand of manufacturing industry for labor because a part of them went to work for small businesses.

These years began the shift of the agricultural work force into industry. Labor supply was greatly increased by the poor masses from the areas re-annexed by Hungary, who migrated toward jobs in the Budapest factories. These figures reveal that between 1939 and 1941, in addition to natural growth, Budapest's population increased by 40,000.[1] The greater part of the population came from rural areas. In the following years, this trend accelerated, becoming the major source of recruitment for the labor force. It would have been impossible to satisfy the sudden increase in demand for labor from any other source. The number of young laborers who had just reached working age was far below the industry's need for labor.

Women in the Work Force

The stagnation of female labor was unique in Europe, since in most belligerent countries, there was a great shift in the proportion of male and female labor due to the shortage of male workers.[2] In Hungary, this shift did not occur because there was no total mobilization and unemployment was very high and could only be offset by conscriptions. The number of workers in search of jobs was further increased by unemployed people from the re-annexed areas who drifted to the industrial heartland. Consequently, the factories were able to employ enough male labor. In 1943, however, the labor demand from the war factories could not be satisfied. One reason was that some work processes could only be carried out by skilled male workers so the employment of women would not have solved this problem.

Women in the Work Force (1938-1943)

Year	Number	% of All Factory Labor
1938	92,731	32.1
1939	105,631	32.2
1940	111,962	32.1
1941	109,916	31.0
1942	120,393	32.1
1943	125,456	32.1

The Need for Labor Increases

After draining the local and neighboring labor, certain provincial centers of the military industry were unable to recruit a sufficient number of laborers. Workers from small businesses couldn't be used because labor had streamed from small business to factories until 1938. Also, the small businesses were in a favorable phase of the business cycle, absorbing large numbers of new employees (approximately 80,000-100,000 people). In Germany, the attempted solution to the labor problem was to close down the small businesses and divert the working force to produce for the war factories. In Hungary, however, no similar measures were taken. As a result, in 1943, there was a grave shortage of labor in nearly all major war factories. The Hungarian Ammunition Works, for example, only worked in one shift in early 1943 for want of sufficient labor. There was no surplus labor force around Veszprém and replacements could not be recruited because there was a shortage of housing for the workers.[3] In the Székesfehérvár plant of the Shotgun Cartridge Factory, 1,695 workers were employed, although another 686 would were needed to keep up with the level of production.[4] During 1943, in the workshops of the Manfréd Weiss Works and the Danube Aircraft Factory, 37,000 workers were employed, but another 2,961 men and 1,451 women would have been needed; another 15,000 were required by the projections for 1944.[5] In 1943, chemical industry needed 20-25% more workers and the shortage increased during the summer months when some of the workers went home to help harvest their crops.[6]

The Use of Forced Labor Battalions

A report by the National Commissioner of War Material Production estimated the shortage of 50,000 laborers in mid-1943.[7] To ease the labor shortage, free, forced labor was introduced. All the large enterprises tried to reduce the shortage by using forced military labor battalions consisting of Jews and other nationalities. the low cost of forced labor was appreciated by industry as indicated by a memorandum from the Manfréd Weiss Works dated March 9, 1943. It projected that the labor force would be increased by 5,000 until the end of June 1943 and another 5,000 until 1944. "It would be most expedient in our view to have those liable to forced labor service providing additional labor." The memo found forced labor service advantageous for other reasons as well. For one thing, "the labor market produces far higher hourly wages than the level set by the price office," whereas the forced laborers cost very little. It was noted that "the great unemployment caused by the transition to the peacetime economy must also be kept in mind and preventive measures should be taken to forestall it. In this regard, too, the most favorable solution was the employment of forced military laborers since they could resume their original work during the transition." The Ministry of Defense soon informed the Manfréd Weiss Works that conscriptions would soon begin and 1,000 people from the nationalities and 500 women would be sent.[8] In most large war production factories, there were several thousand forced laborers. One thing is certain. The use of forced labor could not solve the shortage of labor.

The Work Force Composition Shifts from Skilled to Unskilled Workers

The employment of masses of new labor brought about changes in the proportion of trained and untrained workers. Extensive mass production in the war industry allowed for the employment of a wide strata of unskilled workers. Though there was great demand for the increase of semi-skilled and skilled labor, the rate of skilled workers decreased because of the shortage in skilled labor. This intensified the process to the detriment of skilled labor. What's more, the massive demand for labor decreased the rate of semi-skilled workers.

The Work Force Composition in 1938 and 1943

	1938	1943
Skilled Workers	30.3	27.0
Semi-Skilled Workers	42.2	39.4
Unskilled Workers	23.4	31.0
Apprentices	4.1	2.6

The Percentage Shift in Industrial Branches from 1939 to 1943[9]

Industry	Year	Skilled Labor	Semi-Skilled Labor	Unskilled Labor	Apprentices
Steel & Metal	1939	26.0	37.0	33.0	4.0
	1943	28.5	40.3	26.9	4.3
Machinery	1939	40.7	30.0	20.5	8.8
	1943	36.5	32.5	24.6	6.4
Electric Power	1939	50.0	20.9	27.3	1.8
	1943	48.4	20.3	27.9	3.4
Stone, Clay, Glass	1939	21.5	19.2	57.8	1.5
	1943	18.2	21.5	58.7	1.6
Wood	1939	26.7	24.2	45.9	3.2
	1943	27.5	27.5	42.9	2.1
Leather	1939	18.9	55.5	23.9	1.7
	1943	22.5	52.2	23.4	1.9
Textile	1939	8.1	72.6	18.2	1.1
	1943	9.0	68.6	20.7	1.6
Clothing	1939	49.0	36.3	9.4	5.3
	1943	50.0	35.2	13.3	1.5
Paper	1939	17.8	46.7	29.0	6.5
	1943	18.2	48.0	32.4	1.4
Food	1939	21.0	31.8	45.3	1.9
	1943	20.1	28.4	51.0	0.5
Chemical	1939	15.3	47.5	36.2	1.0
	1943	16.0	43.7	39.0	1.3
Printing	1939	63.6	17.0	13.0	6.4
	1943	53.9	24.5	13.1	7.9

The table clearly reveals the general tendency of a decrease in the number of skilled and trained workers. During the war, the composition of the working class changed to include new, mostly untrained workers from agriculture. At the end of the war, the number of untrained workers came close to one-third of the total factory labor. This change meant a numeric increase in the working class, but at the same time, the earlier generation of workers weakened the traditional organization and class consciousness of the working class. The natural generational change merged the new generation imbued with strong nationalistic and anti-Semitic propaganda with the earlier generation sharply opposed to the Horthy regime.

The Position of the Working Class during World War II

In the first few years, the transition to war economy and the militarization of the economy went together with a rise in real wages and an improvement of the living conditions. Unemployment was quickly reduced and the number of wage-earners within a family increased. During the war boom, the only group adversely affected by the upswing was the skilled laborers of peace industries who were forced to change trades several times. The increase in income also improved the workers' position. In these years, workers employed in war production factories received higher wages. All this helped the position of the working class. After Hungary's entry into the war in 1941, the advantageous changes resulting from the war boom were offset by discouraging military developments limiting consumption, the extension of working hours, military control over the workers, growing inflation and military conscriptions. In the first period of the war, from 1938 to 1942, the position of the working class was characterized by improving employment and the increase of real wages and income this tendency was reversed in the following years of the war.

Wages

Massive increases in employment, the gradual decrease of the unemployed reserves and the extra demand for labor increased wages. A contributory factor was the adjustment of wages due to price rises. The first such move in October 1940 resulted in extra wages amounting to 7% of the basic pay, this figure being 15% of the basic wages in May 1941, 30% in December 1941, with another supplementary pay in July 1943.[10] The following calculations of the Institute for Economic Research clearly show the rise in pay.[11]

Workers and Wages (1938-1943)

Year	Total Annual Factory Wages	Average No. of Workers	Average Wages (In Pengős)	Index
1938	351,227	288,512	1,217.40	100.0
1939	427,527	327,069	1,307.10	107.4
1940	483,581	348,894	1,386.00	113.8
1941	587,610	354,046	1,659.70	136.3
1942	790,726	374,299	2,112.60	173.5
1943	1,068,176	391,838	2,726.10	223.9

Average Hourly Wages

Year	In Pengős	Index
1938	0.50	100.0
1939	0.54	108.0
1940	0.57	114.0
1941	0.69	138.0
1942	0.84	168.0
1943	1.06	212.0

Thus, annual wages earned by a worker more than doubled between 1938 and 1943. This increase was due to the extension of the working time. The gap between the wages of skilled workers and untrained laborers further increased because skilled workers became irreplaceable in most factories since skilled labor was not available from the forced labor camps. There was also a wide gap between the wages of employees in war supply factories and the other workers. While state regulations introduced in July 1943 stipulated a supplementary pay of 60% of the 1939 wages, this figure did not rise above 30-50% for workers employed in factories that did not produce war necessities. Differences between the wages of various worker categories are also noteworthy.

Average Hourly Wages of the Iron and Machine Workers 1938-1942 (in fillérs)[12]

	Skilled Workers	Semi-Skilled Workers	Unskilled Workers	Women Workers
November 1938	87	75	50	42
November 1939	90	76	51	43
November 1940	99	86	58	47
November 1941	116	98	66	52
November 1942	140	120	83	62

While between November 1938 and November 1942, the hourly wages of skilled workers rose by 53 fillérs, the semi-skilled workers received 45 fillérs more, the unskilled workers got 33 and the women received 20 fillérs more per hour. Especially high were the wages in certain industrial branches like precision engineering, machine tool production and electrotechnical industry which were connected with the war supply industry. However, the rise in the cost of living offset the rises in nominal earnings, even surpassing them in the final years of the war. The official figures for the costs of living as estimated in the war period are not reliable. The Statistical Office changed the group of staples in such a way that the calculated price rise was far below the actual rise. These figures do not include the purchase of rationed goods from the black market which considerably increased the cost of living index.

Real Value of Income (1938-1943)

Year	Total Annual Wages/Worker	Subsistence Costs Index Average	Real Value of Wages
1938	100.0	100.0	100.0
1939	107.4	98.5	109.0

Year	Total Annual Wages/Worker	Subsistence Costs Index Average	Real Value of Wages
1940	113.8	106.9	106.5
1941	136.3	126.2	108.0
1942	173.5	154.9	112.0
1943	223.9	203.1	110.2

When evaluating the official real income index, the lengthening of the working hours must be considered. It is therefore more appropriate to consider the real value of the hourly wages:

Real Value Index of Average Hourly Wages

Year	Index
1938	100.0
1939	109.6
1940	106.6
1941	109.4
1942	108.5
1943	104.4

This table reveals that the real income did not exceed the level of 1939 in the subsequent war years and from 1941 there was a decline. Yet, these figures can only be accepted for the period up to 1940-41. In sum, the necessary amount of food could not be acquired without the black market. The staples used for the calculation of the subsistence costs were no longer available at official prices due to various restrictions. These items had to be purchased on the black market at prices which were extremely high. According to the calculations of the Institute for Economic Research, in November 1943, the foodstuffs used for setting the subsistence index cost were 117% more in the black markets than in official prices. They also add that the group of staples fell below the pre-war standards by having 10% less calories as well. But, even in spite of this reduction of consumption, certain foodstuffs had to be bought on the black market which increased the prices by 36%.[13]

As can be seen, the calculations of the cost of living index for 1942-43 presented a far more positive picture than it was in reality. At a session of Committee No. 42 of the Parliament, Károly Rassay, a liberal opposition leader, said: "The Finance Minister presented an index calculation in his Lower House address but, excuse my saying so, I think this index calculation has nothing to do with real life...This I didn't want to tell the House, but here I can say it."[14] Lipót Baranyai, president of the National Bank commented similarly in autumn 1942: "...the purchasing power of wages has decreased considerably from whichever side I look at it. I must realize that our indices show a price rise of 75% whereas, in fact, we are faced with a rise of 100%."[15] Richard Quandt, general director of the National Bank, claimed at a board meeting that while the official figures showed a price rise of 5% between 1942 and April 1943, the rise was actually around 20%. Keeping in mind that 40% of trade was from the black market, the rise was not 20, but 50% in the given period and the growth of the price index was 32%.[16]

Evidently, the calculations for 1942 and especially for 1943 are not accurate. The different computations cited above also reveal that the price rise caused a great decline in real wages. Though there is no statistical data, Finance Minister Lajos Reményi-Schneller admitted in autumn 1943 that compared to 1938, the real wages of the workers dropped from 100 to 91%.[17] Contrary to the published data, the actual decline went slightly below the pre-war real wage level. Around this time, however, the drop in a worker's real wages was offset by a constant labor shortage which enabled several members of a family to work keeping family incomes stable.

It must be stressed that if a comparison of nominal wages and cost of living can never give a realistic picture the working class' wages then during wartime, it is even less indicative of the real value of wages. In these years, it was not the lack of financial resources that posed the major problem but the difficulty of acquiring the necessary goods. Let us note that there were severe restrictions imposed on nearly all the basic foodstuffs. Sugar was rationed in autumn 1940, followed by flour and bread. The daily bread rations per person was reduced to 0.15 kilograms in 1942 and 0.60 kilograms of lard in summer 1942. The per capita rations were often far lower in Hungary than in other European countries. Added to this, was the purchase vouchers for clothes, shoes and even for shoe repair. In other words, a worker's income could satisfy his subsistence needs at the official prices, but he required goods from the black market and encountered restrictions which meant that his income was no longer enough for subsistence at the earlier level.

There were serious grievances concerning the supplies of the working class in 1943. In a petition, the Wolfner Factory protested that their workers were very poorly supplied as they lived around Pest and they only received the regular bread rations, although they did hard physical labor. "They do not get any lard at all for weeks," the petition said.[18] In the autumn of that year, it was also brought up at a meeting of the parliamentary committee: "Physical workers do not see a quarter of a kilogram of pork on their tables for weeks, nay, even for months."[19] As regards manufactured goods, the Hungarian Wagon and Machine Factory, a high-priority war factory, complained that: "for lack of footwear there is a great deal of absence among our workers every day amounting to about 10-15% of the total manpower." The factory asked that its workers in aircraft production should be allotted a pair of shoes a year and a voucher for shoe repairs.[20]

Another factor that cannot appear in real wage calculations is the great deterioration in the quality of manufactured goods after 1940-1941. As a consequence of the halt in raw material imports, various supplementary or artificial materials had to be used especially in the textile and leather goods. These materials were of extremely poor quality as Hungary lacked the technology and the know-how for artificial material production. For instance, the great amount of the artificial fiber blended with natural materials reduced the durability of the textiles to a fraction of the earlier value. Under such circumstances, it is justified to speak of the decline of real income due to the poor durability of goods which required frequent replacements. The quality deterioration of consumer goods was a prime contributor to the plummeting living standards toward the end of the war.

What further aggravated the situation of the working class was the rescission of certain social laws and regulations and the introduction of a series of wartime regulations that created below-standard working conditions.

The deterioration of the working conditions was principally caused by the extension of the working day. The eight-hour work day had been enacted before 1938. Even though Hungary remained neutral after the outbreak of the war, several achievements of the social legislation including the fixed working week were revoked. In 1942, working time was considerably prolonged especially in some branches of heavy industry. In mining, workers worked an average 10 hours a day that year.[21] In summer 1944, plans were considered to introduce a working time of 12 hours a day at the Salgótarján coal mines.[22] In certain Budapest aircraft factory workshops of the Hungarian Wagon and Machine Works the work day was 12 hours.[23] In the Manfréd Weiss Works, the 11-hour shift was introduced in 1944.[24] In most jobs at the Hungarian Chemical Works, a shift lasted 12 hours.[25] Similarly, in certain branches of the woodworking industry where people worked in 10-12 hour shifts in 1942.[26] The Kelenföld Textile Factory introduced the 10-hour day, while in the baking and meat industries the working week was 60-70 hours long.[27] In 1938, the annual per capita working hours were 1,568, rising to 2,439 in 1943. This meant that a worker's workdays increased from 105 to 321 a year, if we calculate an 8-hour working day. In fact, the average length of daily work rose above 9 hours during the war.

By imposing military discipline on the workers, their position deteriorated even further. Under the statutes of the 1939 Defense Act, a considerable proportion of the factories were declared to be war supply factories, placing the workers who worked there under military control. Powerful military commanders were appointed to each of these factories and subjected the workers to the rules of military discipline. The slightest offense was strictly penalized. Reprisals like those at the National Worsted Mill were common where some of the workers charged with absenteeism were sentenced to 3 and 4 weeks imprisonment augmented with weekly one day fasting and a hard berth.[28] Absentees were brought in by force.

Summary jurisdiction was extended to cases of disobedience and sabotaging. The recognition of the senselessness of the war and the increased pressures led to the weakening of labor discipline, especially after 1943.

In October 1943, the military commander of the Salgótarján coal mines declared that money fines and imprisonment for absenteeism were ineffective and so he recommended that "notorious truants" should be sent to the front.[29] In the same vein, the military commander of the National Worsted Mill reported: "The punitive measures applied so far to employees of militarized factories in an effort to maintain labor discipline did not always prove adequate. In order to keep up labor discipline, militarized factory employees who gravely breached the workshop discipline must be detained (interned)."[30] The direct sanctions against the violators of labor discipline were complemented with threats and in many cases, with the actual implementation of internment which meant their despatch to the front. Apart from the pressures of inflation and militarization, the government took other steps to weaken labor resistance. There were incessant attacks on the trade unions from 1938, demanding their abolition and replacement by fascist workers chambers. However, the trade unions were only banned in 1944, though the government had been trying for years to gain full control over the workers. Minister of the Interior, Ferenc Keresztes-Fischer expressed the government's view of the workers in the following way: "We shall die in the field of work if need be, but the aim of the war shall be achieved."

After the political shift to the right and the Italian-German influences in the war years, the Horthy regime used repressive regulations to keep the population under control. They increasingly resorted to extreme nationalist and even fascist demagogy. This was especially powerful during the time of the return of certain territories. From the moment it came to power, the counter-revolutionary government focused its propaganda on the restoration of "Greater Hungary." In schools and forums the minds had been manipulated by the slogan: "Maimed Hungary is No Country, Greater Hungary is Heaven." Propagandists claimed that all the social and economic ills were to be blamed on the Trianon Peace Treaty and only the restoration of Greater Hungary could bring about welfare and prosperity. Between 1938 and 1941 significant territories were ceded back to Hungary. During the same period, the war boom affected an unprecedented upswing which led to the eradication of unemployment and the rise in real wages. The official propaganda profited tremendously by this coincidence. The masses really believed that the return of areas and the improvement of living conditions were directly related. Consequently, they felt that the government was pursuing a successful policy that stressed the interests of the common people. The re-annexation of the territories largely contributed to the consolidation and popularization of the Horthy regime between 1938 and 1941.

All this went together with strong anti-communist propaganda. The military commanders of the factories were heads of propaganda centers at the same time, determined to present the war as a unified mission vital for the nation's survival. They tried to inspire enthusiasm for the war. In Csepel, for example, there was a series of informative lectures on "Sabotage," "The Machinations of Enemy Propaganda," "Red Propaganda and How to Combat It" and "Workers' Life in the Soviet Union." The enthusiasm of the nation roused by the war and the re-annexations reinforced by the regime's propaganda campaign left its imprint upon the new generations of workers. The new generation of workers did not have the historic experiences of their forebearers lacking the decisive collective experience of the workers movement. The democratization after two revolutions, the effective nationalist propaganda of the Horthy administration and after 1938 the propaganda and organizational work of the official and political right wing opposition using anti-Semitism with growing success was very effective. The most important action of the working class, the general miners' strike in 1940 was organized by the fascist Arrow Cross Party, a telling sign of the new tendency of political right wing movements as well as of their temporary success. Nonetheless, through the trade unions and social democracy, the organized working class core was preserved.

The illusions entertained by the political right wing

movements were soon shattered. The Arrow Cross Party's influence on the masses culminated in 1939-40. Following those years, there was a decline in the standard of living. Discontent spread and the hope of change after the war strengthened. By the end of the war, the impact of chauvinistic incitement to war dissipated. All this, however, did not go beyond passive waiting and sabotaging the evacuation orders. As a result, on the day after liberation, immense political energies burst forth.

Notes

1. *Budapest Székesfővάros Statisztikai Évkönyve* [Statistical Yearbook of the Capital City of Budapest] (1940); *Ibid.*, (1943).

2. Considering only the German workers, the rate of female labor in German industry was 25% in 1939 and 35% in 1944; *Die deutsche Industrie im Kriege 1939-1945* (Berlin, 1954), 151-153.

3. Hadtörténeti Intézet Levéltára, VKF-1943, 177-4847.

4. Központi Gazdasági Levéltár, Industrial Secretariat of the Commercial Bank, 190.

5. Központi Gazdasági Levéltár, Manfréd Weiss Papers 51-999/V/10, Vadásztölténygyár.

6. Központi Gazdasági Levéltár, Chinoin material file 36.

7. Hadtörténeti Intézet Levéltára, VKF 1943, 178-5384

8. Központi Gazdasági Levéltár, Manfréd Weiss Papers, 51-999/V/10.

9. Only the years between 1939 and 1943 can be compared as to industrial branches because the sectorial statistics for 1938 were grouped differently from the survey of 1943.

10. Magyar Gazdaságkutató Intézet, Report no. 52. sz. helyzetjelentése, 106.

11. Magyar Gazdaságkutató Intézet Archives, "Gyári munkások keresete," [Earnings of Factory Workers]. According to the *Statistical Yearbook*, in 1943, the total of wages paid was 1,152 million pengős and the average annual income of a worker was 2,840 pengős.

12. *Ungarische Wirtshcafts-Jahrbuch* (Budapest, 1943), 327.

13. Magyar Gazdaságkutató Intézet Archives, 1944, 1-50. In

his comments to Committee No. 42 of the Parliament in Autumn 1943 Béla Imrédy said the black market was thriving more than ever, "the prices today are simply incredible....You see shirts for 250 pengős and ties for 60 pengős in the shop windows...." See: Országos Levéltár, Minutes of Committee No. 42, October 8, 1943, Vol. XXXI, 534.

14. Országos Levéltár, Minutes of Committee No. 42, 1943, XXXI, 239.

15. Központi Gazdasági Levéltár, National Bank board meeting, minutes, September 30, 1942.

16. *Ibid.,* May 21, 1943.

17. Diary of Lower House, October 22, 1943.

18. Központi Gazdasági Levéltár, Wolfner Papers, 149.

19. Hungarian National Archives, Parliamentary Committee, IX, 452. November 6, 1943. Comments by János Szabó.

20. Központi Gazdasági Levéltár, Hungarian Wagon and Machine Factory, October 27-28, 1943.

21. *Bányászati és Kohászati Lapok* [Bulletin of Mining and Metallurgy], June 15, 1947.

22. Központi Gazdasági Levéltár, Salgótartján coal mine, Record of Executive Committee, June 23, 1944.

23. Központi Gazdasági Levéltár, Győr Wagon Factory. 15 Hüsz.

24. Központi Gazdasági Levéltár, Manfréd Weiss Papers Ammunition Factory, 86, October 4, 1944.

25. Chinoin 36.

26. Központi Gazdasági Levéltár, Hungarian National Bank Board Meeting Minutes. August 26, 1942.

27. Központi Gazdasági Levéltár, Keltex, 1940. Rescript of the Ministry of Industry, 54, 616/XIII; Hungarian National Archives, Parliamentary Committee V., November 4, 1941.

28. Központi Gazdasági Levéltár, National Worsted Mill, Hüsz. pk. Order no. 23.

29. Központi Gazdasági Levéltár, Salgótartján Coal Mines, 241, October 7, 1943.

30. Központi Gazdasági Levéltár, National Worsted Mill, Hüsz. pk. November 16, 1943.

III. WAR CASUALTIES

HUNGARY'S CASUALTIES IN WORLD WAR II*

Tamás Stark

Introduction

> On January 31, 1941, as the previous census showed, the number of Hungary's population was 9.316 million. For the years between 1941-48, this number should have risen to about 9.65 million. Instead, the number was only 9.20 million on January 1, 1949 due to war losses, 111,000 or 12% below the corresponding figure for 1941. It aptly illustrates the magnitude of war casualties that during the 80 years following 1869 - the year of the first census in Hungary - 1941-49 was the only period in which the population decreased.

The above passage is quoted from the summary volume of the demographic results of the 1949 census (p. 13). The authors indirectly suggest a deficit of 300,000 people based on the number predicted for 1949 and the actual number of the population. It is, however, not so easy to calculate the Hungary's victims claimed by the war. This is not because the population was profoundly influenced by the migration of people to and from Hungary. Even permitting that, only the casualties in the war zones of the country can be estimated and even these figures can only yield secondary results because this must be considered with the total loss of the country's population. The wartime fate of people in Upper Northern Hungary, Northern Transylvania and Southern Hungary re-annexed by Hungary is an integral part of the country's history. The political events at

* This essay is an abridged and translated version of *Magyarország második világháborús emberveszteségе* (Budapest, 1989).

home and abroad, conscription, bombing, persecution and captivity hit the people of the territory defined by the Trianon Treaty and those of the re-annexed areas alike. Naturally, the relevant extant documents refer to Hungary bounded by the 1941 frontiers, containing the majority of Hungarians living in the Carpathian Basin.

In the preface to the volume of documents about the destruction of the Second Hungarian Army at the Don, Ferenc Münnich wrote: "Tens of thousands of Hungarian peasants, workers and progressive intellectuals were sent to the Don to die by the Horthy regime. We recall the memory of these tens of thousands of Hungarians with a grieving heart." Grieving remembrance, however, does not mean a tribute to the victims and does not replace the objective investigation of their fate.

Tackling the question of prisoners of war was allegedly "injurious to the country's international interests." The guardians of the social sciences were so determined to wipe out this delicate question from the nation's consciousness that the years spent in captivity were often deduced from the length of employment of survivors when calculating old-age pension. By the same token, it was also injurious to the interest of friendly countries, to use the official terms, to estimate the number of refugees.

The material damage caused by the war began the moment the fighting stopped, but hardly any attempts were made to establish the number of war casualties and the size of wartime migration. Although in 1946, the statistician Árpád Snyder, tried to estimate the losses of combatants and civilians for the then area of the country, his results are superficial for lack of adequate sources. The next attempt came at a delay of almost 40 years. The reluctant silence was broken by the pioneering studies of Mihály Korom[1] and Lajos Für[2] who have aroused the interest of a wide reading strata on the subject. The present study is intended to pay tribute to the Hungarian victims of the war. We owe respect to the soldiers who went on fighting and died heroic deaths to ensure the freedom of their comrades.

Almost all the casualties of World War I occurred on the fronts. That World War II was a total war waged on a wider scale is evidenced by the expanded number of casualties. Due to the air raids, the fighting went on at the fronts and in the hinterland. "Hinterland" itself was a temporary concept since in that moving war every town and village became a military target. The aim was to totally destroy the enemy country. That is why tens of thousands of civilians killed in the war increase the final toll, though they were only reluctant, helpless onlookers. The fate of civilians and soldiers was even more tightly connected toward the closing phase of the war. The war was not only waged against countries, but against "races" as well. Hundreds of thousands of Hungarian Jews and several thousand Gypsies died a martyr's death in the concentration camps.

A less-known concomitant of all-out warfare and extreme nationalism was the harassment and arbitrary deportation of national minorities. There were several victorious powers like Czechoslovakia which tried to use their position for the annihilation of Hungarians living in their area. Romanian and Serbian nationalism also claimed many Hungarian victims who were killed by the armed bands or forced to flee their homes. Unfortunately, Hungary was not free from nationalistic intolerance, either. Over 100,000 ethnic Germans were expelled from Hungary. The victims of the war were forced to flee the advancing Red Army.

Military Casualties

Casualties from the Advance of 1941 to the Retreat of 1943

It is only in relation to major campaigns or battles that one finds figures on the losses of the army in military history. The introduction to Miklós Horváth's volume,[3] Pál Kornis' study[4] and the last volume of *The History of Hungary*[5] touch on the losses of the 1942-43 campaigns, giving most diverse figures. Sándor Tóth[6] and Ignác Ölvedi[7] provide some of the casualty figures in Hungary. The most reliable figures can be found in János Csima's highly meticulous endeavor.[8] The confusion in the research is largely due to the contradictory nature of the source materials. The diary of the units at the front, the Casualties Department at the Ministry of Defense and the Staff

Bulletin often state different figures for the casualties of the same period. The records made in 1945 for the Allied Control Commission do not always harmonize with figures in the preparatory material for the peace treaty. Similarly contradictory are the partial figures in documentary volumes. The approach to the hardly accessible material is also hesitant because the authors often fail to differentiate between various types of losses. The numbers of the dead, wounded, missing and prisoners of war are mixed in several studies. The military losses of Hungary in World War II cannot be precisely established. From the moment the country entered the war, the lists of casualties, bulletins of information and many other documents were lost or destroyed.

Although the Hungarian army's first act in World War II was the occupation of Northern Transylvania, the first true military operation came half a year later with the participation in the offensive against Yugoslavia in April 1941 where 65 Hungarian soldiers died and 212 were wounded at Bački Petrovac (Petrőc).[9] They were Hungary's first casualties. For Hungary, the war actually began with the declaration of war on the Soviet Union on June 26, 1941. The first Hungarian casualties on the Eastern front were Lieutenant László Dányai and Ensign István Sallay who disappeared on June 29, 1941 over the Carpathians.[10] On June 30, 1941, the 45,000-strong Carpathian Army Group was set up in Huszt.[11] Their war operations lasted from July 1-7, 1941. Their quick advance into Galicia claimed about 400 lives. When the thrust forward was completed, a motorized corp comprised of the Carpathian Army Group continued attacking under the command of Béla Miklós Dálnoki. By August 1941, this elite corps was fighting east of Dnepropetrovsk in the Donets Basin. During the operations, however, 70-80% of their equipment was lost. Therefore, a decision was made to withdraw the Hungarian troops during Hitler and Horthy's talks in Rastenburg on September 7, 1941. Only a minimum occupying force of a few thousand was left by Hungary in the Eastern theater of war after mid-November.

The final toll of the 1941 campaign against the Soviet Union produced conflicting reports. A 1942 report of the chiefs of staff sets the figure at 4,524 army personnel.[12] The figure specified by the Casualties Department of the Ministry of Defense shows a loss of 3,891.[13] There is no explanation for these conflicting reports other than missing or duplicate figures. Taken within the context of the entire war casualties, either figure is nominal by comparison.

Following the failure of the German high command under Moscow in the winter of 1941, greater tasks were assigned to Germany's allies armies in 1942. During the negotiations between the German and Hungarian governments in Budapest on January 21, 1942, the Hungarians agreed to deploy 9 infantry and 1 armored divisions at the front.[14] The infantry divisions made up the Second Hungarian Army later under the command of Colonel-General Gusztáv Jány. The Hungarians were part of General Maximilian Weichs' Army group in areas of operation.

The manpower to be mobilized for the Second Hungarian Army was selected evenly and proportionately from all over the country. The manpower and equipment available to the armed forces were distributed by the competent organs in such a way that it should affect as little as possible the strength of the Hungarian Royal Honvéd army which they wished to save for after the war. The organization and outfitting of the army and the transport of troops to the front began by early April 1942. By July 27th, all three corps were in place.

The first casualties of the Second Hungarian Army were victims of the partisans. Until May 31, 1942, 30 officers and 469 non-commissioned officers and soldiers lost their lives.[15] The first Hungarian attack started from the direction of the Don on June 28th, before all the troops had been transported. The retreating Soviet units put up the strongest resistance at Tim. By the end of July, all three corps of the Second Hungarian Army had reached the Don. A total of 240,000 Hungarian soldiers were stationed in the Eastern front.[16] The fighting for the destruction of the three Soviet bridgeheads (Suchia, Korotoiak and Uriv) on the west bank of the Don began in late July. This time there were heavy losses; on August 9th, the 8,000-strong 20th Light Division lost 1,400 men.[17] Some battalions lost all four commanders. The Third Corps in the main line of attack suffered a 15-20% casualty rate.[18] Miklós

Horváth estimated the toll at 30,000 men. This number including the dead, wounded and missing based on a report by staff Lieutenant-Colonel Béla Técsői Móricz, head of the panel set up to evaluate the war on the Russian front seems to be exaggerated.[19]

The table of losses issued by the chiefs of the operational staff on May 15, 1944 shows a total loss of 33,763 for 1942.[20] This sum total also includes losses sustained during transportation over the Tim crossing and by the occupation forces. Adding up the figures given by the same source for July, August and September, we get a total of 23,265. From this about 2,000 must be deducted to account for the loss of the occupying forces included in that figure. The remaining 20,000 people can be regarded as casualties of the bridgehead battles. János Csima also estimates 20,000 Hungarian casualties in the attack on the Soviet bridgeheads.[21] The report sent on September 20th by the quartermaster general of the Second Hungarian Army to the army headquarters also claims that there were 20,000 losses in the weeks of the bridgehead fighting.[22] If the report contained the losses for the last 16 days of September, we would probably get the additional 2-3,000 that the table of the chiefs of the operational staff of May 15, 1944 indicates.

The heavy losses surprised the Hungarian and the German top brass. The decisive factor was the technical superiority of the Soviets. In addition to the outdated equipment and the poor training of the Hungarian troops, according to German General Langermann and several leaders of the Second Hungarian Army, the soldiers were unable to penetrate the enemy's defenses undetected.[23] Due to lack of materials, the trenches were flimsy and their air defense was ineffective.

Nearly all the books devoted to Hungary's role in World War II set the number of servicemen in the Second Hungarian Army at 200,000. Undoubtedly, 200,000 soldiers were claimed to be serving in the army in the summer of 1942 by Ministry of Defense documents. The losses of the summer clashes and the increasing operational tasks required new shipments to the front. In his telegram of September 22, 1942, German Ambassador Dietrich Jagow noted that an additional 20,000 people were to go to the front in late September 1942.[24] The telegram of September 29, 1942 sent by the Chargé d'Affairs Karl Werkmeister from Budapest to the German Ministry of Foreign Affairs reveals that in late September, Colonel-General Jány asked the prime minister for a supplementary force of 25,000 and a maximum number of Jewish forced laborers.[25] According to the finance department of the Ministry of Defense, the number of the Second Hungarian Army rose from 204,160 in October 1942 to 237,250 in November and the shipments continued in December.[26] The registration department of the Ministry of Defense reports that 245,000 people were available in the Second Hungarian Army in January 1943.[27] Many of these soldiers were ill-equipped to replace those in the front line. Replacements should have arrived between January 13-20. Indeed, from early December 20,000 soldiers stayed in the support line of the Second Hungarian Army.[28]

From the second half of September 1942 there was no regular military activity on the Soviet-Hungarian front, but the signs of a major Soviet campaign increased dramatically from January 1943. The first Soviet raid was launched from the Uriv bridgehead on January 12, 1943 and on January 14, they also attacked from the bridgehead of Suchei. The next day the front-line was penetrated at several points. By January 24, the Hungarian army resistance had been broken.

As early as the beginning of February, casualty reports began to arrive in Budapest. At a meeting of the parliament's foreign committee on February 19, 1943, Prime Minister Miklós Kállay reported 20,000 dead, 20,000 wounded and 30,000 missing.[29] A report by the Second Hungarian Army dated four days earlier contradicted the prime minister's tally by indicating a loss of over 100,000 men.[30] This figure also includes the victims of the Tim breakthrough and the bridgehead fighting. In his letter of April 3, 1943, Brigadier General Gyula Kovács, the Second Hungarian Army's Chief of Staff, also wrote about a loss of 100,000 men.[31] Similar was the estimate of losses by Andor Szentmiklósi, head of the Ministry of Foreign Affairs' political department in his preparatory notes for Horthy's talks with Hitler on April 16th.[32] In his letter to Hitler on May 7, Horthy set the number of losses at 126,000.[33]

The most extreme figure was published by Pál Kornis who wrote that "a hundred and fifty thousands [were] driven to perdition, tossed off as prey...."[34] Miklós Horváth calculates the number of losses at 147,971 inclusive of the wounded and captives.[35] The *History of Hungary* reports a far smaller number of 110,000 without reference to the sources.[36]

How large was then the loss of the Second Hungarian Army? The most reliable authority should be the figures offered by the casualties department of the Ministry of Defense. After more than a year of processing the incoming lists of losses, their confidential report released on May 15, 1944 reveals the loss for the period between June 26, 1941 and December 31, 1943 was 142,699. Of this number, 18,852 were killed, 40,551 were wounded, 80,549 were missing and 2,747 were in captivity.[37]

Deducing from the 140,000 lost until the end of 1943 the number of casualties sustained before April 1942 and after April 1943 was 127,000. However, the losses of the Second Hungarian Army were less than that amount since it also includes the casualties of the occupation forces which can be roughly estimated at 5-6,000.[38] In the final analysis, it can be estimated that the loss of the Second Hungarian Army totaled 120,000. Of this, 100,000 were killed, wounded, captured or disappeared in the battle of the Don. Another Ministry of Defense report from 1944 also estimates the losses at about 120,000, with a different break-down: dead: 9,977, missing and captured: 55,798; wounded: 25,075; in hospital: 19,989; unknown: 6,791.[39]

Apart from calculating a loss of 140,000 until December 31, 1943, 120,000 of them from the Second Hungarian Army, an exact account is rendered impossible by the extremely large number of the missing (80,549). Due to the chaotic retreat, the victims, especially the dead, could not be counted with precision. To declare someone dead required the presentation of his "identification card" (dog-tag) and two witnesses who confirmed the death with their signatures.[40] Since this procedure was almost impossible during the retreat, the dead and the prisoners of war were ranked in the category of "missing."

Incorporating information from Russian reports for 1943, 1944 and 1946 the Ministry of Defense estimated the number of prisoners of war at 26,000.[41] On the other hand, Ferenc Gallyas, who worded an appeal for the release of Hungarians captured along the Don on February 9, 1943, wrote in the name of 40,000 prisoners of war.[42] According to the *White Book*, published in 1950 by Hungarian émigrés in the West, 87,000 Hungarian soldiers fell into Soviet captivity during the Red Army's breakthrough at Voronezh.[43] In contrast, Miklós Horváth speaks about 30,000 prisoners of war.[44] The preface to "Hungarian Freedom Fighters Against Fascism" contains an estimate of 100,000. This estimate would seem to be erroneous. Out of the 143,699 lost until December 31, 1943, another 40-50,000 deaths could be counted with the 18,852 verified cases. This number also includes victims among forced laborers.

In April 1943, the transports of the Second Hungarian Army back to Hungary were initiated. Until April 1, 1944, there were only occupying forces in the Soviet Union. The Hungarian troops managed to create a "peaceful coexistence" even with the partisans who were mostly Ukrainians. For this reason, the occupying forces had minimal losses in 1943. With the approaching of the front, the higher German command deployed some divisions of the Hungarian forces in the East to fill the gaps. The poorly equipped Hungarian divisions sustained heavy losses against the Soviet forces. In some battalions, only two platoons survived the offensive.[45]

Total Losses in the War Against the Soviet Union (June 26, 1941-December 31, 1943)

Month	1941	1942	1943
January	52	78	533
February	166	12	349
March	648	3	292
April	308	1	873
May	1,143	3	882
June	2	435	553
July	1,310	1,492	711
August	1,016	13,127	1,271
September	1,189	8,646	1,422

Month	1941	1942	1943
October	199	1,907	420
November	88	1,754	411
December	49	2,085	368

Total: 142,699

Source: Archives of Military History, VKF 1944. hdm. cs. f. 437/eln.

Published: May 15, 1944.

The Losses of the Defensive Fights between 1944-45

The mobilization of the First Hungarian Army was ordered after the German occupation of Hungary in March 1944. By then, the front was only 100-150 kilometers away from Hungary's frontiers. The difference between the occupation forces and combat units disappeared completely. The majority of the occupation forces were rearranged as part of the First Hungarian Army, while four divisions were set up as the Second Reserve Corps to be deployed in Poland. The offensive of the First Hungarian Army started on April 17 and ended on April 30, 1944. The better arms of the Soviet troops caused heavy casualties among the Hungarians during the two-week offensive. In the Ministry of Defense report of May 15, 1944, the total loss was set at 15,576. Of that, the dead numbered 1,942, the wounded 10,193 and the missing 3,441.[46]

As a result of the Soviet attack on Tarnopol on July 13, 1944, the front line of the First Hungarian Army was in disarray. The first Soviet raids took place on July 22nd and two days later, the entire battlefield was in utter confusion. The situation could not be stabilized before the retreat to the so-called Hunyadi defense lines at the end of July. Some divisions lost up to 30% of their fighting strength. Reports noted: "No food has been received for four days. The men have not slept for six days. The division represents hardly any combat value....At first, the behavior of the soldiers was excellent, but exhaustion has crushed their power of resistance....The number of deaths is disproportionately high."[47] From July 1944, the daily confidential reports contained fragmented data. The last remark available about the casualties of the First Hungarian Army is found in the report of July 28, 1944. "So far, 20,630 troops including 918 officers of the First Hungarian Army have crossed our frontier."[48] János Csima, an authority on war operations estimates that 20% of the wounded can be assumed to equal the number of deaths and 30% that of the missing — then the 21,548 wounded would imply a total loss of 35,000. This estimate is probably closer to the actual figure than Ignác Ölvedi who put the losses of the First Hungarian Army at 50,000 by the end of July.[49]

Fighting did not cease with the retreat to the Hunyadi line. Clashes claiming heavy losses went on until mid-August when the fighting came to a standstill. Romania's pulling out of the war created a new and more dangerous situation. In September 1944, extensive forces of the First Hungarian Army were ordered to the defense of Southern and Northern Transylvania. The weakened army withdrew from the Hunyadi position to the Carpathian Mountains and the Tatar pass willingly, without fighting. In late September, the army headquarters ordered further retreat to the Árpád position within the borders of the country. In early October, the war was raging behind the army due to the breakthrough at Debrecen and in November the phased withdrawal of the armed forces from the Carpathian Mountains began by stretches of 15-20 kilometers.

Desertion to the enemy was practically non-existent before Hungary's aborted attempt to pull out of the war in early October 1944. Late that month and the following month, when the war losses became evident, the trend was reversed. In his telegram of October 28 to Stalin, Colonel-General Lev Z. Mekhlis, the political commander of the 4th Ukrainian Front reported: "The units of the First Hungarian Army confronting our troops are in the state of collapse and demoralization. Our troops take 1,000-1,500-2,000 or more prisoners of war a day."[50] According to Sándor Tóth, over 20,000 soldiers surrendered to the Soviet forces in two weeks.[51]

Major Ferenc Péchy, M.D., who worked in the Ministry of Defense's headquarters, made notes of the reports sent to the general staff about the losses.[52] In his view, the First Hungarian Army lost 48,000 up to October 31, 1944: 8,000 dead and 40,000 wounded. In the knowledge of the war events, the figure seems inflated. If roughly 35,000 can be estimated as the loss until the end of July 1944, the number of victims is unlikely to have grown by over 10,000 until the end of October. True, heavy losses were claimed in the fighting from late July to mid-August, but September and October passed in relative calm. The total loss of 40,000 seems more likely.

After Romania changed sides on August 23rd, the Second Transylvanian Army was organized from troops of the poorly equipped reserve field divisions and the First Hungarian Army under the command of Lieutenant-General Lajos Dalnoki Veress. The heaviest casualties began on August 26th when the Second Ukrainian Front reached the Hungarian border in the valley of Uz. The fiercest encounters developed around Turda from September 13th, where despite the numeric superiority of the Soviets, the Hungarians maintained their positions until October 8th. In early October, the main targets of Soviet attack became the towns of Arad and Debrecen. To slow down the advance of the Soviet and Romanian troops from Southern Transylvania, the Third Hungarian Army was set up in September 1944, but its fighting force and equipment were no match for the Soviet divisions. In mid-October, the pincer offensive against Debrecen made the withdrawal from Transylvania and the Eastern Carpathians inevitable. Ignác Ölvedi wrote the following about the losses: "The retreating German-Hungarian troops left 13,200 dead on the battlefield."[53]

Chaos overcame the Hungarian corps as they retreated toward Budapest. whenever a regiment reached the vicinity of its recruiting district, it lost the greater part of its effectiveness.[54] Thus, a comprehensive analysis of the losses for 1944 could only be made after the war.[55] The first summary of the losses of the Hungarian army was made in late March 1945 upon the request of the Allied Control Commission. Since the reports of the Casualties Department of the Ministry of Defense were not available yet, the figures of the first statistics are very rough. According to this document, the casualties of the Second Hungarian Army were: 40,000 dead; 65,000 prisoners of war, missing; 15,000 disabled. This statistic contains figures for the losses sustained until October 15, 1944: 20,000 Dead; 50,000 prisoners of war and missing; 23,000 disabled.[56]

The following are two lists of the casualties which were prepared for the Allied Control Commission. the first was delivered in late March while the second, more comprehensive list was delivered in June:

The Hungarian Army's Losses
(July 1943-December 1944)
Presented to the Allied Control Commission March 1945[57]

July 1943-June 1944	73,595 missing, wounded, dead or captured
July 1944-August 1944	22,925 casualties
September 1944-December 1944	35,996 casualties

The Hungarian Army's Losses
(June 26, 1941-December 1944)
Presented to the Allied Control Commission June 1945

Time Period	Officers	Non-Comm Officers	Enlisted Men	Total
June 26, 1941-June 1942	253	106	3,839	4,198
July 1942-June 1943	3,072	839	96,104	100,015
July 1943-June 1944	1,820	554	71,221	73,595
July 1944-August 1944	955	303	21,667	22,925
Sept. 1944-Dec. 1944	1,470	34,526		35,996
Total	**7,570**	**229,159**		**236,729**

Source: Archives of Military History HM 1945 eln. 29055; Report to the Allied Control Commission, June 21, 1945, Budapest.

The casualty report issued to the Allied Control Commission on November 30, 1945 contains the final figures that were adopted by the preparatory material for peace in 1946:

Hungarian Casualties in the War Against the Soviet Union (June 26, 1941-December 31, 1944)

June 26, 1941 - December 31, 1941

Type of Loss	Officers	Non-Comm Officers	Enlisted Men	Total
Dead	8	4	942	954
Wounded	11	6	2,557	2,574
Prisoners of War	---	---	9	9
Missing in Action	---	---	314	314
Total	**19**	**10**	**3,822**	**3,851**

January 1 - December 31, 1942

Type of Loss	Officers	Non-Comm Officers	Enlisted Men	Total
Dead	506	83	8,591	9,180
Wounded	1,247	201	20,036	21,484
Prisoners of War	4	---	148	152
Missing in Action	59	7	2,881	2,947
Total	**1,816**	**291**	**31,656**	**33,763**

January 1 - December 31, 1943

Type of Loss	Officers	Non-Comm Officers	Enlisted Men	Total
Dead	364	120	8,234	8,718
Wounded	838	261	15,398	16,497
Prisoners of War	52	16	2,514	2,582
Missing in Action	990	454	75,844	77,288
Total	**2,244**	**851**	**101,990**	**105,085**

Hungarian Casualties in the War Against the Soviet Union (June 26, 1941-December 31, 1944)

January 1 - December 31, 1944

Type of Loss	Officers	Non-Comm Officers	Enlisted Men	Total
Dead	1,174	488	16,976	18,638
Wounded	2,956	960	43,825	47,741
Prisoners of War	97	45	2,870	3,012
Missing in Action	791	373	43,177	44,341
Total	**5,018**	**1,866**	**106,848**	**113,732**

Hungarian Casualty Totals: June 26, 1941-December 31, 1944

Type of Loss	Officers	Non-Comm Officers	Enlisted Men	Total
Dead	2,052	695	34,743	37,490
Wounded	5,052	1,428	81,816	88,296
Prisoners of War	153	61	5,541	5,755
Missing in Action	1,840	834	122,216	124,890
Total	**9,097**	**3,018**	**244,316**	**256,431**

The total of 113,732 losses in 1944 well indicates the extreme fierceness of fighting, since it comes close to the losses of the Second Hungarian Army. In contrast to the winter of 1942 where the primary cause of death in the army was the extreme cold, in 1944 it was the exchange of bullets on both sides. The number of soldiers missing in action aggravates the attempt to define the death toll. Árpád Snyder considered 75% of the 100,000 people missing to have died.[58] In this way, his estimate for the total deaths is 160,000. Lajos Für declares Snyder's estimate to be unrealistically low, but he didn't offer an estimate of his own. The second note appended to the referred table of the pre-peace material says: "Of those missing 60,000 can be regarded dead. With that, the number of dead can be put at around 100,000."[59] At the same time, a survey made by the Hungarian Statistical Office in 1946 alleged that only 25,000 out of the 125,000 missing were dead.[60] The pre-peace treaty estimate seems to be the most probable. We are likely to get the thinnest margin of error if we assume 100-120,000 deaths in the army between 1941 and 1944. This estimate, similar to Snyder's, refers to Hungary with wartime borders. Snyder set the number of deaths in the present borders of Hungary at 100,000 because the population of the pre- and post-war country was only 64% of the number of inhabitants during the war. This calculation was later adopted by the 1949 census.

All this notwithstanding, we still don't have a complete picture because the figures of the lists of the last losses are incomplete and presumably the 1944 data also fail to precisely reflect the true magnitude of the losses. The Ministry of Defense's preparatory material for peace implies at several points that the loss of 256,431 only includes the casualties until November 1944. There is no estimate available for the military losses from November 1944 to April 1945. Based on references to reports of losses in German and Soviet publications, we can estimate the magnitude of the Hungarian losses. In early November 1944, the bulk of war events shifted to the area between the Danube and the Tisza. The Soviet forces easily broke through the lines of the Third Hungarian Army and came close to Budapest by mid-November. After several unsuccessful Soviet raids, the siege of the capital was completed on December 25th. The report of the German Army Group "South" on combat value dated December 30, 1944, fixed the number of encircled forces at 95,000.[61]

The Hungarian Army's last serious effort was its contribution to the defense of Budapest. The most experienced Hungarian divisions were in the city. The extremely violent house-to-house fighting claimed immense losses on both sides. On February 11, 1945 the German Commander in Chief, General Pfeiffer Wildenbruck reported that he had the following forces at his disposal: "23,900 Germans, 9,600 of them wounded; 20,000 Hungarians, 2,000 of them wounded and 500 Hungarian fascists."[62] Therefore, until February 11, 1945, there were

30,000 Hungarian casualties. Of these, 20,000 were wounded and 28,000 were the dead or prisoners of war. The breakout on February 12, sealed the fate of the forces locked in Budapest. Out of the presumably 45,000 German and Hungarian soldiers participating in the breakout, between 600 and 700 men reached the German lines by February 16.[63] The total number of Hungarian losses amounted to 50,000 soldiers. At least a third of these men were killed. The Hungarian military had not experienced a loss of this magnitude since the battle of the Don.[64]

Hitler considered the defense of Budapest a high-priority. In January 1945, he tried three times to lift the siege of the city. Comparatively few Hungarian forces participated in these fighting, which included the 25th and 23rd infantry divisions and the 1st cavalry division, so the loss was minimal. In the last major German offensive on March 2, 1945, only the 25th and 7th field reserve divisions participated. The German raids which lasted a week and the Soviet counterattack launched on March 15 claimed many victims. A Soviet study claims that the joint German-Hungarian losses of the March operations came to 40,000.[65]

The total loss of the Hungarian armed forces from November 1944 to the end of the war amounted to 50-55,000 which is exclusive of those captured outside the war operations. This number is close to the 45,000 losses estimated by Ferenc Adonyi for the Hungarian casualties in 1945.[66] The 580,000 people registered as soldiers in February 1945 are referred to as prisoners of war by the report of the Hungarian Statistical Office. The statisticians did not evaluate the casualties after February 1945. The number of those killed in action, can be estimated at 20-23,000 which is the number Snyder gives for the dead.

In the military operations of World War II, Hungary lost approximately 300-310 thousand soldiers together with the 256,431 missing until December 31, 1944. But, as noted earlier, this number does not include those hundreds of thousands who lost contact with their units, fell off in the last phase of the fighting in Hungary and were captured by the Soviets. The number of deaths must have been between 120 and 160,000.

This number refers to the wartime territory of the country. Mihály Korom estimated 125,000 men were lost in the present Hungarian borders.[67]

However high the number of military losses may appear, the casualties of the Hungarian army were exceeded by those of the Polish forces, the Yugoslav army led by Tito and by the Royal Romanian army. Romania with a population of 14 million similarly to the Hungary of 1944, lost 624,000 soldiers from the beginning of the war to August 23, 1944. Of them, 71,000 died, 243,000 were wounded and 310,000 disappeared.[68] The larger Romanian loss must be attributed to a more active participation in the war than Hungary's.

Civilian Losses Caused by the Military Operations

Studies dealing with the number of civilians killed in the war have been largely neglected in Hungarian historiography. Besides statistics from county publications devoted to local history, very little has been published on the subject.

The first civilians to be killed were victims of air raids. In the spring and summer of 1944 large formations of American and British aircraft appeared with increasing frequency and with the approaching front, the Soviet air force also joined in the bombing of major industrial centers.

According to a survey of the Central Statistical Office conducted in 1945, 1,024 (32.8%) of the surveyed 3,121 settlements were hit by air raids. "Of these, 847 villages and county towns (82.7%) suffered 1-5 raids and 85 (8.3%) suffered 6-10 raids. Another 29 communities (2.8%) were hit by 11-15 raids, 20 (2.0%) by 16-20 raids and 43 (4.2%) were struck by the bombs of the flying fortresses."[69] Budapest was the hardest hit since it was the political and industrial center. It was the target of nearly all the air raids. The first bombing on April 3, 1944 claimed 1,073 deaths.[70] One reason for the high number of casualties was that the population of Budapest did not conduct air raid drills before the war. During air raids many civilians fled to the streets instead of running to air raid shelters.

On April 12, 13 and 16, Budapest was bombed again. In May, there were only two air raids against Angyalföld, Újpest and

Rákospalota in the north-eastern part of the capital. The second major wave of bombing came in June 1944. In August, there was a break, followed by eight raids on Budapest in September. "From December 2nd, the air raids were no longer sounded. So called sporadic "nuisance flights" were only announced on the radio. When less than 12 planes flew over the city, a minor alarm was sounded. it was only when more than twelve aircraft were sighted that civilians went to the air shelters."[71]

The exact number of Budapest civilians who were killed by bombings is unknown. By comparing the number of deaths in 1943 with the respective figure for 1944, Árpád Snyder calculated 6,500 casualties.[72] This number is hardly tenable, though. Snyder ignored the fact that in 1944 mortality did not only increase because of the air raids, but also because soldiers and residents of Budapest were killed on the fronts and Jews in the city were being killed by the Hungarian fascists. According to the documentation, "the killing of 1,630 Jewish inhabitants of Budapest was reported to the Committee set up to investigate the Atrocities caused by German and Hungarian Nazis."[73]

The population of country towns also suffered in Western and South-eastern Hungary. Bomb raids killed 574 people in Győr;[74] In Sopron, over 500 civilians were killed[75] and 423 civilians were killed in Szombathely;[76] in Szeged, the air raids claimed 116 lives.[77] The gravest losses of the civilian population, however, were caused by the land war. According to the June 1945 survey of the Central Statistical Office, "out of the surveyed 3,121 villages and towns 1,617 (51.8%) were besieged for a shorter or longer period, 29.1% only for a day. 60.7% of them were involved in land fighting for less than a week. In 273 villages and county towns (16.9%) the siege lasted for 2-3 weeks; in 362 (22.4%) were under siege for over a month. 139 (8.3%) settlements were besieged for over three months.[78]

The largest losses were suffered by the population of Budapest which was in the theater of war for over six weeks. The ruthless fighting claimed lives among soldiers and civilians. In January, the mortality indices was 172.8%. The heaviest fighting occurred in that month with an average of over 400 people killed a day.[79] The Central Statistical Office set the number of war deaths at 8,568.[80] In preparing for the peace talks in Paris, the mayor of Budapest fixed the number of losses "expressly caused by military activity" during the siege at 7,121.[81] The difference of roughly 1,000 people is attributed to the different interpretation of the categories "war deaths" and "losses expressly caused by military activity."

The Statistical Office table includes the only figures available for the losses of the civilian population. According to this source, the war took the largest toll in Fejér county with 3,940 deaths. The reliability of these figures is confirmed by the sporadic lists of losses in more recent works of local history. Agreeing with the Statistical Office, Alajos Németh estimated the casualties of Sopron at roughly one thousand.[82] In Gabriella Molnár's study on the war years of Székesfehérvár where she mentions 714 deaths.[83] The corresponding figure from the Statistical Office is 700. The victims of Szombathely are estimated at 423 by János Papp which is very close to the 450 cited by the Statistical Office.[84] Recently published figures for Veszprém and Borsod-Abaúj-Zemplén counties coincide with the Statistical Office's figures.[85]

According to a Statistical Office survey, 44,490 lost their lives in the war due to air raids and land operations. The scarce food supplies, the rapid spread of epidemics and poor sanitary conditions caused 1.5 - 2 times as many deaths as the fighting. In Budapest, 12,000 more people died of illnesses in the spring of 1945 than in the corresponding period in 1944. The civilian casualties can be estimated at around 80-100,000. Mihály Korom set the loss of Budapest at 28,000 and that of the rest of the country at 16,000. Numerically, this equals the figure of 44,000 given by the Statistical Office table, although the components are different.

The Losses of Hungarian Jewry in World War II

Historiographic Overview

No book on Hungary's history in World War II can and does, evade the tragedy of the Hungarian Jews. The student of this topic is at first dazzled by the profusion of relevant literature. A second glance, however, reveals that with a few exceptions, the relevant parts are highly similar, hence they have little informative value. What accounts for the similarity is the fact that the writings on the wartime fate of the Jews are all based on works like those by Jenő Lévai and Ernő Munkácsi which were published during the short-lived, post-war, intellectual boom. The scholar who improved on the early results was an American, Randolph Braham.

During the period of Stalinism in Hungary, the designation and identification of Jews and other cultural and religious groups were prohibited in the name of proletarian internationalism. The row of works concerned with the persecution of those who violated the Soviet's "proletarian nationalism" were interrupted for many years. The works of fiction and poetry with relevance to Jewry also became rare. The only exceptions were the books of Elek Karsai published by the National Agency of Hungarian Jewry which printed a very small number of copies. A slow change began to unfold from the mid 1970s. The works of György Száraz, György Ránki and later László Varga and Sándor Szenes broke the depressing silence of the Stalinist period. Yet, the central questions have not been clarified to this day. How could over 800,000 Hungarian citizens be excluded from society? How was it possible to send hundreds of thousands to be slaughtered? What ideological, socio-psychological antecedents led to the tragedy? Even today, this subject stirs up passionate storms. The stifling of an open exchange of views for decades reinforced the inhibitions and prejudices. Consider the following contradiction: the Arrow Cross Party claimed that no Jews were killed in Hungary, while 600-700,000 martyrs were estimated by Jewish sources after the war.

The purpose of this work is not only to establish that thousands of Jews were killed in Hungary, but to provide an unbiased elaboration of the Jewish plight during the war. The largest group of source material is made up of tables including the victims of all the countries occupied by the Germans. The first work completed was a study by Jacob Lestchinsky, an associate of the World Jewish Congress.[86] The author sets the number lost by the Hungarian Jews at 200,000. A report in 1946 by the Anglo-American Committee of Inquiry arrived at the same figure.[87] The figure was adopted by Imre Benoschofsky, the editor of the book *Remnants of the Jewry* published in 1946.[88] In his book, the noted holocaust researcher, Raul Hilberg, devoted a whole chapter to the wartime fate of the Jews in Hungary in which he also quoted the above number.[89] The *American Jewish Yearbook* for 1949 estimated the number at 220,000.[90] In his book on wartime migration of peoples, Michael Proudfoot only writes about a loss of 180,000.[91]

Substantially different is the finding of the Joint Distribution Committee's inquiry which reports that 123,000 Hungarian Jews were killed. This figure was published by *Egyleti Élet* and and *Új Élet*, two Hungarian papers, the first from New York and the second from Hungary.[92] A similar figure — 110,000 — is given by Ariel Tartakower in his study of 1949.[93] At the furthest extreme is the summary table of the "Statistics of Jewish Casualties during the Axis Domination" published by the Institute of Jewish Affairs which estimated 294,000 Jewish victims from Hungary. By the end of the 1940s, most of the published works on this subject draw on one or more of the listed sources. Despite the variety of results, there is far greater similarity than a difference between the listed calculations. Their first common feature is that they all refer to the present-day territory of the country. The original documents all refer to the administrative division of the region as it was during the war. The way of defining the loss is also similar in all the listed works. The authors deduced the post-war number of the Jewish population from the pre-war number.

In Hungary, the Jewish population before the war was estimated at around 400,000. The figure itself is misleading, because it refers those affiliated with Jewish institutions. The anti-Jewish laws affected all Jews regardless of their affiliation.

After the war, the assessment of the Jewish casualties began in Hungary. Árpád Snyder was one of the statisticians who launched a comprehensive investigation.[94] One of the limitations of his study is that he only studied the Jews who were killed in the present-day borders of Hungary. Similar to western researchers, Snyder used the method of deduction by setting the pre-war number of the entire Jewish population at 481,000 and counted 220-260,000 survivors after the liberation.

He therefore reasoned that 220-260,000 Jews were killed during the war. The Hungarian statistical literature accepted the lower limit: 220,000.[95] Lajos Thirring and Jacob Siegel also accepted this figure.[96]

Another group of casualty figures was calculated by the Hungarian Jewry. The treatments by Béla Vihar, Szigfrid Róth and the World Jewish Congress are far more detailed and elaborate than the previously mentioned ones. The first common feature of the three is that they also calculated the losses for the entire wartime area of Hungary and not only for the present-day territory. The method of research also became subtler. Not only the simple method of deduction was used, but the authors also registered the losses directly, in detail.

In the epilogue to his volume of collected documents, Vihar gave a detailed account of the Jewish casualties during the Holocaust.[97] He cites that until March 1944, 81,000 people had been killed during the deportation in Kamenets Podolskii and forced labor. During the German occupation, 710,000 Jews were deported, of which 70,000 returned. The total loss is therefore 720,000. He arrived at this figure from the total of Hungarian Jews estimated in 1941 at 900,000 and then deduced the 120,000 registered in 1945 and the 70,000 expected to return from deportation. This calculation also produced 710,000 as the final sum. Szigfrid Róth used a different method of calculation by estimating the casualties before the German occupation at 63,000. The deported numbered 730,000, of whom 120,000 survived. Thus, the victims of the Hungarian genocide totaled 673,000. Remarkably, this is very close to the sum that was arrived at using Vihar's deductive method.

The study published by the Statistical Information Office of the World Jewish Congress in 1946 seems to be one of the most scientifically reliable.[98] They have been adopted without modification by the most outstanding researcher of Hungary's period of disaster, Randolph Braham. This work is also drawn on by Yehuda Z. Moor and László Varga for their research. According to Péter Várdy, of all the existing statistics the figures from the World Jewish Congress are the most accurate.[99] But even more important is that this number was established in the mind of the public. Every year 600,000

Hungarian Jewish martyrs killed in the war are commemorated.

The reasoning used by Vilmos Sándor and Artur Geyer, the presumed authors of the World Jewish Congress' figures were that up until the spring of 1944, 63,000 died in forced labor, in deportation to Kamenets Podolskii and in the massacre at Újvidék. During the German occupation a total of 618,000 were deported, 502,000 never returned, and 565,000 were killed. The report defined the number of the Jewish population in Hungary in 1941 as 825,007. In the same area, 255,500 survivors were registered in 1945. The difference of 569,507 is almost identical.

The Number of Jews in Hungary Before and After the War

	Present-Day Area		Detached Area		Total of	Total of
	Budapest	Present Area	Detached Area	Enlarged Area	Present Area	Enlarged Area
Affiliated Jews According to the 1941 Census	184,453	216,528	324,026	540,554	400,981	725,007
Unaffiliated Jews (Act IV: 1939, Act XV: 1941)	62,350	27,290	10,360	37,650	89,640	100,000
Total Number of Jews	246,803	243,818	334,386	578,204	490,621	825,007
Jews Killed by Forced Labor 1941-March 1944	12,350	12,500	17,150	29,650	24,850	42,000
KEOKH Deportation July 1941	3,000	2,000	15,000	17,000	5,000	20,000
Massacre in Újvidek	---	---	1,000	1,000	---	1,000
Decreased Number of Jews March 19, 1944	231,453	229,318	301,236	530,554	460,771	762,007

	Present-Day Area		Disannexed Area		Total of	Total of
	Budapest	Present Area	Disannexed Area	Enlarged Area	Present Area	Enlarged Area
Deported, Killed or Died During the German Occupation	105,453	222,318	290,236	512,554	327,771	618,007
Jews that Fled Abroad During the German Occupation	2,000	1,000	2,000	3,000	3,000	5,000
Liberated as Forced Laborers	5,000	6,000	9,000	15,000	11,000	20,000
Liberated in Budapest	119,000	---	---	---	119,000	119,000
Number of Jews at the Time of Liberation	124,000	6,000	9,000	15,000	130,000	139,000
Percentage of 1941 Number	(50.25)	(2.46)	(2.69)	(2.59)	(26.51)	(16.84)
Returned from Deportation until the end of 1945	20,000	45,000	56,500	101,500	65,000	121,500
Number of Jews on 12/31/45	144,000	51,000	65,500	116,500	195,000	260,500
Percentage of 1941 Number	(58.35)	(20.92)	(19.58)	(20.15)	(39.75)	(31.57)
Of these Affiliated Jews	96,480	45,000	---	---	141,480	---
Expressed in Percent	(67.00)	(88.23)	---	---	(72.55)	---

Source: Jenő Lévai, *Zsidósors Magyarországon* [Jewish Fate in Hungary], (Magyar Téka, 1948), 463.

The similarity of the results computed with the direct and indirect methods in all three statistics seems to confirm the reliability of the data. Instead of confirmation, however, the exact coincidence of the final scores arouses suspicion. It appears likely that the component items were calculated in view of the total loss, which in turn was computed with the deductive method. This is supported by the fact that the direct data of Szigfrid Róth and the Statistical Information Office increase or decrease according to the number of the deported and the size of the Jewish population in 1941.

It is only theoretically possible for the final sums of the direct and indirect computations to coincide exactly, for in practice, there is no precise information available on the subtracter or the subtrahend. During the 1941 census, only the Jews belonging to Jewish associations were counted precisely. The number of Hungarians categorized as Jews was always controversial. Estimates ranged from 750,000 to 1 million.[100] Their number in 1945 is even more uncertain. After the liberation from Nazi occupation, there were no reliable and comprehensive surveys made about the number of the Jewish population. The simple deductive method ignores the number of those who survived the deportations but never returned to Hungary.

Deportation to Kamenets Podolskii

Until 1940 the Germans wanted to expel the Jews through forced emigration. Between 1940 and 1942, they resettled the Jews in ghettos set up in the eastern territories. The deportations took place amid pogroms and violence throughout Eastern Europe. The Jews of Croatia were driven to forced labor and in Yugoslavia they had to wear a yellow arm-band and a yellow star. In the Bohemian Protectorate, the Polish province and the Baltic states, terror raged. Mass murders became common practice in Romania.

Hungary could not exempt itself from German pressure either. The first deportation took place in the summer of 1941. Upon the suggestion of the Chief of Staff Henrik Werth, Defense Minister Károly Bartha proposed to the Council of Ministers in late June 1941 to resettle the Polish and Soviet Jews residing in

Hungarian territory over the Carpathians under Hungarian military administration. The proposal was ratified and the Central National Office for Controlling Aliens (KEOKH) was put in charge of the selection and collection of Jews to be resettled.

Thousands of Jewish refugees, most of them Polish citizens, were in Hungary at that time. An act of the Polish government passed in 1936 revoked the citizenship of the 8,000 Jews in Hungary, calling them "stateless."[101] Following the *Anschluss*, the Germans exiled several thousand Jews of Polish origin from Austria, some of whom came to Hungary since the Polish government refused them re-entry. The bulk of the nearly 100,000 Polish refugees reaching Hungary after the German attack on Poland in 1939 were Jewish.

There was a confidential instruction in Hungary whose aim was "to get rid of Polish and Russian Jews infiltrating the country as quickly and in as large numbers as possible."[102] The police authorities were instructed to transport these Jews to a camp at Kőrösmező and hand them over to the military authorities. Actually, many Jews with Hungarian citizenship were also deported from the Sub-carpathian region by the local authorities. The victims brought to Kőrösmező were first taken to transit camps where truckloads of them were transported beyond the border and then released. The Jews were scattered in various villages of Eastern Galicia, most of them in Kamenets Podolskii. The authorities subjected them to forced labor but they had to find their own subsistence without permission to leave the precincts of the village.

In the second half of August, the Ukrainian police collected the Jews that were deported under the pretext of making the area Jew-free. The mass slaughter that followed was carried out by an SS squad, the Ukrainian militias and Hungarian sappers, according to Hungarian sources. Other sources claim that Einsattzgruppe C alone was responsible for the massacre.[103] Similar atrocities occurred in Stanislau and Horodinka. The World Jewish Congress estimated the death toll from these incidents at 20,000.[104] The source for the figure was the registry kept by the Bureau of Protection of Hungarian Jews [Magyar Izraeliták Pártfogó Irodája].

The leader of KEOKH at that time, Sándor Siménfalvy, estimated the victims transported past the border at 18,500. According to a senior KEOKH official, Ámon Pásztói, 16,000 were deported.[105] Contemporary German sources put the number of Jews deported to Galicia at 11,000.106 The number of deaths were probably between 15-16,000, since at least 2,000 managed to survive the massacres.[107] The survivors fled back to Hungary and reported to the Bureau of Protection the horrors they had lived through. The Bureau then informed Ferenc Keresztes-Fischer. The minister of internal affairs took steps and deportations soon stopped. Even those on the road were ordered back. According to German sources, in early January, Brigadier General József Heszlényi conveyed the wish of the Hungarian government to resettle the Jewish refugees staying in Hungary in areas east of the Dniester.[108] The matter was protracted until September 1942 when Adolf Eichmann declared:

> Experience has shown that preparing and executing such partial actions require just as much effort as the performance of a general plan aimed at the entire Jewry of a country. Therefore, I do not think it justified to mobilize the entire deporting mechanism for the Jewish refugees without getting an inch closer to the solution of the Jewish question in Hungary, stop this mechanism again. It is generally maintained here that this action should be postponed until Hungary was willing to extend this regulation to the Hungarian Jews as well.[109]

Another incident illustrating the anti-Semitism of the Hungarian army elite was the raid in Újvidék. In early January 1942, the general staff ordered Lieutenant-General Ferenc Feketehalmy-Czeydner, commander of the 5th corps of Szeged, to wipe out the partisan forces in Southern Hungary. Nearly 4,000 people were slain during the operation directly headed by Brigadier General József Grassy. This number was established by the military inquiry of the Hungarian army in 1943.[110] About 1,000 of the victims were Jews who were killed simply because of their origin.

Losses of Forced Laborers

The anti-Semitism permeating the army found its most peculiar outlet in the establishment of forced labor formations. From 1941, following the anti-Jewish laws of 1938 and 1939, the liability of Hungarian Jews for military service was also changed. Instead of regular service, they were obliged to render labor in the military. The draftees in the first labor companies were treated humanely, but after spring 1941 the situation changed. In June, they were given the yellow star and an identifying uniform. Officer ranks for Jews in the labor formations were abolished. "Aryan" officers and skeleton staffs were assigned to the units. The number of men mobilized for labor at the beginning of the aggression against the Soviet Union was 15-18,000 which was decreased to 4-5,000 by autumn.[111] Few of the laborers were attached to the Carpathian Army group and the Motorized Corps, hence Jewish losses in their area of operation were not considerable.

On March 17, 1942, Defense Minister Károly Bartha instructed the appropriate authorities to draft all the Jews of military age for forced labor if they were in a military district that mobilized troops for the front. When combat troops went to fight, they took the respective labor units with them. Thus, when the Second Hungarian Army was deployed to fight, several labor battalions were also transported there. Besides the overwhelming majority of Jews, the laborers included people deemed politically unreliable by the government, such as the communists. A few Nazarenes and Jehovah's Witnesses who objected to armed service for conscientious reasons were also used as laborers.

Elek Karsai, György Ránki and Randolph Braham put the number of conscripted laborers at 50,000.[112] They cite the estimate in Vilmos Nagybaczoni Nagy's memoirs as their source. There is, however, no Ministry of Defense document to confirm this figure. The general staff deployed 69 forced labor companies in February 1942 which meant approximately 14,000 people.[113] Peter Gosztonyi, a military specialist of the period, estimated of 25-30,000 laborers.[114] In proportion, the Jews in labor companies lost fewer people than the combat forces. In

1942, the death toll of forced laborers was 2,149, which was less than 8% of all the draftees. The corresponding figure for combatants was 13%.[115]

The Soviet breakthrough on January 12, 1943 and the ensuing retreat incurred heavy losses by the forced labor companies. The confidential statistics of the Ministry of Defense issued in May 1944 registered the loss of 23,308 people in January and 2,003 in February.[116] According to the Ministry of Defense, the labor companies lost a total of 25,451 people between January 1942 and December 1943. Of these formations, 3,786 died, 1,035 were wounded, 1,633 were taken as prisoners of war and 19,003 were missing.[117] The true death toll is probably closer to 15,000 since half of those missing were regarded as dead and the other half as prisoners of war. C. A. Macartney drew on contemporary sources yielding similar totals.[118] The total loss of 43-44,000 stated by Vilmos Nagybaczoni Nagy and accepted by Elek Karsai appear somewhat exaggerated.[119]

Ironically, after the German occupation in March 1944, the only refuge for Jews became the very Hungarian army that previously caused them most of the suffering. They joined because the overall situation for the Jews deteriorated below the army's treatment. By joining the army, Jews were at least saved from deportation to the German extermination camps.

To boost the army's strength as required by the Germans entailed the increase of labor formations. As a result, the draft boards conscripted masses of Jewish men, many of which came from the Jewish ghettos. The order of May 15, issued under German pressure to stop conscriptions was sabotaged by some Hungarian officials. Adolf Eichmann and SS General Otto Winkelmann tried, but failed to interfere with these conscriptions. The number of Jews saved from deportation in this way was about 150,000. This number is confirmed by the German Ambassador Edmund Veesenmayer's reports as well as contemporary Ministry of Defense documents. During the German occupation, labor units included about 506,000 people.[120] In early May, however, the strength of a company was raised from 210 to 575 which more than doubled the total number of conscripts.[121]

Until the fascist Arrow Cross Party was placed in power by the Germans in mid-October 1944, 1,656 were killed during the battles of the First, Second (Transylvanian) and Third armies; 571 were injured; 1,039 were taken as prisoners of war; 10,471 were missing in action; approximately 7,000 people died.[122] Before October 1944, the total loss of forced labor consisting almost exclusively of Jews was about 25,000. The information released by the World Jewish Congress in 1946 seems to be exaggerated as it estimates the death toll until March 1944 at 42,000.[123]

Preparations for the Deportation of Hungarian Jews

By the end of 1941 and early 1942, Germany's approach to the Jewish question had changed radically. At the start of the war, the aim was resettlement., but at the Wannsee Conference in January 1942 the decision was made to exterminate the Jews. The declaration of the *Endlösung* put an end to former uncertainties and directed "the final solution" during the war. Accordingly, 70,000 of Slovakia's 90,000 Jews were transported to Germany and 24-25,000 Jews in Croatia were slaughtered. Some of the Jews in Romania escaped by emigrating and bribing the authorities, but the Jews in Bukovina, Transnistria and Odessa fell victim to Romanian terror. According to the post-war Romanian people's tribunals, 400,000 Jews were extermintaed.[124] Prime Minister Miklós Kállay tried to delay the German demands to destroy the Jews. He did this because of his humane conviction and for foreign policy interests in which he counted on the benevolence of the Anglo-Saxon powers. In his policy speech the prime minister declared: "there is no other final solution than deporting the 800,000 Jews, but this cannot be done before the end of the victorious war."[125] Hungary was the only state in the German sphere of control where no systematic deportations took place and the Jews lived in guarded safety.

On September 24, 1942, however, German Foreign Minister Joachim von Ribbentrop gave instructions for preparing the deportation of Hungarian Jews. Döme Sztójay, Hungary's ambassador to Berlin, reported on October 8, 1942 that Deputy

Foreign Secretary Martin Luther, head of the *Inland II Department* in charge of the Jewish question, asked him "to start the deportation of Hungarian Jews, which would mean that these Jews would be taken over by the German authorities and deported to eastern territories."[126]

Prime Minister Kállay, however, declared again that the Jewish question was Hungary's internal affair. In his official note issued on December 2, 1942, he refused the German demands which required, besides deportation, the confiscation of Jewish property and requiring them to wear the yellow star. In his talks in Klessheim in April 1943, Horthy refused the German solution to the Jewish question. After the talks, Sztójay sent the following message to his government:

> ...let me kindly draw Your Excellency's attention to the fact that as I see it, the Germans have reached the climax of earnestness in the Jewish question. In view of the mentality of the German leading circles and their resolute ideas and deeds in the time of life-and-death fighting, I should propose, fully aware of my responsibility, that the question be solved to prevent a possible third intervention at all costs.[127]

While German pressure increased, the plight of Jews in Hungary was temporarily alleviated. During the spring of 1942, Hungary received refugees from neighboring countries, especially from Slovakia. The Zionist leader, Rezső Kasztner estimated the Jewish refugees at 6-8,000.[128] Another source names 15,000, while in his memoirs Miklós Kállay estimated 24,000.[129] Together with those who had arrived earlier, the Jewish refugees must have totaled between 40,000 and 50,000. During the Hitler-Horthy talks on April 10, 1943 in Klessheim, the Germans ruefully noted that Prime Minister Kállay had sent a message to the American ambassador in Turkey saying that he was "protecting 70,000 Jewish refugees in Hungary."[130]

According to the German Ministry of Foreign Affairs, every month 300-600 people emigrated until March 19, 1944. Thus, the total of Jewish emigrants between the 1941 census and the

German occupation can be put at 16-17,000.[131] It becomes more difficult to establish the exact number of Jews that were killed since we do not know what eventually occurred to the Jewish refugees in Hungary or the composition of emigrants.

During 1943, the condition of the men in the labor battalions got better. The number of conscripts had risen to 65-70,000, but their strength of 25-30,000 dropped to 14,000 by December in the occupied areas.[132] Of all the mitigating regulations, the one forbidding corporeal punishment and verbal abuse was especially important.[133] The declaration of war in early 1943 exhausted much of the German labor reserves. The industrial plants and mines desperately needed manpower in the occupied areas. The Germans asked the Hungarian government to put Hungarian forced laborers at the disposal of the Ministry of Armaments in charge of the copper mines of Bor in Yugoslavia. After several refusals, Kállay complied with the request in July by surrendering 15 forced labor companies, one of them consisting of Jehovah's Witnesses, totaling about 4-4,500 people. Jenő Lévai estimated 6,600 were supplied while Elek Karsai calculated 10,000.[134] Hard working conditions and brutal treatment claimed many lives. Those still alive were to have been transported to German labor camps in autumn 1944. However, few arrived at the destination, because at least 1,000 were killed on the way by their guards and others were freed by Yugoslav partisans.

The first concrete German measures for the deportation of Hungarian Jews were taken in early March 1944. Karl Adolf Eichmann later admitted that "he was sent to Mauthausen to organize a special commando (Sondereinsatzkommando)." The instructions from Himmler were: "Comb the country (Hungary) from the east to the west, deport all Jews to Auschwitz as soon as possible. Start with the eastern counties which the Russians are approaching; make sure that no incident similar to the ghetto uprising of Warsaw shall occur."[135] Although Germany's plenipotentiary, Edmund Veesenmayer remarked during his talks after the occupation of the country that "the new government will have to solve the Jewish question," the actual demand for deportation was not yet voiced.[136] Accordingly, the new prime minister, Döme Sztójay, stressed in the first Council of Ministers meeting that the Germans were demanding orders to differentiate the Jews from Hungarians.[137] During a Ministry of Foreign Affairs meeting on April 7th, the Hungarians discussed the methods of isolation and enclosure of the Jews in ghettos with members of the Eichmann group. They agreed to carry out the plan by gendarmerie districts. On April 18th, the ghettos were set up throughout Sub-carpathia. A total of 42 ghettos were created in the country.

Veesenmayer first proposed the implementation of deportations during his talks with Sztójay. In early April, the representatives of German war industry requested a Jewish labor force of 100,000 from Hungary. Veesenmayer relayed this request to Sztójay, who agreed to surrender 50,000 and promised to conscript another 50,000 Jewish laborers in May. In response, the Hungarian Ministry of Defense promised to transport 5,000 people immediately, followed by shipments of 5,000 every 3-4 days. These promises, however, never took effect.

On April 24th, a Gestapo memorandum declared: "...their free employment in the factories of the Reich is out of the question for reasons of principle." It noted, however, that "there is no objection to taking over the Jews in question for the labor camps in the territory of the Empire which are subordinated to the Reich Führer of the SS."[138] The labor camps "subordinated to the Reich Führer of the SS" were in fact concentration camps, which were designed to exterminate the Jews. Veesenmayer's action suggests that at the beginning, not even the highest-ranking German leaders in Hungary were aware of the true aim of Eichmann to destroy the Jews. The direct precedents of the deportations have not been clarified to this day. According to one version, in the last days of April, Veesenmayer asked Sztójay to transport the Jews from the northern and southern parts of the country to Germany for military reasons. Sztójay forwarded the request to Andor Jaross, who turned to László Endre. In his report, Endre declared that complying with this request was impossible for the large number of Jews. At the same time, he noted that "otherwise, the Germans have offered their willingness to transport the able-bodied young men and women to labor camps in Germany and those incapable of work to concentration camps."[139] Endre recommended accepting the German offer and Jaross mediated this proposal to Sztójay.

In another version proposed by the Zionist leader, Rezső Kasztner, who held negotiations with Eichmann, the idea of deportation was raised by the commander of the Máramarossziget ghetto (Sighetu Marmaţiei).[140] According to this account, the Máramarossziget ghetto commander recommended the transportation of Jews to Germany and the closing down of the ghetto. The proposal reached State Secretary László Baky, who agreed with Eichmann.[141] In fact, no pact was ever signed allowing the deportation of hundreds of thousands of Hungarian Jews. In the confession of State Secretary István Bárczy given to the war crimes tribunal, he admitted that after the deportations "Imrédy shrewdly remarked that a written agreement should have been made and the responsibility should have been shared between the Hungarian government and the Parliament, since Defense Act of 1939 stipulated who can be interned, not deported, mind you."[142]

The Number of Jews Deported in Summer 1944

Defining the number of the deported is of key importance in the process of uncovering the total loss. The most detailed statistics of the deportations can be obtained from Veesenmayer's daily reports. He gained his information directly from Eichmann's Sondereinsatzkommando group in charge of the deportation and the Hungarian gendarmerie. Between May 15th and June 7th, 289,357 people were deported from Sub-carpathia and Northern Transylvania. In northern Hungary, 50,805 victims were deported between June 14-16. From June 25-28, 41,499 people were taken away from south-eastern Hungary. Of the Jews who were deported from the western part of the country and from the outskirts of Budapest, 55,741 were taken to Auschwitz between June 4-8. The total number of deported Jews was 437,402.[143]

Giving support to Vessenmeyer's figures on the number of deported Jews, the following is a list of concurring sources. In his report dated October 31, 1944, Horst Wagner, a successor to Luther in the *Inland II Department* of the German Ministry of

Foreign Affairs, reported the same number of Jews deported until June 14th. In addition, László Ferenczy, the Hungarian officer in charge of deportation, reported to the minister of the interior that he handed over 434,351 Jews. A June pamphlet of the Jews of the capital addressed "To the Christian Hungarian Society" mentions 500,000 deported.[144] A far more reliable figure can be found in the petition of the Executive Committee of the Jewish Alliance (Zsidó Szövetség): "According to reports we have received, 427,400 Jews - that is, about half of the Hungarian Jewry - were hit by the dire fate of deportation."[145] The June 24th memorandum of the Jewish Council (Zsidó Tanács) set up by Eichmann shows the figure of 500,000.[146] Rezső Kasztner, who negotiated with Eichmann, wrote about the deportation of more than 500,000 Jews.[147]

The relevant documents of the war crimes trials are also contradictory about the number of deported Jews. Eichmann's deputy in charge of Hungary, Dieter Wislyczeny, mentioned at the Nüremberg trial that 458,000 Jews were deported.[148] In his confession on January 3, 1946, he repeated that "the operation affected about 450,000 Jews."[149] Explaining the verdicts of László Endre, László Baky and Andor Jaross, the People's Tribunal referred to the figure given by László Ferenczy (434,351).[150] Two members of the Eichmann group, Hermann Krumey and Otto Hunsche, were accused of complicity in deporting 443,351 Jews during their trial in Frankfurt in 1969.[151] The Auschwitz trial held between 1963-65 in Frankfurt in also contained references to these figures. From September 1942, Willi Hilsche was the deputy station master at Auschwitz. In his testimony, he stated that between May and mid-June over 400,000 Hungarian Jews were transported to concentration camps by 120 trains. He calculated this number from the waybills sent with the consignments.[152] This figure was also confirmed by Selection Officer Wilhelm Bogert.

A recently discovered document published in the January 1988 issue of *Kritika* contains the notes by Miklós Gaskó, a lawyer in Kassa (Košice) during the summer 1944. With the help of István Vrancs, who served at the station headquarters, he kept records on the deportation trains. The sealed carriages arriving in Kassa with a gendarme escort were opened by the local authorities and handed over to the Germans and the Slovakian railway staff after counting. This was done so that they could ascertain the place and date of origin of each train and the number of Jews transported. The first consignment arrived on May 14 from Nyíregyháza and the last one came from Rákoscsaba on July 20th. A total of 137 trains stopped in Kassa. The number of victims packed in cattle cars was 401,439.[153] Not all of those who were taken to Auschwitz passed through Kassa; the Huszt-Lemberg-Tarnow-Auschwitz and Érsekújvár-Auschwitz routes were also used to transport the Jews. Also, for technical reasons a group of 20,000 ghetto dwellers were transported to Strasshof.

With this information it is possible to establish how many people were indeed deported in the summer of 1944 and the reliability of Ferenczy and Veesenmayer's figures. Not only were they referred to in the war crimes trials but also because the railway transports also confirm them. The similar figures in Ferenczy's and Veesenmayer's statistics attests their authenticity.

In László Endre's report to the Council of Ministers on June 24th, 615,416 Jews were alleged to have been deported by the state secretary for internal affairs.[154] Based on the verifiable evidence stated before, this figure seems to be grossly exaggerated; yet, it was widely circulated after the liberation. In his *Yellow Book*, Béla Vihar estimated the number of deported Jews during Sztójay's rule at 620,000. In the indictment against László Endre, László Baky and Andor Jaross 700,000 deported Jews was mentioned as the number of Jews that were deported at this time.[155] This figure probably includes the number of deported Jews after June 24th. This figure features in contemporary publications, articles in *Új Élet*, which includes statistics by Szigfrid Róth.[156] *Egyleti Élet*, the Hungarian Jewish daily and *Világ* published in Hungary went even further, writing about 780,000 deported.[157]

Other source material on the Jewish deportations also draw on Veesenmayer's data. Professor Macartney wrote about 450,000 deported.[158] Raul Hilberg puts the number of deported Jews at 438,700 subtracting 1,700 to account for those that were sent through Kistarcsa.[159] A publication of the Holocaust

Research Center at Yad Vashem in Israel[160] contains similar figures as the *Encyclopedia Judaica*,[161] as does Martin Gilbert's *Atlas of the Holocaust*.[162] and the works of György Ránki and Elek Karsai.[163]

The World Jewish Congress relies on Ferenczy's data which is similar to Veesenmayer's. However, in addition to the 434,351 people deported from the gendarmerie districts, another 21,000 were added to account for the deportations from southern Hungary. According to a report from the World Jewish Congress, the deportation of 21,700 Jews from southern Hungary was carried out by the German-Hungarian military forces "in the second half of May 1944 independently of the gendarme deportations and not belonging to the jurisdiction of the gendarmerie, it was not included in Gendarme Lieutenant-Colonel Ferenczy's report."[164]

The examined works of Jenő Lévai and Randolph Braham touch on the deportation from southern Hungary and reveals that there were two actions launched in southern Hungary. The first was begun at the same time as the operation in Sub-carpathia when some parts of the southern border were proclaimed operational areas to forestall the influence of Tito's partisans. Ghettos and labor camps were created in the second half of April, the largest of them being in Nagykanizsa, Horgos, Barcs and Baja where Jews from these localities were gathered. According to Braham, the deportations affected 21,700 people. This American researcher of Hungarian origin borrowed the figure of the Statistical Information Office, though a few lines below he also presented a figure indirectly refuting this data. Referring to Jenő Lévai's *Black Book*, he alleged that the head of the first operation was gendarme Lieutenant Colonel Ferenc Zalasdy (Zalostyán).[165] Consequently, the action was probably executed by the gendarmerie and included in the figure given by Gendarme Lieutenant Colonel Ferenczy. It gives the figure of 288,333 for those deported between May 15 and June 7th from Sub-carpathia and Northern Transylvania. Under this figure 274,415 is written in brackets. The difference of 13,000 must be the number of the deported during the first action. Professor Macartney noted that 13,000 from the southern areas were added to the 275,415 deported from the first and second zones.[166] Braham and Lévai wrote that between May 25-27, 8,000 people were deported from Baja.[167] At the same time, 4,000 people were deported from Nagykanizsa.[168] Thus, 12,000 of the 13,000 can be identified. The remaining 1,000 victims probably came from Barcs or Horgos.

The second southern action took place in late June and early July. The tens of thousands deported from the ghettos of Szeged, Szabadka, Nagykanizsa, Bácsalmás and other places which are clearly indicated in the lists of Ferenczy and Veesenmayer. Thus, the number of those deported in the summer of 1944 was indeed around 440,000 including the 1,700 transported from the internment camp in Kistarcsa. The latter are not mentioned either by Ferenczy or Veesenmayer.

As a result of Horthy's intervention, the Jews of Budapest were saved from deportation. The regent was forced to take a firm action under pressure from the news of mass slaughter in concentration camps, foreign protests and the news of the allied invasion of Normandy. Though the plight of Budapest's Jewry was further aggravated by new regulations in July, the legal position of converted Jews improved with the establishment of the Association of Christian Jews in Hungary. However, the German government and the Hungarian political right did not cease to call for the continuation of deportations. Negotiations and bargaining lasted until August 19th. On August 29th, the Hungarian Minister of Internal Affairs agreed with Eichmann to gradually transfer the Jews of Budapest to three camps in the country as of August 25th. Some days later, the date was postponed by a declaration that prohibited deportations. The number of the Budapest Jews temporarily saved again is debated. The government calculated between 250-280,000,[169] while the Jewish Council reported 200,000.[170] The latter figure, however, only includes those who were gathered in buildings marked with the Star of David. The estimate of 250,000 seems to be more realistic, since at the start of the deportations, thousands of Jews from the countryside hid in the capital.

Deportation of the Jews under Szálasi

On October 16, 1944, the puppet government of Germany led by the Hungarian fascist, Ferenc Szálasi, rose to power marking the beginning of a new phase in the sufferings of the Hungarian Jews. As early as 1936, Szálasi envisaged a "Jew-free" Hungary. However, he wished to achieve this goal through resettlement and not the German final solution (Endlösung). His government's program made it explicit: "after the termination of the war, the Jews will be removed from Hungary to a location determined by an international agreement."[171] Under the general mobilization proclaimed by Szálasi, the Jews were assigned the task of constructing Hungary's fortifications.

Colonel-General Károly Beregfy, the defense minister of the Szálasi cabinet, ordered on October 21, 1944, all Jewish civilians, men under 60 and Jewish women under 40 were to be mobilized until October 23rd under the Defense Act of 1939. The women and men who joined by October 26th are estimated at 35,000.[172] The forced laborers grouped in teams were called "trench-diggers" to differentiate them from those rendering labor service for the military.

But the plan of putting the Hungarian Jews to work at home was only partially fulfilled. In October, the Germans asked on two occasions for 50,000 laborers to be employed in their fighter-plane project. During the talks Szálasi mentioned that he could only lend Jewish labor and only a limited amount. Finally, he agreed to surrender 25,000 men between 16 and 60 and women between 16 and 40. The details of the agreement are still unknown.[173] As part of the agreement, the defense minister issued order 975/M 42 of 1944 stipulating that the government "puts on loan, at the disposal of the German authorities, an auxiliary military force for military construction."[174] The World Jewish Congress must have had this order in mind when they wrote that practically all forced laborers were deported during Szálasi's regime. They put the number at 59,000. Jenő Lévai probably drew on this source for his books when he wrote about 50,000 and 60,000 forced laborers employed by the army.[175] Randolph Braham adopted Lévai's former figure without revision.[176] Actually, Beregfy's order affected 70 forced labor companies amounting to 15-17,000 people. Szabolcs Szita and Randolph Braham discussed the particulars of the companies lent to the Germans.[177]

The Jews that were sent were ordered to the fortification line at the German-Hungarian border—not to war factories. The first labor groups were handed over on November 2, 1944 at Hegyeshalom. To meet the promised number, the "trench-diggers" and other Jews had to be used. Issuing a new order on November 3rd, Defense Minister Beregfy obligated the Jews of Budapest to render forced labor. The order issued on October 21st had to be repeated because many had escaped back from trench-digging or refused to join. For lack of transport vehicles, the Jewish laborers had to reach their destination on foot. From November 6th, 2,000 Jews set out every day on the death march to Hegyeshalom. The Hungarian fascists of Szálasi applied increasingly brutal methods to keep up the flow of transports. On November 4th, the Jewish men and women refusing to heed the call-up were rounded up with the help of the police. On November 9th, a three-day curfew for Jews was ordered. During the extensive raids, 30,000 Jews were dragged to the brick factory of Óbuda.[178]

By this time Szálasi had accepted the German demand of raising the labor force from 25,000 to 50,000. As Eichmann reported, 27,000 people marched toward the German-Hungarian border until November 13th. Veesenmayer noted that "another 40,000 able-bodied Jews can be counted on in the daily contingents of 2-4,000."[179] On November 20th, Szálasi declared that women could only be transported by vehicles followed by an order to stop the forced marches. He probably did this because of the incessant protest by the neutral powers and the papal nuncio. Some German officers who saw that the exhausted Jews could not be used for labor also expressed their concern about the forced marches. SS General Hans Juttner wrote of the "shocking processions" during his supervision.[180] He sent a critical note to Himmler, among other people. SS Lieutenant Colonel Kurt Becher went further and declared that driving them on foot was "pure murder."[181] Rudolf Hoess, who was in charge of receiving the Jews, also protested, "the miserable people arrived at Hegyeshalom so exhausted that the former commander of the Auschwitz camp considered turning them back from the frontier of the Reich."[182]

These Jews, unfit for forced labor escaped the extermination camps as Heinrich Himmler, commander of the SS, ordered a halt to the extermination of Jews in the concentration camps to reinforce his feelers for a separate peace.[183] After that, it was an "unsolvable problem" and extra burden for the Germans to put up the deported incapable of work. This did not affect Eichmann who concentrated all his efforts on the total annihilation of the Jews of Budapest.[184] German Foreign Minister Joachim von Ribbentrop supported him on this issue. In Ribbentrop's telegram of November 25th to Veesenmayer, he wrote, "Szálasi must see clearly that the more Jews he can remove from Budapest as quickly as possible, the more easily the city will be defended."[185] There is no proof that Szálasi accepted Ribbentrop's proposal, but the forced marches continued until November 28th.

On November 29th, the head of the Budapest Gestapo, Hans Geschke, demanded another 17,000 Jewish laborers from the Hungarian government.[186] Although Eichmann had managed to obtain trains from Vienna, it was no longer possible to carry out the order in full. Only 1-2,000 Jews from labor battalions were taken out of the country. The action was to come to an end soon. The last deporting train pulled out of Budapest in the first days of December with 30,000-36,000 Jews who had found shelter in buildings under the protection of the International Red Cross.[187] The building of the *Südostwall* lasted until March 1945 and then the Jewish laborers from Hungary were transported to German concentration camps to remove them from the advancing troops of the Red Army. The third and last phase of deportations was over.

The autumn deportations were less organized. With the front approaching, the administration gradually withdrew to the countryside. The police, gendarme and military authorities were transferred and reorganized so detailed statistics were not made of the surrendered Jews, the military losses and the Hungarian units deployed in Germany. In addition, the evaluation of deportations was not carefully documented in Hungary and Germany. Due to the dispute between Himmler and Eichmann and the hesitation of Szálasi, the whole action was disorganized.

Finally, geographic division also made statistical summaries difficult. A fragment of the deported Jews traveled by train but those who marched on foot arrived at the German border from three directions. The "trench-diggers" came along main roads, the companies from Budapest and Transdanubia marched south of them and the labor units back from the front walked to the north.[188] The transports were received at Kőszeg, Sopron and Hegyeshalom.

On November 21st, Veesenmayer reported that the 50,000 Jews that were promised by Szálasi could not be delivered. As far as he knew, 30,000 had been handed over by that date.[189] During his secret negotiations with representatives of neutral embassies on November 22nd, Chief of Police Nándor Batizfalvy reported that 9,800 Jews crossed the border, 13,000 Jews were on the road and were expected to arrive in the next three days. "10,000 Jews disappeared on the roads...some of them escaped and others died or were shot dead."[190]

In late November, Eichmann regretfully noted that as few as 38,000 Jews reached their destination, though another 20,000 were needed.[191] On December 8th, following the deportations, Raul Wallenberg, secretary of the Swedish embassy, registered 60,000 Jews who went by foot, 15,000 of whom were brought back to Budapest.[192] Thus, the number of Jews given over to the Germans was about 45,000. Dieter Wisliczeny, the second-in-command of the Eichmann brigade, admitted in Nüremberg that in "October and November 1944, about 30,000 people or a few thousand more were deported from Budapest to Germany."[193] In his testimony in Nüremberg, Rezső Kasztner mentioned 45,000.

These accounts suggest that the number of victims surrendered to the Germans was a maximum of 50,000. This is confirmed by the documents of the German command in charge of the fortification works which mention 35,000 Hungarian forced laborers.[194] Adding up the numbers given by Szabolcs Szita for the major camps, we calculate about 30,000 laborers.[195] It must be noted that some of the Jews were not taken to the zone of the *Südostwall* construction, but to the Dachau concentration camp so 50,000 laborers is not unrealistic. Macartney's final figure is also similar, though he differed with the proportions of those transported by train and those who marched on foot: "20,000 were taken by train, 20,000 marched, 10,000 were not sent at all."[196] Gerald Reitlinger,

Martin Gilbert, Leopold Banny and György Ránki also estimated the number of deported at 50,000.[197] Only the report of the World Jewish Congress diverges from these figures significantly by reporting 59,000 laborers. It is also improbable that 76,209 Jews were taken from Budapest and handed over to the German authorities during the Szálasi regime.[198]

The Number of Jews Killed under the Reign of the Arrow Cross Party and During the Siege of Budapest

Although the deportations were halted in early December, it did not put an end to the suffering of the Jews of Budapest. An order was released on December 2nd about the establishment of the ghetto in Pest. All Jews incapable of forced labor had to move there, except those having safe conduct pass issued by a foreign country and those in hiding. At least 70,000 people were forced to move to the ghetto in the 7th district of the city. The number of those with safe conduct pass and in hiding cannot be established. The plight of Jews in the ghetto was disastrous. Mortality was very high since feeding the people became impossible: the Arrow Cross Party activists stopped even those food contingents that were officially allocated by the capital.[199] In addition to those who starved to death were the victims Hungarian fascist raids. Packs of Arrow Cross men slaughtered Jews in hospitals, homes, in the streets and along the Danube. As the front was approaching, SS General Otto Winkelmann set up an SS guard to protect the ghetto fearing a ghetto revolt which would endanger the defense of the capital.

The number of the victims of the Arrow Cross Party and the casualties of the siege cannot be established exactly and separately. According to the available documentation, "the murder of 1,630 inhabitants of Budapest considered Jews by Hungarian fascists was reported to the Committee of Inquiry into German and Hungarian Fascist Atrocities until the end of April 1945."[200] According to Jenő Lévai, "in the first months of its operation the People's Tribunal had to hear cases of 6,200 murders proved to have been committed by Hungarian fascists."[201] 2,600 victims are buried in the area of the ghetto.[202] Post-war mortality statistics show an excess of 8,000 Jewish deaths.[203] In view of the non-recorded deaths and the number of religiously unaffiliated Jews, this figure implies at least 15,000 victims.

The Sum Total of the Losses

Apart from the formerly established numbers of the victims of Kamenets Podolskii, Újvidék, Budapest and the forced labor camps, reasonable estimates are very difficult to assess. The total number of Jews killed in these incidents amount to 55,000 (Kamenets Podolskii: 15,000, forced labor until October 1944: 25,000, Budapest: 15,000).

Until October 31, 1944, the number of missing was 29,474 and 2,674 were prisoners of war, according to Ministry of Defense records.[204] Since about half of the missing were normally considered dead, about 18,000 were taken into captivity. A specialist of the issue, George Bárány states that until summer 1945 20-30,000 fell into Soviet captivity where they were treated similarly to the combat troops. Considering the fact that several Jewish inhabitants of Budapest and many of those returning from deportation were captured by soldiers of the Red Army, the upper limit seems realistic. Only half of the Hungarian prisoners of war returning from the Soviet Union were registered.[205] In 1947, 817 former forced laborers, in 1948 337 were registered in the Debrecen camp after returning. The overwhelming majority of prisoners of war from forced labor units lost their lives (at least 25,000).

Far more uncertain information is available about the fate of the 490,000 deported (440,000 in summer 1944, 50,000 in autumn 1944). Before the publication of the reports by the World Jewish Congress, Jenő Lévai concluded:

> No authentically exact number can be established for the loss suffered by the Hungarian Jewry, since no authority has exact figures about the number of people "of the Jewish race" who were affected by the Sztójay-Szálasi regulations, persecuted, deported and exterminated. Likewise, we have no verified data at our disposal showing how many "Jews"

> according to fascist laws are alive at the moment, since no such survey is possible. Another insurmountable problem is that the figures for the former territory of the country cannot be checked now that the imperium of the country was reduced.[206]

The survivors were taken care of by the National Committee To Care for the Deported (Deportáltakat Gondozó Országos Bizottság). According to their figures first published in the report of the Statistical Information Office, 20,000 returned to Budapest and 45,000 to the countryside (present area) from various concentration camps in 1945.[207] According to the daily *Világ*,[208] 76,657 people returned until September 20th while *Egyleti Élet* published an article estimating 75,000.[209] The December 20, 1946 issue of *Egyleti Élet* revised its figures to 85,000 and then in the January 3, 1947 issue, it updated its figures, reporting that 90,000 survivors had returned.

The Committee to Care for the Deported registered every returning person on a separate card which amounted to 100,000 people. The cards also reveal that several Jews from Transylvania and Sub-carpathia set out for their homeland after a transit stay in Budapest. Probably the above-mentioned figures also imply deported from detached areas who were registered in the capital upon returning. The World Jewish Congress estimated that 56,500 returned to Transylvania and Sub-carpathia.[210] According to some sources, 15,769 deportees returned to Northern Transylvania until September 1945.[211] The Romanian section of the World Jewish Congress registered 44,706 people.[212] An American Jewish source estimated the total Jewish population in Transylvania at 80,000 at the end of 1946.[213] In 1940, the Jewish population of Southern Transylvania was around 40,000.[214] The survivors who returned to Sub-carpathia can be estimated at 15,000.[215]

Based on these figures, we can estimate that there were 60,000 survivors of the deportations in the re-annexed areas. If the approximate number of those returning to the present-day area of the country is 70,000, a total of 130,000 returned to their original homeland. Of the 490,000 Jews who were deported,

360,000 never returned. In addition, 80,000 lost their lives in Kamenets Podolskii, forced labor, fascist atrocities, the siege and captivity. The total of those who never returned is 440,000. If we take the mean value of all the individual estimates for the Jewish population in 1941 which comes to 800,000, then after subtracting the 20,000 emigrants during the war years, we get 340,000 for the number of Jews who must have returned to their original homelands by 1946. From the newly re-annexed areas theoretically all Jews had been deported; therefore, the post-1945 Jewish population practically tallies with the 60,000 who returned. Thus, the Jewry in the present-day area probably numbered about 280,000.

Two attempts were made to survey the remaining Jewry in post-war Hungary which was headed by Pál Zsigmond Pach of the World Jewish Congress in the summer of 1945. In Budapest, a registration staff was sent around and in rural towns and villages.[216] In early 1946, Jenő Lévai wrote that the survey began enthusiastically and collected 120,000 questionnaires "from those 'of the Jewish race'," remarking that the questionnaires "cannot provide any clue, however approximate, as to the authentic number of the losses of the Hungarian Jewry."[217] Pál Zsigmond Pach, the leader of the inquiry commented that "We never believed we had covered the entire Jewry."[218] Questionnaires failed to reach several rural communities and not all those concerned could be found in Budapest, either.

In July 1945, the Central Statistical Office tried to register the war-related changes in the population with questionnaires. Unfortunately, only a small portion of their findings was published in *Magyar Statisztikai Szemle*. The rest of the material was inaccessible to researchers. Western sources, on the other hand, usually estimate the Hungarian Jewry at 200-220,000. Árpád Snyder and Lajos Thirring estimated the Jewish population of Hungary at 260-270,000.[219]

The differing figures and the theoretical number of 280,000 presented by this study must be analyzed in light of *alia* or Jewish emigration. From 1946 and especially in 1947, masses of Jews left the country, due to reviving anti-Semitism. According to a March 1946 memorandum of Zionist organizations, 63,500

Hungarian Jews wished to emigrate to Palestine and 45,000 were headed to other parts of the world.[220] A report dated November 7, 1947 in Vienna says: "in the past five days at least 5,000 Hungarian Jews came here in various ways, ready to go anywhere."[221] No official statistic is available on the number of Jewish emigrants from Hungary, but they must have numbered several tens of thousands. The inclusion or exclusion of this large mass would have significantly influenced the population estimates. In would seem that 280,000 includes everyone who could potentially emigrate from the country's present area.

When trying to calculate the total loss, the most important question one is face with is what happened to the 360,000 of the 490,000 deported Jews who did not return. How many of those died in concentration camps and elsewhere? The problem of estimating the loss is equally unresolved for all the Jews that were deported across Europe. Historians estimate that 1-4 million Jews were taken to Auschwitz and killed there.[222]

There will never be exact data available, for the camp officers did not file identification cards for many of those who were executed and only a fragment of the files recorded has survived.[223] The dilemma of the loss could be solved if the number of survivors who did not return were known. Between 1945-46, Europe's main roads were crowded with former inmates of concentration camps wandering back to what was left of their homes. Upon returning, many turned westward again to wait out their immigration permits in Germany. A few of the newcomers in the western zones of occupation had managed to evade deportation. Those who remained and those who arrived more recently were completely mixed in the Anglo-American zones.

The official Western statistics are highly fragmentary considering the hundreds of thousands of Russians, Ukrainians, Poles and Hungarian displaced persons (DP's) that migrated, besides the Jews. In summer 1945, the UNRA registered a total of 90,000 Jewish displaced persons.[224] By July 1947, when refugees were taken over by the International Refugee Organization (IRO), the number had risen to 186,000.[225] The historian-demographer, Jacques Vernant, is of the opinion that far more displaced persons were in the Western zones of occupation.[226] As the director of the Jewish Agency and later the prime minister of Israel, Ben Gurion claimed in August 1946 that there were at least 500,000 displaced Jews in Europe.[227] There is only one IRO report on Hungarian Jews in the Anglo-American zones of occupation. It registered 8,445 Hungarian Jews on September 30, 1947.[228] In the July 21, 1945 issue of *Mai Nap*, a correspondent from Germany wrote that the deported who did not return home yet numbered 80-100,000. The author noted that "no official statistics were made. However, the presumed data and estimates made available to me by various authorities were comparatively homogeneous."

In November 1945, the Committee to Care for the Deported stated that "undoubtedly there are still tens of thousands of deported Hungarian Jews in Germany."[229] The same organization presented a more exact figure in *Új Élet* on January 10, 1946. According to their survey, 34-37,000 Jews deported from Hungary were in Austria and Germany.[230] Ten thousand of them were in the Soviet zone. That was a partial figure because the search for survivors continued. In February 1946, the Jewish Agency calculated the number of survivors from Sweden and Italy in the several thousands.[231] Several thousands were identified in Switzerland as well.[232]

The September 1947 issue of *Utunk* and several other papers asked help for 40,000 "Hungarian-speaking Jews".[233] At the same time, 8,000 Hungarian Jews were detained in Cyprus internment camps by the British authorities.[234] The Jews who arrived in Palestine numbered more than 30,000.[235] By 1948, the majority of Jews remaining in the refugee camps left to live in the newly established state of Israel. According to Gyula Borbándi, "some 115,000 of the Jews remaining in the West or returning to Hungary emigrated."[236] The Israeli immigration statistics put the number of Jews arriving from Hungary between 1945 and 1954 at 18,000.[237]

During the late 1960s, the daily with the largest circulation in Israel, excluding those in Hebrew and English daily was the Hungarian, *Új Kelet*. According to a Hungarian statistician living in England, Eugène Csocsan de Várallja, the 20,000 copies *Új Kelet* circulated in 1968 suggests a Hungarian-Jewish readership in Israel of 200,000.[238] The March 1951 issue of

Egyleti Élet provides more concrete information. Out of Israel's population of 2,200,000, 12% or 260,000 were Jews with Hungarian origin. Today, the Hungarian-speaking Jews claim to number 300-350,000.[239]

Many Hungarian Jews found a new home in Canada, the United States, Australia and Argentina. The Hungarian Jews who emigrated after the Holocaust must have numbered about 300,000. Some emigrated from the present-day area of Hungary, others from Sub-carpathia, Transylvania, southern Hungary or from the concentration camps. The number of Jews who survived the concentration camps without returning to Hungary is at least 50,000. Fewer than 310,000 of the 360,000 that were deported perished. The highest number of Hungarian Jews that died in the Holocaust was 390,000 including 15,000 that were killed in Kamenets Podolskii, 25,000 in the army's labor battalions, 15,000 killed during the terror of the Hungarian fascists and 25,000 who died as prisoners of war in the Soviet Union.

Prisoner of War Casualties

The Number of Hungarian Citizens Taken as Prisoners of War

Until recently, information was not released about the number and fate of Hungarian prisoners of war. Mihály Korom's work was the first to present an estimate about the number of Hungarian prisoners of war. A thorough study of the prisoners of war was very difficult since a larger part of the relevant archival material is missing or inaccessible. Only the Archives of the Institute of Military History has a significant stock of material about prisoners of war. In the New Hungarian Central Archives research was limited by administrative obstacles. The prisoner of war material in the archives of the Ministry of Foreign Affairs was still blocked as of this writing.

As it was mentioned, between July 26, 1941 and October 31, 1944 there were 256,431 prisoner of war casualties. 37,490 of them died, 88,296 were wounded, 124,890 missing and 5,755 taken captive. In his article, Árpád Snyder approximates that 25%, or 30,000 of the missing were prisoners of war. A supplementary note to the preparatory material for peace suggests that 65,000 were taken captive[240] while a short study by the Hungarian Statistical Office in 1946 indicates 100,000.[241] The most probable estimate is that 70,000 must have been taken as prisoners of war before November 1944.

From November 1944, the central registration of losses practically ceased. The information of prisoners of war preserved in the Archives of the Institute of War History contain data for specific companies, regiments or batteries at most. For lack of printed forms and typewriters, the reports often reveal a disintegrating army. The greatest part of the loss includes those missing. During the winter retreat, the missing either died or fell captive. After November 1944, the report entries explaining the absence of the soldiers from duty contained notations like "deserter" and "not returned from leave." Another indication of mass desertion is the fact that the Arrow Cross authorities recorded 200,000 deserters until February 1945. The effective strength of the Hungarian army quickly decreased, in view those who died. A Ministry of Defense report dated January 31, 1945, suggests the magnitude of the prisoners of war. Those actually in service numbered 487,677 (20,211 officers, 467,466 private soldiers).[242] Together with the reserves, the armed forces personnel well exceeded 500,000. The last muster was on February 2, finding 216,191 people (13,685 officers, 199,698 soldiers, 2,808 civil employees).[243] Several Hungarian historians including Sándor Tóth and József Gazsi equate this number with the full strength of the military.[244] However, the count of 216,191 only refers to the combat troops and not to the training and other non-combatant corps who are included in the total of 478,677. The total of 211,000 is also rejected by Manfréd Rauchensteiner since "this estimate only refers to the combat troops then fighting on the side of the Germans, but ignores the fact that the military units transported to the German Reich numbered almost as many as the units remaining in Hungary."[245] The preparatory material for peace compiled after the war by the Ministry of Defense confirms that the Hungarian army was actually over half a million strong.[246] Former Staff Sergeant Ferenc Adonyi, estimated the size of the army at 555,000.[247]

The rapid disintegration of the army is also illustrated by the fact that at the beginning of 1945, the full strength was over 500,000. In autumn 1944 the Hungarian armed forces numbered around one million.[248] Half a million troops simply dropped out from November 1944 to February 1945. The number of Hungarian corps also shows the degree of disintegration within the army. In summer 1944 26 divisions and brigades were obeying the military elite. In late autumn 1944 18-20 corps, heavily reduced in personnel and armament were deployable against the advancing Red Army. After the liberation of Budapest, a mere 8 Hungarian divisions were left at the disposal of the German headquarters.[249]

One of the most difficult questions to answer is what happened to the 500,000 missing soldiers. The note entitled: "Data about the Approximate Number of Prisoners of War" written in 1946 for the Hungarian peace delegation sent to Paris proposed the following hypothesis: "If about half of these (the 500,000) are taken as captured in action or fallen prisoners of war while in military service, then their number can be estimated at 250,000."[250] The 250,000 includes the majority of those civilians who were picked up in various parts of the country on the pretext of performing three days of public labor; instead were transported to the Soviet Union.

The total of prisoners of war until February 1945, together with the 70,000 estimated before November 1944 and the 250,000 captured during the fights in Hungary is 320,000. Large though this sum may be, it is only a part of the Hungarians taken captive during World War II. Most of the prisoners of war consisted of the 530-540,000 reported in late January 1945 as the effective force of the army. Little information is available of their fate and of the tens of thousands conscripted later. About one third of the more than half a million left Hungary by January. Their transfer to Germany began the previous October.

An increasing part of the country became liberated thanks to the Red Army's autumn offensive. There was no room to house the army or the people to be drafted. It became clear that the Germans and the Hungarian fascist leadership wished to continue the war. The reorganization of the disintegrating army and the deployment of new corps would only be possible in Germany. Szálasi himself declared in November 1944 that Hungary would be able to organize 20 new divisions by spring 1945 provided that it happened in German territory. He declared, "Only outside Hungary does the true spirit imbue the troops."[251]

On behalf of the Szálasi government, Colonel-General Feketehalmy-Czeydner signed a written agreement with the Germans in November 1944, which stipulated that:

> For the setting up of new military units,...the Hungarian government should send to Germany:
>
> a) the youths aged 21-23 years liable for military service,
> b) the youths aged 24-25 years without military training,
> c) 100,000 men over 35 for auxiliary services (horse grooming, labor units, sanitary and other services),
> d) the youths aged 18-20 years as a supplement to the fighting force,
> e) adolescents of 15-17 years to be trained and used together with the children of the Hitler Jugend.[252]

Owing to the quick deterioration of the situation, the transfer was faster and more extensive than the one originally planned for in late November 1944. In place of the two border crossing points available for the transfer of troops and freight toward German territory, nine had to be opened in December. By December 1944, three transit camps housing 7,000 had to be opened for the Hungarian troops near Vienna. These, however, being transit camps, each transport could only stay for a day or two.[253]

At Christmas 1944, it became necessary for the Ministry of Defense to appoint an Inspector General, Colonel-General Jenő Major, to take stock of the units evacuated to Germany. His endeavors revealed that by the end of January 1945 well over

100,000 Hungarian soldiers had been evacuated.[254] By the end of March 1945, when the Soviet troops were approaching the German border, the orderly retreat changed into disorganized flight. German units, Hungarian soldiers and civilians, people employed by the government or the gendarmerie, tried to leave the country in a panic. Even so, some units of the Hungarian army fell into Soviet captivity before reaching the German border. Soviet sources reveal that in the last days of March, 45,000 Hungarian soldiers were captured.[255] Seeing that all further fighting was senseless, many voluntarily surrendered to the Red Army and became prisoners of war.

Since nearly all the evacuated units fell into captivity, it would be very important to establish their number. But no exact number is available. Even the most competent authority on the issue, Colonel-General Major could not keep a precise record. In his memoirs, he gives the following reasons for the failure to precisely register the Hungarian units deployed to Germany:

> 1. Being dispersed, a part of our general headquarters was still in the capital, the larger part, however, was scattered in villages in Transdanubia or in the process of being transferred, with hardly any telephone links between them. As a consequence:
>
> 2. Most of the transferred troops were not briefed at all about who to turn to in Germany for instructions; many did not even know about the inspectorate....
>
> 3. The inspector general was refused the transport data and information on further German-Hungarian agreements.[256]

Under such circumstances, by the end of April, 300,000 Hungarian soldiers were registered by the inspector general. As Colonel-General Major wrote, however, "their number must have been far higher for many units were impossible to contact."[257] The question of the number of troops evacuated to Germany was brought up during the preparations for the peace talks. Two sets of figures can be found in the preparatory material for peace compiled by the Ministry of Defense:

Estimates of Hungarian Troops Evacuated to Germany

	I	II
Training Corps	131,687	161,120
Combat Troops	184,400	213,383
Non-Combat Troops	264,339	487,677
Total	**580,426**	**862,180**

With regard to the 530-540,000 kept on record in January 1945, the first version — 580,000 — appears to be more realistic. The other version of 862,180 was considered unrealistically high by the statistic compilers who felt that the non-combat troops of 487,677 might also include the 213,383 combat troops. Even with this explanation, there is still a difference of 70,000 men between the two estimates.

In the light of the January 1945 survey, even the 580,000 of the first version might seem excessive. It must be remembered, however, that in the last phase of the war, thousands joined the Hungarian SS corps and the Slovene population was also conscripted. The total of 580,000 probably contains the thousands that were taken as prisoners of war during the great retreat in late March.[257] The probability of the first estimate is also supported by other sources. According to German scholar, Andreas von Weissenbach, the number of Hungarian troops retreating to Germany in March and April was around 170,000, excluding the German SS units with Hungarian recruits and the Hungarian SS "Hunyadi" and "Hungaria" divisions.[258] These formations were organized following the Hungarian fascist take-over and were 20,000 strong.

In the appendix of János Csima's book, he lists the battalion and regiment personnel training recruits which exceeded 90,000. But, as he notes, his data is incomplete. One can assert with certainty that the entire force including the missing units must have numbered something nearer to the 130,000 of the first version than the 160,000 of the second.

Regarding the non-combatant troops, a note made in 1944 by the registration department of the Ministry of Defense is available under the title "Grouping plan for the staff, supplementary and hinterland units to be transferred to Germany."[259] 280,000 out of the 300,000 registered belonged to auxiliary and hinterland units who were not equipped with weapons which is slightly more than the roughly 260,000 estimated by the first version. But this note of 1944, shows only an approximate number of the evacuated troops.

Hungarian historical research does not discuss the number and fate of Hungarian soldiers taken to Germany and captured there in detail. In the *History of Hungary*, it is said that over 100,000 soldiers were taken to Germany.[260] In his book, János Csima estimates the transferred troops are at 400,000.[261] Another specialist of the period, Mrs. Tamás Morva, estimates the number of Hungarian soldiers ordered into Germany at 580,000.[262] This is also the number mentioned by Mihály Korom.[263]

If the most probable estimate of 560,000, is accepted as the number of soldiers transferred to Germany, then the total number of Hungarian soldiers and civilians captured in World War II, together with the 350,000 taken captive before February 1945, was about 830,000. The number of Hungarian prisoners of war was probably between 800,000 and 900,000.

Nearly all the literature touching on the question presents similar figures. The *Fehér Könyv* estimates the number of prisoners of war at 900,000.[264] Among the researchers in Hungary, Mihály Korom enlarges upon this question in more detail. He writes, "From the present area of the country, 850-900,000 Hungarian soldiers fell into the hand of the victorious powers."[265] It is to be noted, however, that the army units were conscripted from various parts of the country so this number must refer to the territory of the country as it was in 1944 and not today.

Lajos Für left this point out when he elaborated on Mihály Korom's argumentation, concluding that the prisoners of war of the territory in 1944 was between 1.3-1.4 million.[266] After surveying the number of prisoners of war the question that arises is: how many were in Anglo-American, French and Soviet captivity respectively? The 300,000 verified until February 1945 were captured by the Red Army. The distribution of the 580,000 evacuated to German territory cannot be established. A clue to solving this problem is the report made by the Hungarian Statistical Office for the peace delegation in Paris. The report stated that the training units of 130,000

> ...were settled in the area of Germany under calm conditions...their exact training points are also known. Considering the separation of the zones and the fact that the units were hardly mobile at all, of the 130,000, 40,000 fell into the American, English and French zones and 90,000 to the Soviet Russian zone...The transfer of non-combat troops of whom, 150,000 might have fallen into the American zone in Bavaria, while 90,000 into the Soviet-Russian zone took place in spring 1945.
>
> Regarding the combat troops, about 110,000 reached the American and British zones and about 80,000 fell into Soviet Russian captivity due to the quick pace of the Soviet's advance...[267]

Out of the 580,000 deployed in the last months of the war, 300,000 fell into Anglo-American and 260-280,000 into Soviet captivity. The total of Hungarians captured by the Red Army amounted to 600,000. The *Fehér Könyv*[268] and other discussions of the subject published in the West[269] present similar figures. Mihály Korom gives a similar data in size (350-570,000), but he adds that "together with them, another estimated 150,000 Hungarian ex-soldiers were taken captive from the areas attached to the country before and during the first phase of the war." The prisoners of war from re-annexed areas are included as part of the 600,000 which is confirmed by figures from the Prisoner of War Department in the Ministry of Defense.[270] In

May 1945, 130,000 were reported to have been detained at the prisoner of war camp at Cegléd. There were approximately ten prisoner of war camps with a capacity of over 20,000 and 10,000 survivors in the Slovakian camps.[271]

The Transportation of the Prisoners of War Back Home

According to Article 75 of the Geneva Convention, dated July 27, 1929 and enacted in 1936, "the belligerent parties were obliged to return the prisoners of war as soon as an armistice was signed." The armistice agreement signed on January 20, 1945 and enacted as statute 1945.V included no provisions concerning the return of Hungarian prisoners of war. In spite of that, the Red Army began freeing the Hungarian soldiers and civilians captured in Hungary even before the war ended. For lack of registration, their number is not known. Although the Hungarian provisional government in Debrecen set up a prisoner of war department in the Ministry of Defense to register and care for the prisoners of war, there was much to hinder its work. Added to this, the lists of casualties compiled in the earlier phases of the war were missing, financial resources were insufficient and the Allied Control Commission refused to give consent to an organization under the aegis of the army to oversee the repatriation of the prisoners of war.[272]

However meager its resources, the Ministry of Defense ran a few receiving stations and kept records on the number of those who returned. Although incomplete, the Ministry of Defense documents from the in the spring 1945 are useful since no other agency dealt with the prisoners of war at that time. A Ministry of Defense memorandum in August reveals that 2,400 captives of the 24th division were released in April 1945.[273] Another group of 4,000 captives were released in April which constituted the 5th division of the new army. The number of prisoners of war received by the Hungarian army for the organization of railroad, road and bridge construction units can be estimated at about 5,000. Therefore, about 11,500 were released from captivity and joined the work of reconstruction after the transfer of the government to Budapest. At the same time, on February 3, 1945, Minister of Defense János Vörös told the Council of Ministers that 20,000 soldiers had been released by the Soviet authorities.[274] Although the two estimates are not too far apart, the difference illustrates the gaps in registration.

At the beginning, the release of prisoners of war took place in the presence of the representatives of the Hungarian town nearest the prisoner of war camp and the local agent of the Allied Control Commission. Apart from a pass in Russian stating that the prisoner of war was traveling to his locality, there were no documents that were issued, which often led to the capture of the newly freed person. Later, the Ministry of Defense managed to have representatives present at prisoner of war releases. Official releasing documents were issued to establish the degree of the disability, requirement of allowances, and to register the men as prisoners of war. The number of prisoners of war that were discharged and recorded by the army is 18,000.[275] It is still questionable if the Ministry of Defense representatives registered the released civilians as well. (Most of those who died in Hungarian prisoner of war camps were buried in nearby plow fields in unmarked graves).[276]

In the summer of 1945, the transportation of prisoners of war began from the Soviet Union and Romania. For want of a centralized administration besides the Ministry of Defense, their registration and care was carried out by prisoner of war bureaus of social organizations and political parties. These organizations included: the National Association of Families of Prisoners of War, National Aid, Social Mission Society and the Democratic Association of Hungarian Women. They were in contact with the Ministry of Defense through the Central Executive Committee of Prisoner of War Service which tried to coordinate their activity without much success. A report by the Ministry of Welfare in 1945 described the tribulations of those who returned:

> The most gravely afflicted victims of the war imposed upon us are undoubtedly the returning prisoners of war. Completely crushed in body and soul, run down, gravely wounded, maimed, paralyzed, starving and freezing, in rags, without hope, thousands and thousands of them are roaming the countryside. Many were robbed of all their

> belongings while they were away, their apartments were given to others. They are walking the thorny path of life embittered, looking for their families and loved ones who had fled from the specter of war. Exhausted by starvation, in utter despair, many find shelter in doorways, reduced to the humiliating act of begging, asking for charitable handouts and try to hang on to their life of misery and suffering.[277]

The limited ability of the army to act was further curtailed by the reduction of personnel ordered in autumn 1945. Upon the decision of an intra-ministerial meeting, the administration of prisoner of war affairs was taken on by the Hungarian Red Cross. Still, the search for prisoners of war in the Soviet Union and the registration and care for those who returned remained an unsolved problem.

From the summer of 1945, the number of prisoners of war returning from the Soviet Union clearly indicate the chaos caused by the lack of a centrally coordinated prisoner of war service. The available estimates are highly contradictory including the estimates from the Prisoner of War Department of the Ministry of Defense. A memo in May 1947,[278] for example, claimed that not a single prisoner of war returned home from the East before summer 1946 while the Ministry of Welfare reported in January 1947 that in 1945, the prisoners of war were returning sporadically.[279] Yet, a report by the Hungarian Mission in Bucharest that was sent to the Ministry of Defense and was dated December 20, 1945, referred to a large number of prisoners of war transported through Romania. Relying on information by the Hungarian Popular Alliance and other sources, Consul György Varga asserted that "between January 21 and October 31, 1945, 66,240 prisoners of war were cared for in Kolozsvár (Cluj) and about the same number in Arad. In November their number was 11,546. In addition, 40-50,000 were not attended to since they were transported through these cities at night."[280] On the basis of this report, the number of home-comers can be put at 190,000. Another Ministry of Defense report also confirmed the mass influx of prisoners of war from the direction of Romania.[281] "Having removed the bottom planks of trains near the border crossing at Biharkeresztes, many prisoners of war escaped from the trains and dispersed throughout Hungary individually or in groups. Those who arrived said many trains from the Soviet Union were on Romanian territory. The author of the report concluded that the large influx of returning prisoners of war at the reception camps in Szeged and Debrecen required that new reception camps had to be opened."[282]

The study by the Ministry of Defense in its preparatory material for peace, estimated the number of prisoners of war returning from the East before September 1946 at 108,000 on the basis of registers kept at demobilization centers.[283] Another document of the preparatory material for peace dated a few days later, on September 30, 1946, arrived at a very different conclusion on the basis of the daily reports of district centers. "In October, November and December 1945, 192,812 prisoners of war returned; in January, February and March 1946, 30,655 prisoners of war returned; in April, May and June 19,514 prisoners of war returned; in July, 1,261 prisoners of war returned to the area of the country."[284] Based on these figures, the total number of returning prisoners of war equaled 244,242. Another Ministry of Defense report of April 3, 1947 registers as few as 120,000 returnees from the East between June 1945 and March 31, 1946. The returnees in summer and autumn 1946, however, is about the same in this report as in the formerly mentioned document: 30,000.

The public was officially informed by the *Magyar Hadirokkant és Hadifogoly Híradó* [Hungarian War Disabled and Prisoner of War News] published by the prisoner of war office of the Hungarian Communist Party. Unfortunately, the 1945 volume of this source is no longer to be found, only the daily papers are available for this period.[285] The August 12, 1945 issue of *Szegedi Hírlap* reported on the Red Cross nurses looking after the prisoners of war passing the railway station. The *Szabad Szó* of Győr estimated the returned prisoners of war at 100,000 on October 14, 1945. The *Szegedi Hírlap* wrote on November 18, 1945, "Masses of prisoners of war have started toward home from all the camps of the Soviet Union: 3,000 arrived from Sevastopol, 5,000 from Kiev, 8,100 from

Stalingrad, 2,000 from Komarchiko and 3,000 from the camp near Moscow."

The replies of the National Aid to the questions of *Új Szó*, the paper published for the Hungarians by the Red Army. The National Aid welcomed 17,000 prisoners of war in Gyoma and the Szolnok center welcomed 81,000.[286] A brief report on December 25 revealed that between September 1st and December 16th, 149,973 returning prisoners of war were given lunch by the prisoners of war kitchen in Szolnok.[287]

The first news item concerning the number of returnees in the 1946 volume of the *Magyar Hadirokkant és Hadifogoly Híradó* was published on March 18. It stated, "At least 100,000 prisoners of war returned." Three days later, *Kossuth Népe* wrote about 200,000 returns. The March 25th issue of the *Magyar Hadirokkant és Hadifogoly Híradó* confirms this number. Two months later, it wrote that 250,000 returned from the Soviet Union, although no mass returns were reported in April and May. Erik Molnár, the Minister of Welfare, reported on November 16, 1946, "260,000 prisoners of war had returned from the East."[288]

There are many reasons to account for the great divergence in the mentioned estimates and figures. Before June 1946, the POWs' return was not centrally coordinated, their registration and care was organized *ad hoc* at the thirty reception and care stations for prisoners of war all over the country. Although the figures of the Ministry of Defense are based on the records about former prisoners of war kept by the district military offices and discharging centers, they are not fully reliable.

In theory, the registration of returning prisoners of war took place in the following manner: the reception or welcoming committees at the major railway stations supplied the returnees with a temporary pass that entitled them to free railway travel and free tram use in Budapest. At home, the former prisoners of war had to report to the nearest recruiting center where they were given their back pay for the duration of their captivity upon presenting their pass. A detailed bulletin of information was issued by the Ministry of Defense in September 1945 for prisoners of war arriving from the East, which was published in the September 18, 1945 issue of *Világ* as well.

The process of demobilization explains the main divergence in the data. Those who arrived in Hungary on their own could not be registered. It is also possible that due to hyper-inflation, the promised pay was not large enough to attract many of them to the recruiting centers. At the same time, one pass could be used by several people since the Ministry of Defense did not have a complete list of the former Hungarian army in autumn 1945.

Under such circumstances, the differences in the figures of regional recruiting and discharging centers are evident. It is also probable that the Ministry of Defense did not keep a record of the civilian prisoners of war who returned with the soldiers. Theoretically, these were accounted for by the *Magyar Hadirokkant és Hadifogoly Híradó*. For want of a unified database, the best estimate of the total number of prisoners of war returning until summer 1946 is about 200-250,000.

Those Who Returned from the West

The release of the 280-300,000 soldiers captured by British or American forces began in summer 1945. The Ministry of Defense was in charge of receiving, discharging and transporting those who returned. Owing to difficulties caused by the Allied Control Commission, the Ministry of Defense was unable to fulfill the increasing demands, so it utilized the Hungarian Red Cross and other voluntary social organizations.

The first group of prisoners of war in Austria had already come home when in mid-August 1945, a Hungarian delegation headed by Mihály Farkas, Secretary of State for Internal Affairs, visited the American headquarters in Salzburg to discuss the details of transportation. The delegation included several representatives of the Allied Control Commission as well as Gábor Péter who was head of the security police and György Pálffy, head of the Office of Political Affairs in the Ministry of Defense. The Americans promised to start the mass transportation of prisoners of war home within ten days. The trains were arranged by the American army and transportation was free. Upon returning home, Mihály Farkas declared, "no exact figures are available of the number of prisoners of war because the Hungarians do not live in one place or in huge internment camps, but they are divided into small groups in villages and estates....As far as it can be estimated, the Hungarian prisoners of war in Austria number somewhat over 100-110,000."[289] Paris radio also reported this mass transportation home on September 6, 1945.[290]

Even with the cooperation of the Red Cross the organizers of reception could not absorb the increasing number of returnees. Therefore, the government set up the Government Commission for Repatriation [Hazahozatali Kormánybiztosság] within the prime minister's office to answer for the affairs of prisoners of war returning from the West. The screening camps at Komárom, Kaposvár, Székesfehérvár and Szentgotthárd established by the army were placed under police control and the Ministry of Defense's role was thereby reduced to discharging.[291]

The prisoners of war returning from the Anglo-American zones included several people accused of war crimes. Their recognition and arrest depended on the precise registration of the returnees. The figures of registration by the Government Commission for repatriation which began in August 1945 were later adopted by the Defense and Welfare Ministries. According to these reports, 114,900 passed through he screening camps and arrived home until March 31, 1946.[292] Records were not kept of those returning home before August 1945. The rest can only be estimated.

According to a January 1946 broadcast of the Hungarian Service of the BBC, there were 75,000 Hungarian prisoners of war in Germany.[293] This number probably does not include the 60,000 paramilitary troops whose transport to Canada was offered by Colonel Antal Vattay to the British headquarters, without success.[294] De Bartillet, the head of the prisoner of war department in the French Ministry of Foreign Affairs, put the number of those in France at 40,000 in an interview with *Magyar Hadirokkant és Hadifogoly Híradó*.[295] French sources, however, record only 30,000 prisoners of war, half of them under American surveillance in Mailly-le-Camp.[296] As for the 8-10,000 Hungarian prisoners of war detained in Italy, unfortunately, there is very little information available.[297]

Hungarian prisoners of war detained in Sweden numbered 1,700,[298] while those held in Belgium numbered 2,000.[299] The survey is still incomplete since some of the Hungarian soldiers drifted to other European countries during the retreat in 1945; at least 2,000 of the training corps reached Denmark. Many members of the "Hunyadi" and "Hungarian" SS squads remained in Switzerland until the end of the war.

After the winter of 1945, mass transports resumed in spring 1946. In March, 7,000 prisoners of war came home from France.[300] The Hungarian press reported that in April and May, prisoner of war trains arrived from Hegyeshalom every day. In July, 19,000 soldiers came from the British zone in Germany.[301] By that time, most of those who wished to return had arrived. In 1946, the prisoner of war camps in Austria and Germany were dismantled. According to a report of the Welfare Ministry, 5,544 arrived in August, 3,660 in September, 1,234 in October, 1,214 in November and only 474 in December.[302] With these figures, the number of returnees rose to 187,889 until December 16, 1946.[303] In 1947, only a few hundred arrived: 680 in January, 76 in February. In March, the number rose to 905, followed by 114 in April and 329 in May.[304] The daily reports of the Government Commission for Repatriation conclude in May. The final total of prisoners of war returning from the West is 189,993.[305] In view of those not registered before the Government Commission and those arriving after May 1947, the total number can be put at about 200,000. Out of the officially registered 189,993 returns, 15,552 were officers, 174,441 soldiers. The overwhelming majority - 182,813 - were collected in screening camps. After identification, 12,205 (1,712 officers, 10,493 soldiers) were handed over to the authorities for further investigation.[306]

Of the 280,000 troops taken to Germany, 30-35% never returned. This rate is confirmed by Bálint Botár, head of the prisoner of war department of the Welfare Ministry. "I often talked to Sándor Millok, head of the Government Commission for Home Transportation and people around him...they often reiterated that unfortunately, 30-40% of the soldiers, especially the officers, did not return."[307] The press also often reported about the prisoners of war deceived by Nazi propaganda in the

West and refused to return.[308] Apart from being unfamiliar with the changed situation at home, fear from arrest and the drive for adventure motivated those who remained abroad. Many of those that didn't return made up the 20,000 mercenaries of Hungarian origin in the foreign legion who fought in Indo-China in 1952.[309]

Organized Transports from Soviet Captivity

July 1, 1945 marks a turning point in the resolution of the prisoner of war question. Upon the request of the government and the Supreme Economic Council, the Welfare Ministry took over the task of receiving and registering the prisoners of war since the help provided by the Red Cross was not sufficient to fulfill the task. Welfare Minister Erik Molnár set up the prisoner of war department IV/5 which merged with Department I/2 in charge of welfare on February 15, 1947. With a central administration in place, precise registration became possible; therefore, the sources and figures for those arriving after July 1, 1946 do not significantly vary.

Lieutenant-Colonel V. P. Sviridov informed the Hungarian government that until September 3rd, 25,000 people would be transported home from the Soviet Union.[310] To organize the exchange, General Bielianov arrived from Moscow in August 1946. The Soviet authorities were in constant contact with the embassy in Bucharest and informed the Romanian and Hungarian authorities when a transport train left Foksany or Máramarossziget (Sighetu Marmaţici).

The report of the Welfare Ministry recorded 4,807 returnees in August, followed by 7,484 in September.[311] In October 3,311, in November 498, and in December 222 prisoners of war crossed the border from the East.[312] Out of the promised 25,000, 16,322 arrived. This number is consistent with the relevant statistics of the Ministry of Defense. 65% of the received prisoners of war were soldiers, 8.75% were officers.1.85% were paramilitary soldiers, 3.77% were women, 15.15% were civilian men and .15% infants under a year old.[313]

On February 10, 1947, Minister of Foreign Affairs, János Gyöngyösi, signed the peace treaty for Hungary in Paris. The provisions for prisoners of war in Article 21, Title II, Part III ran as follows:

1. As soon as possible the Hungarian prisoners of war are to be transported home, according to agreements between the power retaining the prisoners of war and Hungary.

2. All costs including the cost of maintenance of Hungarian prisoners of war under transportation from the assembly points which is determined by the government of the concerned Allied or Associated power to the point of entry into Hungary are to be born by the Hungarian government.[314]

The proposal of the Hungarian delegation to have all prisoners of war transported home within six months after signing the peace treaty was rejected by the conference. Neither did the Hungarian government get guarantees that the Hungarian prisoners of war living in neighboring countries could return to their homes.

The winter and spring of 1947 witnessed political crisis triggered by the arrest of the prominent centrist political leader, Béla Kovács, and by the concern "for the cause of the Hungarian community." The Hungarian communist leader, Mátyás Rákosi, and his circle resorted to the prisoner of war question to channel off the unleashed passions. On behalf of the Democratic Association of Hungarian Women one of its leaders, Mrs. Károly Döbrentei headed a delegation of a hundred women asking Mátyás Rákosi to intervene with Stalin to expedite the return of the prisoners of war. Mátyás Rákosi forwarded the women's request on May 9, 1947. The positive reply from Stalin arrived within a week: "The Soviet government studied Mátyás Rákosi's letter and in response to the request therein, ordered the release and transportation home of prisoners of war in May, before the ratification and the date of entering into force of the peace treaty with Hungary."[315]

Before the prisoner of war transports resumed in June, the Hungarian authorities made a survey of prisoners of war still in the Soviet Union. The results varied because of different definitions of the people captured by the Red Army and those who returned by the summer of 1946. According to *Magyar Hadirokkant és Hadifogoly Híradó*,150-200,000 people were still in the Soviet Union.[316] In a joint ministerial meeting with the Ministry of Foreign Affairs, the representatives of the Welfare Ministry counted between 200-250,000 prisoners of war in spring 1947.[317] Another senior official of the Welfare Ministry set the number of expected returnees at 350,000.[318] The Hungarian Red Cross also reckoned with 350,000,[319] while the Ministry of Defense estimated 400,000.[320] Hermann Pokornyi, the head of the Ministry of Foreign Affairs' Prisoner of War Department felt that there were about 400-500,000 prisoners of war.[321] If we accept that the number of returnees until summer 1946 was between 200-250,000, then the second estimate of the Welfare Ministry and the figure given by the Red Cross appear to be most realistic.

In the month of June 1947, 16,000 prisoners of war arrived home and in July over 30,000 returned. On October 30th, the 100,000th prisoner of war returned.[322] From June 4th to October 31st, a total of 100,288 were freed from captivity. Of them, 7,171 were officers, 9,984 non-commissioned officers, 72,751 soldiers, 817 from the labor battalions, 5,829 interned men, 3,596 interned women, 124 paramilitary soldiers and 16 infants.[323] 8,000 were to have arrived in November 1947, to be released on the 30th anniversary of the Bolshevik Revolution. Cold weather, however, only made the transportation of 1,557 prisoners of war possible. The Hungarian public, however, kept the fate of the prisoners of war in the fore. To put the people's minds at rest, Mátyás Rákosi said in a speech delivered in Csepel that: "each and every prisoner of war is going to be taken home this year."[324]

The Hungarian-Soviet Agreement of Friendship, Cooperation and Mutual Aid signed on February 18 largely facilitated the resumption of transports. During a dinner Stalin with the Hungarian delegation in Moscow, he promised that the return of the prisoners of war would resume on April 1. The first train arrived on May 1, 1948. The returnees numbered 10,000 by May 21.[325] Another seven trains arrived in Debrecen in June, with a total of 8,074 prisoners of war.[326] By August 15, the number of released prisoners of war rose to 42,892.[327] Staff officers were 337, officers 1,350, non-commissioned officers 8,376, soldiers 2,827, laborers 337, civilians 2548, and 1,171 women.[328]

Until November, the transports home were similar. The records of the Prisoner of War Reception Committee at Debrecen contain 84,310 entries until that date. At that point, the government officially declared the question of prisoners of war to have been solved, saying that only war criminals convicted by the Soviet authorities would remain in the Soviet Union. Soon after, the organizations and parties caring for the prisoners of war and the prisoner of war departments were soon disbanded, although 30,000 people were still missing.[329] The prisoner of war question, however, was only removed from the public agenda. The Ministry of the Interior and the State Security Authority still kept attending to the prisoner of war transports. The register of the Prisoner of War Reception Committee of Debrecen has 5,055 entrees for 1949. According to the western press, another 20,000 prisoners of war arrived from the Soviet Union between 1950-51.[330]

Number of Hungarian Troops Captured by the Allies

	Soviet	Anglo-American	Total Captured
June 26, 1941-October 31, 1941	70,000	---	70,000
November 1944-February 1945	250,000	---	250,000
After February 1945	280,000	300,000	70,000
June 26, 1941-end of the war	**600,000**	**300,000**	**390,000**

Number of Hungarian Returnees from Allied Captivity

	Soviet	Anglo-American
Until July 1946	200-250,000	---
July 1946-January 1947	16,000	200,000*

	Soviet	Anglo-American
January 1947-January 1948	102,000	---
January 1948-January 1949	84,000	---
From 1949 to 1951	20-25,000	---
From 1945 to 1951	422-477,000	200,000

* Out of the 300,000 in Anglo-American captivity, 200,000 returned until May 1947.

All things considered, it can be established with great probability that the prisoners of war who returned numbered about 400-450,000. This number also includes those men who were processed in Debrecen, but lived in northern and southern Hungary, areas that were ceded to Hungary's neighbors. Most were not allowed by the Czechoslovakian authorities to return, forcing many to stay in Hungary or go home illegally. Those from the south were comparatively easily taken over by the Yugoslav authorities. This was simpler since only 400 asked to return home after 1947.[331] Those Transylvanians who wanted to return to their families were separated in the transit camps of Foksány and Máramarossziget and transported home directly. In view of their proportion within the army, they cannot have been more than 15-20,000. Out of the 600,000 prisoners of war in the captivity of the Red Army, 450,000 appears to be a realistic number of returnees. Those who did not return numbered about 150,000. The majority probably died of contagious diseases. The precise death toll is unknown, for Hungarians were not registered separately in the prisoner of war camps. Most authors in the West estimate the loss of prisoners of war at 200,000.[332] Mihály Korom evaded the question, but if we subtract from the 550-570,000 prisoners of war the total of 500,000 returnees - both his calculations -, then he implicitly gives 50-70,000 for those who did not return.[333]

Relying on Mihály Korom's figures, Lajos Für draws completely different conclusions: "prolonging as it were the conditions of war, hundreds of thousands perished in the prisoner of war camps due to miserable, often inhuman circumstances."[334] This author's estimate of 150,000 is the mean of various calculations. Of course, its reliability is not due to this but to the fact that it is based on a far richer stock of sources than that of any work published in Hungary or abroad. The 80,000 prisoners of war who remained in the West and 150,000 who did not return from the East meant a far larger cut in the population than the casualties of the actual war, which amounted to 120-140,000.

Painstaking research is still needed to answer the so-far unsettled questions and put forth a more precise figure. More of the answers to these questions can probably be found in the unexplored archives of the Hungarian Railways, Red Cross and Pension Office and personal recollections of the former prisoners of war could also largely contribute to the creation of a more realistic picture.

Summary

In theory, there are two ways to establish the loss of lives in World War II. One calculates either indirectly, comparing the result of the census of 1941 and that of 1949, or directly, taking into account everyone who died. The passage quoted in the introduction of this manuscript summing up the demographic results of the 1949 census takes the indirect course. It may lack an analysis of the migration and the 330,000 people to account for the natural growth of the population. Some paragraphs later, the authors of the same volume could assume a natural growth of 400,000-500,000.

Thirty five years later, Lajos Für further improved on this method. "...in our view, it cannot be too unrealistic to assume that the sum total of the loss of Hungary's population within the borders established at the Trianon Peace Treaty comprises the missing natural growth (520-600,000), the absolute decrease of the population between 1941 and 1949 (110,000) and the surplus of the balance of migration with 200,000 that emigrated and 70,000 who immigrated. The shocking and alarming figure is somewhere between 750,000-900,000."[335] Since the population of the wartime territory was 58% larger than that of the post-Trianon area, Lajos Für increased the figures by this percentage to arrive at the final loss. His result ranged between a minimum of 1.2 million (750,000 + 450,000) and a maximum of 1.43 million (900,000 + 530,000).[336] The authenticity of his figures is weakened by the uncertainty about defining the balance of migration and the natural growth.

Hungary's Total Loss Within Its Post-1947 Borders[337]

Military Losses in the Area of the Soviet Union	100,000
Bombing Casualties in Budapest	6,500
Bombing Casualties Outside Budapest	9,500
Military Losses in the Area of the Country	24,000
Prisoners of War Captured in the Country Who Died	12,000
Civilians Killed in the Siege of Budapest	28,000
Loss of Civilian Jews	220,000
Total:	**400,000**

What accounts for the imprecision of his data is the lack of available sources when he wrote his work in 1946. Regrettably, later statistical works including Mihály Korom, adopted this calculation with some corrections.[338] The basic principle of direct approach by computing the total loss from each component item was correct. If the total loss is calculated item by item, one can avoid the problems due to the inefficient calculations of natural growth. This picture could also offer a more subtle picture of the wartime migrations.

Summing up the previous chapters, the following can be said of Hungary's total loss in World War II and of the migration:

Military Casualties:	140,000-160,000
Hungarian Soldiers and Civilians Who Died in Soviet Captivity:	150,000
Civilian Casualties in the Present Area:	80,000-100,000

Several thousand Hungarian civilians must be added to this number if the areas detached from Hungary after the war are also to be covered. These thousands were the victims of the chauvinistic bands. The number of Hungarian Jews from

Hungary's 1941 borders that were killed is approximately 400,000. The Gypsy casualties were not discussed separately for lack of sufficient sources; the World Organization of the Gypsies put the number of Hungarian Gypsy victims at 50,000.[339] The total loss is therefore between 810,000 and 900,000.

Hundreds of thousands of displaced refugees constitute another group of war victims. 120,000 Hungarians in minority status in Czechoslovakia were forced to leave their homes; the corresponding figure for Romania is 100,000, for Sub-carpathia 10,000, for Yugoslavia 65,000 which totals 300,000. The refugees fleeing to the West are not discussed here since no archival material on this subject was accessible in Hungary. Gyula Borbándi, one of the authorities on those who fled to the West, claims that 350,000 Hungarians left the Carpathian Basin including the Jewish concentration camp survivors who did not return.[340] The ethnic Germans of Hungary deported between 1947-48 numbered 190,000.[341] The Slovaks resettled in Czechoslovakia under the population exchange agreement numbered 60-70,000. All in all, 900,000 people were affected by migration.

The figures for the present area were calculated by taking 64% of the previous row of data, since the Hungarian population of the areas re-annexed between 1938 and 1941 came to 36% of the entire country. In this way, the loss of the army was 80-100,000 and the victims of captivity were 150,000. According to some sources, 80,000-100,000 civilians lost their lives. The corresponding figure for the Jewry is around 180,000. In fact, a far larger ratio of Jews survived in the present-day area than in the area added to Hungary between 1939 and 1941. The total loss of the Hungarian population was below 500,000. The population loss due to migration is 160,000. Some 460,000 moved out of the country by calculating the 210,000 who emigrated to the West and 190,000 Germans and 60,000 Slovaks who were resettled from the present area. Immigrants to Hungary numbered 300,000.

It is commonly accepted that there were 50 million casualties of World War II. Forced migration in Europe affected 22 million people compared to the total, Hungary's loss of roughly 600,000 and 1 million, as well as the 600,000 migrants seems small. The sad fact is, however, that this loss represented one-tenth of Hungary's population. The impact of this loss is still felt, almost fifty years after the war.

Notes

1. Mihály Korom, "A magyar népi demokrácia első évei" [The First Years of the Hungarian People's Democracy], *Valóság*, n. s. 3, (1984), 1-9.
2. Lajos Für, "Magyarország emberveszteségе" [Hungary's Loss of Lives], *Magyar Hírlap*, June 23, 1984.
3. Miklós Horváth, *A 2. magyar hadsereg megsemmisülése a Donnál* [The Destruction of the 2nd Hungarian Army at the Don] (Budapest, 1958).
4. Pál Kornis, "A voronyezsi front támadó hadműveletének előkészítése a német "B" hadseregcsoport déli szárnyának szétzúzására" [The Preparations for the Offensive of the Voronezh Front to Crush the Southern Wing of the German Army Group "B"], *Hadtörténelmi Közlemények*, 3 (1982), 432-463.
5. György Ránki, ed., *Magyarország története* [A History of Hungary] (Budapest,1984), Vol. 8, 1090.
6. Sándor Tóth, *Budapest felszabadítása 1944-45* [The Liberation of Budapest 1944-45] (Budapest, 1975).
7. Ignác Ölvedi, *A budai vár és a debreceni csata* [Buda Castle and the Battle of Debrecen] (Budapest, 1970).
8. János Csima, *Adalékok a Horthy-hadsereg szervezetének és háborús tevékenységének tanulmányozásához 1938-45* [Some Additions to the Study of thc Organization and Military Activity of the Horthy Army 1938-45] (Budapest, 1961).
9. Péter Gosztonyi, "Magyarország katonai története a második világháborúban" [Hungary's Military History in World War II], Part II, *Katolikus Szemle*, (Rome), 2 (1982), 117.
10. Norbert Csanádi, Sándor Nagyváradi and Lajos Winkler, *A magyar repülés története* [The History of Flying in Hungary] (Budapest, 1977), 233.
11. Hadtörténeti Intézet Levéltára [Archives of the Institute of Military History], *Békeelőkészítő anyag* [Preparation for Peace], box 1, A 4/37161.

12. Hadtörténeti Intézet Levéltára, 692/VKF eln. 1. oszt. - 1942, bundle 231.

13. Hadtörténeti Intézet Levéltára, VKF 1944. hadm. cs. f. 437/eln., appendix no. 3.

14. Horváth, *op. cit.,* 17.

15. Csima, *op. cit.,* 158.

16. Hadtörténeti Intézet Levéltára, HM 1944. eln. 6. K. oszt., bundle 6675.

17. Gosztonyi, *op. cit.,* Part IV, *Katolikus Szemle,* (Rome), 4 (1982), 329.

18. Horváth, *op. cit.,* 25.

19. *Ibid.*, 29.

20. Hadtörténeti Intézet Levéltára, VKF 1944 hdm. cs. 437/eln. appendix no. 3.

21. Csima, *op. cit.,* 165.

22. Horváth, *op. cit.,* 98-100. Adding up the items between July 1 - September 15, the loss totals 20,406. From this, I deducted 728 losses suffered on July 1 and 2 before the bridgehead fighting, during the breakthrough at Tym.

23. Gosztonyi, *op. cit.,* 332 (n. 53). The "lecture" of the Chief of the Hungarian Army Staff to the Supreme Defense Council's meeting on October 5, 1942.

24. György Ránki, *et al.*, eds., *A Wilhelmstrasse és Magyarország* [Wilhelmstrasse and Hungary] (Budapest, 1968), 693.

25. *Ibid.,* 695.

26. Hadtörténeti Intézet Levéltára, HM 1944/eln. 6. K. oszt., bundle 6776.

27. Hadtörténeti Intézet Levéltára, HM 1944 eln. /1/ny., bundle 6768.

28. Gosztonyi, *op. cit.,* Part V, *Katolikus Szemle* (Rome), 1 (1983), 47.

29. Ránki, *et. al.*, eds., *op. cit.,* 707.

30. Horváth, *op. cit.,* 197.

31. Horváth, *op. cit.,* 343.

32. Miklós Horthy, *Horthy Miklós titkos iratai* [The Secret Papers of Miklós Horthy] (Budapest, 1965). 373.

33. Ránki, *et. al.*, eds., *op. cit.,* 721.

34. Kornis, *op. cit.,* 447.

35. Horváth, *op. cit.,* 42.

36. Ránki, ed., *Magyarország története* 1090.

37. Hadtörténeti Intézet Levéltára, VKF 1944. ham. cs. f. 437/eln. appendix no. 3 and Hadtörténeti Intézet Levéltára, HM, *Békeelőkészítő anyag,* box 3, A/II. 31. 309. 1.

38. Estimate on the basis of Hadtörténeti Intézet Levéltára, VKF 1944. ham. cs. f. 437/eln., appendix no. 3.

39. Hadtörténeti Intézet Levéltára, VKF 1944. eln. 1/ny oszt. no. 52 and bundle 6768.

40. *Harcászati Szabályzat* [Tactical Rules], Part II, "Alaki határozmányok" [Technical Regulations], (Budapest, 1939), 82.

41. Horváth, *op. cit.,* 343, Letter of György Kovács, chief of staff of the Second Army to Colonel Zeitzler, Hadtörténeti Intézet Levéltára, HM box 3, A/II. 31, 309.

42. Ferenc Gallyas, "Az érzelmek és az értelem szerepe hadifogoly-magatartásunkban" [The Role of Emotions and Reason in Our Behavior as Prisoners of War], *Hadtörténelmi Közlemények,* (1973), 547.

43. *Fehér könyv a Szovjetunióba elhurcolt hadifoglyok és polgári deportáltak helyzetéről* [White Book About the State of Prisoners of War and Civilians Deported to the Soviet Union], (n. p., 1950), 17.

44. Horváth, *op. cit.,* 43.

45. Csima, *op. cit.,* 132.

46. Hadtörténeti Intézet Levéltára, VKF 1944. 1. oszt. eln. 4567-6375

47. Hadtörténeti Intézet Levéltára, VKF 1944. 1. oszt. box 298, "Bulletin" July 8, 1944.

48. Hadtörténeti Intézet Levéltára, VKF 1944. 1. oszt. box 298, "Bulletin" July 28, 1944.

49. Ignác Ölvedi, "Adalékok Horthy és a Lakatos-kormány katonapolitikájához" [Some Additions to the Military Policy of Horthy and the Lakatos Cabinet], *Századok,* (1969), 31.

50. Tóth, *op. cit.,* 21 (n. 10); Stymenko, "V'szerdce Jeprovi," *Znamia,* 2 (1972).

51. Tóth, *op. cit.,* 22.

52. Hadtörténeti Intézet Levéltára, HM At the bottom of the page, there is a note with the date, November 30, 1945.

53. Ölvedi, *op. cit.,* 213 (n. 187).

54. Jenő Czebe and Tibor Pethő, *Magyarország a második világháborúban* [Hungary in World War II] (Budapest, 1946), 66.

55. The bulk of the DM documentation for the period up to October 15, 1944 was taken along by the Szálasi government to western Transdanubia. The material left behind almost completely perished in the siege of Budapest.

56. Hadtörténeti Intézet Levéltára, HM 1945. eln. 20. 312.

57. Hadtörténeti Intézet Levéltára, HM 1945. eln. 29. 055.

58. Árpád Snyder, "Becslés Magyarországnak a második világháború következtében elszenvedett emberveszteségéről" [An Estimate of Hungary's Loss of Lives in World War II], *Magyar Statisztikai Szemle*, (1946), 2.

59. Hadtörténeti Intézet Levéltára, HM; *Békeelökészítö anyag*, box 3, A/II 31.

60. Hadtörténeti Intézet Levéltára, HM; *Békeelökészítö anyag*, box 2, A/I 94/4766.

61. Tóth, *op. cit.*, 206-207.

62. *Ibid.*, 261.

63. *Ibid.*, 262.

64. Soviet sources state different figures for the German-Hungarian losses. In a translated multi-volume publication, the following can be read: "In their fight for the eastern part of the city the fascists lost 36,000 lives and 63,000 fell into captivity... In Budapest, another 29,000 soldiers were taken prisoners of war... During the fighting in Budapest, a total of 188,000 soldiers of the enemy were killed or taken captive." With the knowledge of the size of the forces enclosed in Budapest, the above figures seem unrealistic. See: Dmitrii F. Ustinov, *et al.*, *A második világháború története 1939-1945* [The History of World War II 1939-1945] (Budapest, 1981), Vol. 10, 216-217.

65. V. V. Gurkin, "Osvobozhdenie vengrii" [The Liberation of Hungary], *Voenno Istoricheskii Zhurnal*, (1981), 65-71.

66. Ferenc Adonyi, *A magyar katona a második világháborúban* [The Hungarian Soldier in World War II] (Klagenfurt, 1954), 1.

67. Korom, *op. cit.*, 3.

68. G. Zaharia, *et al.*, "A román történetírás Közép- és

Délkelet-Európának a második világháború előestéjén és a háború alatt betöltött szerepéről" [The Role of Central and South-Eastern Europe Before and During World War II as Reflected in Romanian Historiography], *Történelmi Szemle*, (1973), 383 (n. 3).

69. "Tájékoztató gyorsfelvétel a községek, városok közérdekű viszonyairól" [An Informative Quick Survey of the Public Relations of Villages and Towns]. *Magyar Statisztikai Szemle*, (1946), 16.

70. Miklós Horváth, ed., *Budapest története a forradalmak korától a felszabadulásig* [A History of Budapest from the Age of Revolutions to the Liberation] (Budapest, 1980), 571.

71. *Ibid.*, 571.

72. Snyder, *op. cit.*, 3.

73. József Szekeres, ed., *Források Budapest múltjából* [Sources on the Past of Budapest] (Budapest, 1972), Vol. 3, *Források Budapest történetéhez* [Sources on the History of Budapest 1919-1945] (Budapest, 1972), 569.

74. Dávid Lajos, *A népi demokratikus forradalom Győr-Moson megyében 1945-48* [The People's Democratic Revolution in Győr-Moson County 1945-48] (Győr, n. d.), 9-10.

75. Németh Alajos, "Sopron könnyes, véres dátumai" [Days of Tears and Blood in Sopron], Manuscript, 323.

76. János Papp, "Légitámadások Szombathely ellen" [Air Raids on Szombathely], *Vasi Szemle*, (1975), 227.

77. János Rácz, ed., *Válogatott dokumentumok Csongrád megye munkásmozgalmának történetéből 1944-45* [Selected Documents on the History of the Labor Movement in Csongrád County 1944-45] (Szeged, 1970), 33.

78. For a quick statistical survey, see: *ibid.*, 16.

79. *Városi Szemle*, (1945), 54-55.

80. *Ibid.*

81. Tibor Zinner, "A Horthy-Magyarország fasiszta maradványainak felszámolása az 1950-es évek második felében, különös tekintettel az ország fővárosára" [The Eradication of the Fascist Remnants of Horthy's Hungary in the Second Half of the 1950s, With Special Regard to the Capital of the Country], Manuscript.

82. Németh, *op. cit.*

83. Gabriella Molnár, "Hogyan hatott Székesfehérvár életére a második világháború" [How World War II Affected Székesfehérvár], *Fejér Megyei Szemle*, (1975), 173.
84. Papp, *op. cit.*, 227.
85. Béla Beszteri, ed., *Veszprém megye fejlodése, 1945-70* [The Development of Veszprém County, 1945-70] (Veszprém, 1970), 13; Ms. Gábor Varga, ed., *Borsod-Abaúj-Zemplén megye története és legújabbkori adattára* [A History and the Most Recent Archives of Borsod-Abaúj-Zemplén County] (Miskolc, 1970), 173.
86. Jacob Lestchinsky, "Balance Sheet of Extermination," *Jewish Affairs* (1946); Louis Finkelstein, ed., *The Jews. Their History, Culture, and Religion* (London, 1961), 1534; *A Zsidó Állam* [The Jewish State] (Budapest, 1948), 209.
87. *Report of the Anglo-American Committee of Inquiry Regarding the Problems of European Jewry and Palestine. Lausanne, April 20, 1946* (London, 1946), 58-59.
88. Pál Zsigmond Pach, "A magyarországi zsidóság mai statisztikájának szembetűnő jelenségei" [The Conspicuous Features of the Present-Day Statistics of the Hungarian Jewry], in Imre Benoschofsky, ed., *A maradék zsidóság* [The Remnants of the Jewry] (Budapest, 1946), 33.
89. Raul Hilberg, *The Destruction of the European Jews* (Chicago, 1961), 670.
90. The Jewish Publication Society of America, *American Jewish Yearbook 1947-48* Vol. 49, (Philadelphia, 1948), 740.
91. Malcolm Proudfoot, *European Refugees 1939-52* (Evanston, 1956), 336-337.
92. *Egyleti Élet*, (New York), December 29, 1945; *Új Élet*, March 14, 1946.
93. Arieh Tartakower, "The Problem of European Jewry (1939-1945)," Finkelstein, ed., *op. cit.*, 290.
94. Snyder, *op. cit.*, 3-4.
95. Lajos Thirring, "Terület és népesség" [Area and Population], in Elekes Dezső, ed., *Mai Magyarország* [Today's Hungary] (Budapest, 1947), 72; "Magyarország károsodása a második világháborúban" [Hungary's Damage in World War II], *Statisztikai Szemle*, (1955), 183.
96. József Kovacsics, ed., *Magyarország történeti*

demográfiája [An Historical Demography of Hungary] (Budapest, 1962), 236; Jacob Siegel, *The Population of Hungary* (Washington, 1958), 33.

97. Béla Vihar, *Sárga könyv. Adatok a magyar zsidóság háborús szenvedéseiből 1941-45* [Yellow Book. Data on the Sufferings of the Hungarian Jewry 1941-45] (Sao Paulo, 1945), 223-224.

98. Jenő Lévai, *Zsidósors Magyarországon* [Jewish Fate in Hungary] (Budapest, 1948), 464-469.

99. See: Sigfrid Róth's study in *Új Élet*, November 15, 1945; Randolph Braham, *The Politics of Genocide. The Holocaust in Hungary* (New York, 1981), 1144; Yehuda Zoltán Moor, "Budapest 1944, a magyar zsidóság sorsa a második világháborúban" [Budapest 1944, the Fate of the Hungarian Jewry in World War II], Manuscript, National Széchényi Library, 109-111; László Varga, "A magyarországi zsidóság megsemmisítése 1944-45" [The Annihilation of the Hungarian Jews 1944-45], in *MIOK Évkönyv*, (Budapest, 1984); Péter Várdy, "A magyarországi zsidóüldözések a hazai történetírásban" [The Persecution of Jews in Hungarian as Reflected in Hungarian Historiography], in Péter Kende, ed., *Zsidóság az 1945 utáni Magyarországon* [Jews in Hungary After 1945], (Paris, 1984), 191-193.

100. At the Wannsee Conference (Jan. 20, 1942) where the extermination of European Jews was decided upon, 742,000 Hungarian Jews were reckoned with. Dezső Schön, *A jeruzsálemi per* [The Jerusalem Trial] (Tel Aviv, n. d.), 221-223; In his policy speech, Miklós Kállay mentioned 800,000 Jews, Lévai, *op. cit.*, 43. Other German sources including the notes of the Plenipotentiary Veesenmayer, Embassy Counsellor Thadden and Foreign Affairs Counsellor Wagner estimated the number of Hungarian Jews at 900,000-1 million, in Ránki, *et al.*, eds., *op. cit.*, 867, 908.

101. Lévai, *ibid.*, 40.

102. Artur Geyer, "Az első magyarországi deportálás" [The First Deportation in Hungary], in *Új Élet Almanac 1960-61* (Budapest, 1960), 77.

103. Gideon Hausner, *Itélet Jeruzsálemben* [Verdict in Jerusalem] (Budapest, 1984), 195.

104. Lévai, *op. cit.*, 465.
105. Geyer, *op. cit.*, 80-81.
106. Hilberg, *op. cit.*, 520.
107. Geyer, *op. cit.*, 81.
108. Ránki, *et. al.*, eds., *op. cit.*, 675.
109. *Ibid.*, 694.
110. See: Varga, *op. cit.*, 402, n. 3.
111. Hadtörténeti Intézet Levéltára, HM eln. 6/k 48481 1942.
112. Elek Karsai, *Fegyvertelen álltak az aknamezőkön... Dokumentumok a munkaszolgálat történetéhez Magyarországon* [They Stood Unarmed on the Minefields... Documents to the History of Labor Service in Hungary] (Budapest, 1962), Vol. 1, LXXV; Ránki, ed., *Magyarország története* Vol. 8, 1079; Randolph Braham, *The Hungarian Labor Service System 1939-1945* (New York, 1977), 28.
113. Hadtörténeti Intézet Levéltára, HM VKF 1. oszt. no. 268.
114. Péter Gosztonyi, *A magyar honvédség a második világháborúban* [The Hungarian Honvéd Army in World War II] (Rome, 1986), 110.
115. Hadtörténeti Intézet Levéltára, HM VKF 1944/eln. 299.
116. *Ibid.*
117. *Ibid.*, VKF. 1943. 708/eln.
118. C. A. Macartney, *October Fifteenth. History of Modern Hungary 1927-1945* (Edinburgh, 1961), 135.
119. See: "The Recollections of Vilmos Nagybaczoni Nagy," in Karsai, *op. cit.*, 278.
120. Hadtörténeti Intézet Levéltára, HM 1944. eln. 1/ny. bundle 6768.
121. Szabolcs Szita, "A fasizmus végnapjai Nyugat-Magyarországon, különös tekintettel a munkaszolgálat és a hadimunka történetére 1944-45" [The Last Days of Fascism in Western Hungary, With Special Regard to Labor Service and Military Labor 1944-45], Manuscript, (Budapest, 1987), 54.
122. Hadtörténeti Intézet Levéltára, HM 1945. 47. 675 eln.
123. Lévai, *op. cit.*, 467.
124. Jenő Lévai, *Fekete könyv a magyar zsidóság szenvedéseiről* [Black Book About the Sufferings of the Hungarian Jews] (Budapest, 1946), 79-84.

125. *Ibid.*, 64.
126. Horthy, *op. cit.*, 444.
127. *Ibid.*
128. Livia Rothkirchen, "Hungary, An Asylum for the Refugees of Europe," in *Yad Vashem studies on the European Jewish Catastrophe and Resistance VII* (Jerusalem, 1968), 134.
129. *Ibid.*
130. Lévai, *Zsidósors,* 48.
131. Varga, *op. cit.*, 400.
132. Hadtörténeti Intézet Levéltára, HM 1/ny 16/d-16/h.
133. Karsai, *op. cit.*, LXXVII.
134. Lévai, *op. cit.*, 53; Karsai, *op. cit.*, LXXXVI.
135. Hausner, *op. cit.*, 198.
136. Jenő Lévai, *Fekete Könyv,* 96.
137. *Ibid.*
138. Ránki, *et. al.*, eds., *op. cit.*, 837.
139. Lévai, *Fekete Könyv,* 107; Braham, *The Politics of Genocide,* 599.
140. *Der Kastner-Bericht über Eichmanns Menschenhandel in Ungarn* (Munich, 1961), 299.
141. C. A. Macartney, *op. cit.*, 281.
142. Karsai Elek, *Itél a nép* [The People Pass Judgment] (Budapest, 1977), 207.
143. Ránki, *et al.*, eds., *op. cit.*, 881.
144. Lévai, *Zsidósors,* 164.
145. *Ibid.*,175.
146. *Ibid.*, 260.
147. Randolph Braham, *The Destruction of the Hungarian Jewry* (New York, 1963), 913.
148. *Ibid.*, 927-929.
149. Elek Karsai, *Országgyarapítás, országvesztés* [Increasing the Country, Losing the Country] (Budapest, 1961), Part II., 221.
150. Karsai, *Itél a nép*, 214.
151. Miklós Gárdos, *Nemzetvesztők* [Destroyers of the Nation] (Budapest, 1971), 151.
152. Bernd Naumann, *Az Auschwitz-per* [The Auschwitz Trial] (Budapest, 1966), 333.

153. Ferenc Vadász, "Nappalok és éjjelek egybefolytak" [Days and Nights Were Washed In One], *Kritika*, January 1988.
154. Lévai, *Zsidósors,* 217.
155. Karsai, *Itél a nép,* 192.
156. See: *Pictures of the Deported* (Budapest, 1945).
157. *Egyleti Élet*, October 27, 1945; *Világ*, July 28, 1945.
158. Macartney, *op. cit.,* 286.
159. Hilberg, *op. cit.,* 547.
160. *The Catastrophe of European Jewry* (Jerusalem, 1976), 735.
161. *Encyclopaedia Judaica* (Jerusalem, 1971), Vol. 8, 1101.
162. Martin Hilbert, *The Atlas of the Holocaust* (New York, 1982).
163. György Ránki, *1944. március 19* (Budapest, 1978), 275.
164. Lévai, *Zsidósors,* 467.
165. Braham, *The Politics of Genocide,* 608; Lévai, *Fekete Könyv,* 149.
166. Macartney, *op. cit.,* 286.
167. Braham, *The Politics of Genocide,* 643-644.
168. Horthy, *op. cit.,* 446.
169. At the September 21, 1944 meeting of parliament, Tibor Korody mentioned 250,000 Jews living in Budapest. See: Lévai, *Zsidósors,* 286, and Ránki, *1944,* 293.
170. Lévai, *Zsidósors,* 261.
171. Lévai, *Fekete Könyv,* 217.
172. Ránki, *et. al.*, eds., *op. cit.,* 907.
173. Raul Hilbert writes about a Veesenmayer-Vajna Agreement (See: *op. cit.*, 552). In Randolph Braham's view, the agreement was between Eichmann and Vajna (See: *The Politics of Genocide,* 834). Macartney named Jury and Kovarcz as the signatories (*op. cit.,* 450); Szabolcs Szita mentions an agreement between Eichmann and Kovarcz (*op. cit.,* 68).
174. Szita, *op. cit.,* 70.
175. Lévai, *Fekete Könyv,* 275.
176. Braham, *The Politics of Genocide,* 844.
177. *Ibid.,* 1187-1188; Szita, *op. cit.,* 72.
178. Szita, *op. cit.,* 74.
179. Ránki, *et. al.*, eds., *op. cit.,* 910.
180. Hausner, *op. cit.,* 226.

181. Szita, *op. cit.,* 82.
182. *Ibid.,* 102.
183. Hausner, *op. cit.,* 227.
184. *Ibid.*
185. Ránki, *et al.*, eds., *op. cit.,* 912.
186. Gerald Reitlinger, *Die Endlösung* (Berlin, 1961), 504.
187. Szita, *op. cit.,* 104.
188. *Ibid.*, 75.
189. Hilberg, *op. cit.,* 553.
190. Lévai, *Zsidósors,* 342.
191. *Ibid.*, 353.
192. *Ibid.*, 366-367.
193. Karsai, *Országgyarapítás, országvesztés* 223.
194. Unterlagen BAM Freiburg - RM 11111/289, in Banny, *op. cit.,* 89.
195. Szita, *op. cit.,* Chapter V, "A Niderdonau erődvonal munkatáborai" [Labor Camps Along the Fortification Line of Niderdonau] and Chapter VI, "A Steiermark Nord erődszakasz építése" [Construction of the Steiermark Nord Fortification Section].
196. Macartney, *op. cit.,* 450.
197. Reitlinger, *op. cit.,* 504-507; Gilbert, *op. cit.,* 211; Banny, *op. cit.,* 62; Ránki, ed., *History of Hungary* Vol. 8, 1194.
198. Lévai, *Zsidósors,* 466-467.
199. Ránki, ed., *History of Hungary* Vol. 8/2, 1195.
200. Szekeres, ed., *op. cit.,* 569.
201. Lévai, *Zsidósors,* 386.
202. *Ibid.,* 400.
203. *Budapest Statistical Yearbook 1948,* 32.
204. Hadtörténeti Intézet Levéltára, HM 1845-47. 675/eln.
205. George Barany, "Jewish Prisoners of War in the Soviet Union During World War II," *Jahrbücher für Geschichte Osteuropas*, 31, (1983), 199.
206. Lévai, *Fekete Könyv,* 313.
207. Lévai, *Zsidósors,* 468.
208. *Világ*, September 28, 1945.
209. *Egyleti Élet,* November 17, 1945.
210. Lévai, *Zsidósors,* 468.
211. Béla Vágó, "The Destruction of the Jews of Transyl-

vania," in Randolph Braham ed., *Hungarian-Jewish Studies* (New York, 1966), 209.

212. *Ibid.*

213. *Egyleti Élet*, November 1, 1946.

214. Vágó, *op. cit.*, 196.

215. Randolph Braham, "The Destruction of the Jews of Carpatho-Ruthenia," in *Hungarian-Jewish Studies*, 232-233.

216. Personal communication by Zsigmond Pál Pach.

217. Lévai, *Fekete Könyv*, 313.

218. Personal communication by Zsigmond Pál Pach.

219. Snyder, *op. cit.*, 4. Central Statistical Office Demographic Department, Thirring Papers 85/a.

220. Viktor Karády, "Szociológiai kísérlet a magyar zsidóság 1945 és 1956 közötti helyzetének elemzésére" [A Sociological Attempt to Analyze the Position of the Hungarian Jews Between 1945 and 1956], in *Zsidóság az 1945 utáni Magyarországon* (Paris, 1984), 100.

221. *Egyleti Élet*, November 7, 1947.

222. Neumann, *op. cit.*, 11.

223. One-time registration cards are preserved at the center of the Jewish congregation on Síp Street in Budapest.

224. Kurt Grossmann, *The Jewish DP Problem* (New York, 1951), 10.

225. *Ibid.*, 15-19.

226. Jacques Vernan, *The Refugee in the Post-War World* (Geneva, 1951), 57.

227. *Egyleti Élet*, August 23, 1946.

228. Grossmann, *op. cit.*, 19.

229. *Új Élet*, November 13, 1945.

230. *Új Élet*, January 10, 1946.

231. *Egyleti Élet*, February 2, 1946.

232. *Ibid.*

233. *Egyleti Élet*, September 29, November 28, October 31, 1947, January 23, April 2, 1948.

234. *Egyleti Élet*, November 28, 1947.

235. *Egyleti Élet*, August 1, 1947.

236. Gyula Borbándi, *A magyar emigráció életrajza 1945-1985* [A Biography of the Hungarian Emigration 1945-1985] (Munich, 1985), 77.

237. Lestchinsky, *op. cit.,* 1582.

238. *Area Handbook for Israel* (Washington, 1970); Eugène Csocsán de Várallja, *La population de la Hongrie au XXe siècle* (Paris, 1977), 110.

239. The figures concerned were mentioned in a TV film of Hungarian Television about Israel, shown in April 1988.

240. Hadtörténeti Intézet Levéltára, HM box 3, A/II. 31.

241. Hadtörténeti Intézet Levéltára, HM box 2, A/I. 94/4766.

242. Hadtörténeti Intézet Levéltára, HM box 3, A/II. 31.

243. *Ibid.*

244. Sándor Tóth, *A szovjet hadsereg felszabadító harcai Magyarországon* [The Liberating Fights of the Soviet Army in Hungary] (Budapest, 1965), 30; József Gazsi, "Adatok és dokumentumok a Szálasi-hadsereg történetéhez" [Data and Documents to the History of the Szálasi Army], *Hadtörténelmi Közlemények* (1960), 227.

245. Manfréd Rauchensteiner, "A második világháború vége Ausztriában, különös tekintettel a magyar honvédség sorsára" [The End of World War II in Austria, With Special Regard to the Fate of the Hungarian Army], *Hadtörténelmi Közlemények* (1974), 316.

246. HM box 2, A/I. 94/4766.

247. Adonyi, *op. cit.,* 104.

248. HM Eln. 1944 1/ny. bundle no. 6768, and Hadtörténeti Intézet Levéltára, HM box 1, A/4/37161 eln.

249. Csima, *op. cit.,* 275, 322-329.

250. Hadtörténeti Intézet Levéltára, HM box 2, A/I. 94/4766.

251. Andreas Hillgruber, *Staatsmänner und Diplomaten bei Hitler* (Frankfurt, 1970), 522.

252. Lajos Dálnoki Veress, *Magyarország honvédelme a második világháború elott és alatt* [Hungary's Defense Before and During World War II] (Munich, 1972), 251.

253. Rauchensteiner, *op. cit.,* 308.

254. Dálnoki Veress, *op. cit.,* 275.

255. *A Nagy Honvédő Háború története* [A History of the Great Patriotic War] (Budapest, 1967), Vol. 5, 175.

256. Dálnoki Veress, *op. cit.,* 255.

257. *Ibid.,* 307.

258. Andreas von Weissenbach, *Magyarország és a fegyveres*

SS [Hungary and the Armed SS], (Munich, 1978), 110.

259. Hadtörténeti Intézet Levéltára, HM 1944 eln. 1/ny.

260. Ránki, ed., *A History of Hungary* Vol. 8, 1213.

261. Csima, *op. cit.,* 333.

262. Mrs. Tamás Morva, "Dokumentumok a Horthy-Szálasi hadsereg utolsó hónapjainak történetéhez," [Documents to the History of the Last Months of the Horthy-Szálasi Army], *Hadtörténelmi Közlemények* 1970, 281.

263. Korom, *op. cit.,* 3.

264. *Fehér Könyv,* 18.

265. Korom, *op. cit.,* 3.

266. Lajos Für, "Mennyi a sok sírkereszt?" [How Many Are the Graves?] *Alföld* no. 9, (1984), 39.

267. Hadtörténeti Intézet Levéltára, HM box 2, A/I. 94/4766.

268. *Fehér Könyv,* 18; Sándor Krupa, *A sarló-kalapács rémtettei* [Atrocities of the Sickle and Hammer] (De With, Michigan, 1979); László Juhász, *Magyar rabok idegenben* [Hungarian Prisoners in Alien Land] (Munich, 1982), 200; *Nyugati Hírnök,* May 30, 1950, 30; Ferenc Fiala, *Zavaros évek...* [Troubled Years...] (London, 1966).

269. Korom, *op. cit.,* 3.

270. Hadtörténeti Intézet Levéltára, HM box 2, A/I. 95/6792.

271. Hadtörténeti Intézet Levéltára, HM box 2, A/I. 94/4766.

272. Hadtörténeti Intézet Levéltára, HM box 2, A/I. 95/6792.

273. Hadtörténeti Intézet Levéltára, HM 1945. eln. 35. 328.

274. Sándor Mucs and Ernő Zágoni, *A magyar néphadsereg története* [A History of the Hungarian People's Army] (Budapest, 1984), 66.

275. Hadtörténeti Intézet Levéltára, HM 1945. eln. 35. 328.

276. Hadtörténeti Intézet Levéltára, HM 35 214/eln. 1945.

277. Report on the POW question by the Welfare Ministry. Compiled by Bálint Botár, counsellor to the head of the ministerial department; In the compiler's possession.

278. Hadtörténeti Intézet Levéltára, HM box 2, A/I. 95/6792.

279. Report to the Welfare Minister on the care for POWs; In Bálint Botár's possession.

280. Hadtörténeti Intézet Levéltára, HM 1659 1946/eln.

281. Hadtörténeti Intézet Levéltára, HM 1945 eln. 44014.

282. *Ibid.*

283. Hadtörténeti Intézet Levéltára, HM A/I. 94/4766.
284. *Ibid.*
285. The issues of *Magyar Hadirokkant és Hadifogoly Híradó* are available in the Parliament Library, only from 1947 and in the Széchényi Library from 1946.
286. *Uj Szó*, September18, 1945.
287. *Uj Szó*, December 25, 1945.
288. *Magyar Hadirokkant és Hadifogoly Híradó*, November 16, 1946.
289. *Világ*, August 18, 1945.
290. *Világ*, September 7, 1945.
291. Hadtörténeti Intézet Levéltára, HM box 2. A/I, 95/6792.
292. Hadtörténeti Intézet Levéltára, HM box 2. A/I, 94/4766.
293. *Magyar Hadirokkant és Hadifogoly Híradó*, January 7, 1946.
294. *Magyar Hadirokkant és Hadifogoly Híradó*, January 28, 1946.
295. *Magyar Hadirokkant és Hadifogoly Híradó*, February 11, 1946.
296. Hadtörténeti Intézet Levéltára, HM 1946. eln. 10415.
297. *Kossuth Népe*, March 21, 1946.
298. *Ibid.*
299. *Kis Újság*, September 15, 1946.
300. Hadtörténeti Intézet Levéltára, HM 1946. eln. 10415.
301. *Magyar Hadirokkant és Hadifogoly Híradó*, July 3, 1946.
302. Report on the 1946 Work of the I/2 Department For the Social Care of Refugees, Prisoners of War and Deported People; In Bálint Botár's possession.
303. Hadtörténeti Intézet Levéltára, HM 1947. eln. 1333.
304. *Ibid.*
305. *Ibid.*
306. *Ibid.*
307. Oral communication by Bálint Botár.
308. Referring to PI Arch. 283. 31/43, Mihály Korom writes in his article (*Valóság*, 1984) that in October 1947, there were only 41,000 Hungarian Prisoners of War in the western zones of Germany and Austria. This number is only part of those staying abroad since many had already left the Anglo-American zones,

drifting westward. At the same time, there were still prisoners of war in France and Italy.

309. *Hungaria*, February 1, 1952.

310. *Fehérvári Hírek*, July 19, 1946; *Esti Szabad Szó*, July 21, 1946.

311. *Magyar Hadirokkant és Hadifogoly Híradó* delayed the deadline given by Svirodov of September until October for unknown reasons. The Soviet Union had promised in July to transport 25,000 POWs home until the end of October 1946; See: *Magyar Hadirokkant és Hadifogoly Híradó*, September 21, 1946.

312. Report on the work of the department in care of the POWs. In Bálint Botár's possession.

313. *Ibid.*

314. *1947. évi törvénycikkek* [Statutes of 1947], (Budapest, 1947), 152.

315. Hungarian Ministry of Foreign Affairs, *Magyar-Szovjet Kapcsolatok 1945-1948. Documentumok* [Hungarian-Soviet Relations 1945-48 Documents] (Budapest, n. d.), 197.

316. *Magyar Hadirokkant és Hadifogoly Híradó*, March 8, 1947.

317. Hadtörténeti Intézet Levéltára, HM 1947. eln. 10903.

318. Report for April 1947 of the work of the Welfare Ministry's Department I/2 for the Social Care of Refugees, Prisoners of War and Deported People. In Bálint Botár's possession.

319. Hadtörténeti Intézet Levéltára, HM 1947. eln. 10903.

320. *Ibid.*

321. Hadtörténeti Intézet Levéltára, HM Hermann Pokornyi's estate. Diary of events.

322. Kálmán Benda, ed., *Magyarország Történeti Kronológiája* [Hungary's Historical Chronology] (Budapest, 1982), Vol. IV, 1040.

323. Hadtörténeti Intézet Levéltára, HM 1948. eln. III. Informative bulletin.

324. *Kiskunság*, February 6, 1948.

325. *Világ*, May 21, 1948.

326. *Világ*, July 2, 1948.

327. *Világ*, August 15, 1948.

328. *Ibid.*
329. Hadtörténeti Intézet Levéltára, HM Hermann Pokornyi Papers. "Életem munkálkodásának története," [The History of My Life's Work], Manuscript.
330. *Hungaria*, (Munich), April 17, 1953.
331. Hadtörténeti Intézet Levéltára, HM 1948. eln. III, Informative Bulletin.
332. *Fehér Könyv* 18; *Nyugati Hírnök*, May 30, 1950.
333. A semi-official letter by Erik Molnár, Welfare Ministry, UMKL V/2 stated that "Out of the prisoners of war wishing to join the new Hungarian army, the Soviet government released at least 20,000 in spring 1945, and gradually freed 259,222 from October 1945 to October 1946"; "thus, together with the thousands transported home before the signing of the Peace Treaty, they totaled 300,000 people," *Magyar Hadirokkant és Hadifogoly Híradó*, May 17, 1947; "...from spring 1947, after the ratification of the Peace Treaty until the end of the year 120,000 (were released by the Soviet government), until the end of October 1948...another 80,000 were released by the Soviet government," in Korom, *op. cit.*, 3-4.
334. Für, *op. cit.*, 39.
335. Lajos Für, *Mennyi a sok sírkereszt?* [How Many Are the Many Graves], (New York, 1987), 49.
336. *Ibid.*, 55.
337. Snyder, *op. cit.*, 4.
338. Thirring, *op. cit.*, 72; Kovacsics, *op. cit.*, 357.
339. Menyhért Lakatos, "A cigányok sorsa 1944-ben" [The Fate of Gypsies in 1944], in *Magyarország 1944-ben* [Hungary in 1944] (Budapest, 1984), 58; According to the estimates of László Karsai, the losses of the Hungarian Gypsies were several thousands. László Karsai, "Cigánykérdés Magyarországon (1919-1945)," [The Gypsy Question in Hungary (1919-1945)], Manuscript, 1991.
340. Borbándi, *op. cit.*, 67-68.
341. Balogh, *op. cit.*, 101-102, 131.

Maps

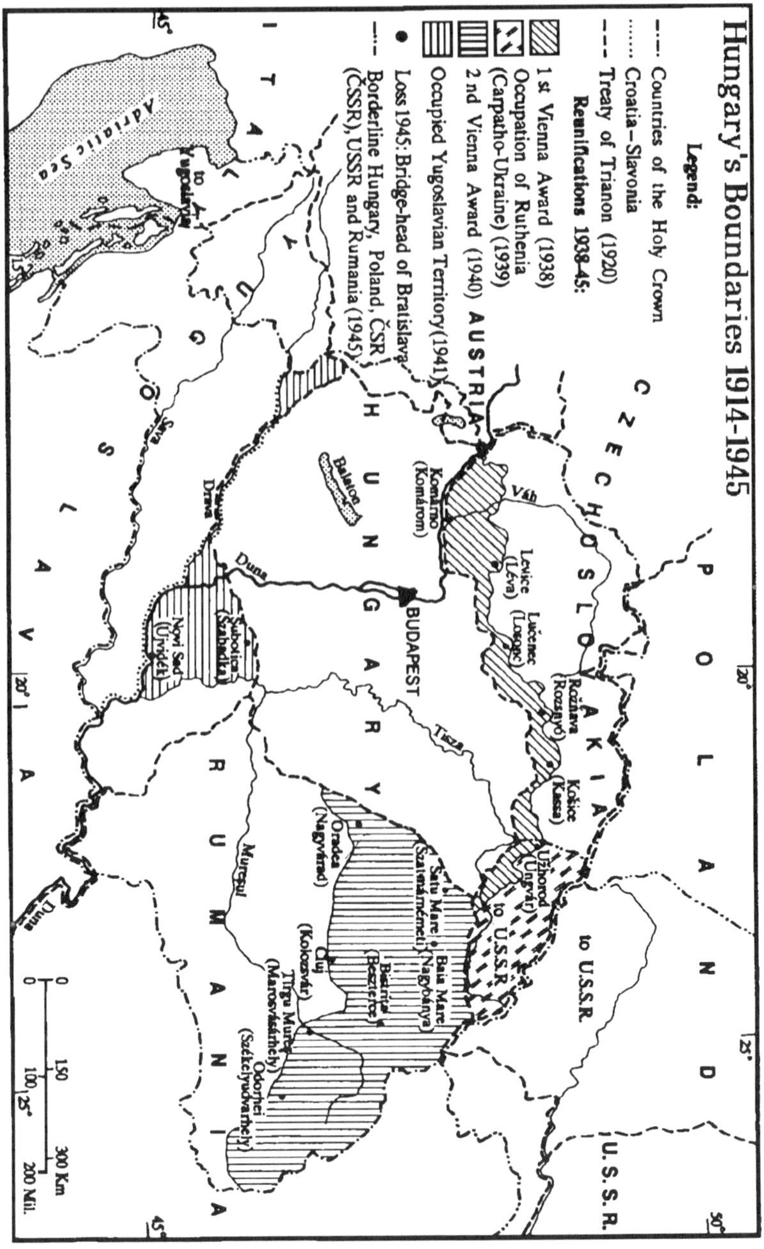
Hungary's Boundaries 1914-1945
Legend:
Countries of the Holy Crown
Croatia–Slavonia
Treaty of Trianon (1920)
Reunifications 1938-45:
1 st Vienna Award (1938)
Occupation of Ruthenia (Carpatho-Ukraine) (1939)
2 nd Vienna Award (1940)
Occupied Yugoslavian Territory (1941)
Loss 1945: Bridge-head of Bratislava
Borderline Hungary, Poland, ČSR (ČSR), USSR and Rumania (1945)
AUSTRIA
CZECHOSLOVAKIA
POLAND
U.S.S.R.
to U.S.S.R.
HUNGARY
RUMANIA
YUGOSLAVIA
ITALY
Adriatic Sea
to Yugoslavia
BUDAPEST
Komárno (Komárom)
Levice (Léva)
Lučenec (Losonc)
Rožňava (Rozsnyó)
Košice (Kassa)
Užhorod (Ungvár)
Satu Mare (Szatmárnémeti)
Baia Mare (Nagybánya)
Oradea (Nagyvárad)
Cluj (Kolozsvár)
Bistrita (Beszterce)
Tîrgu Mureş (Marosvásárhely)
Odorhei (Székelyudvarhely)
Subotica (Szabadka)
Novi Sad (Újvidék)
Balaton
Duna
Dráva
Sava
Váh
Tisza
Mureşul
0 150 300 Km
0 100 200 Mil.
45°
50°
20°
25°

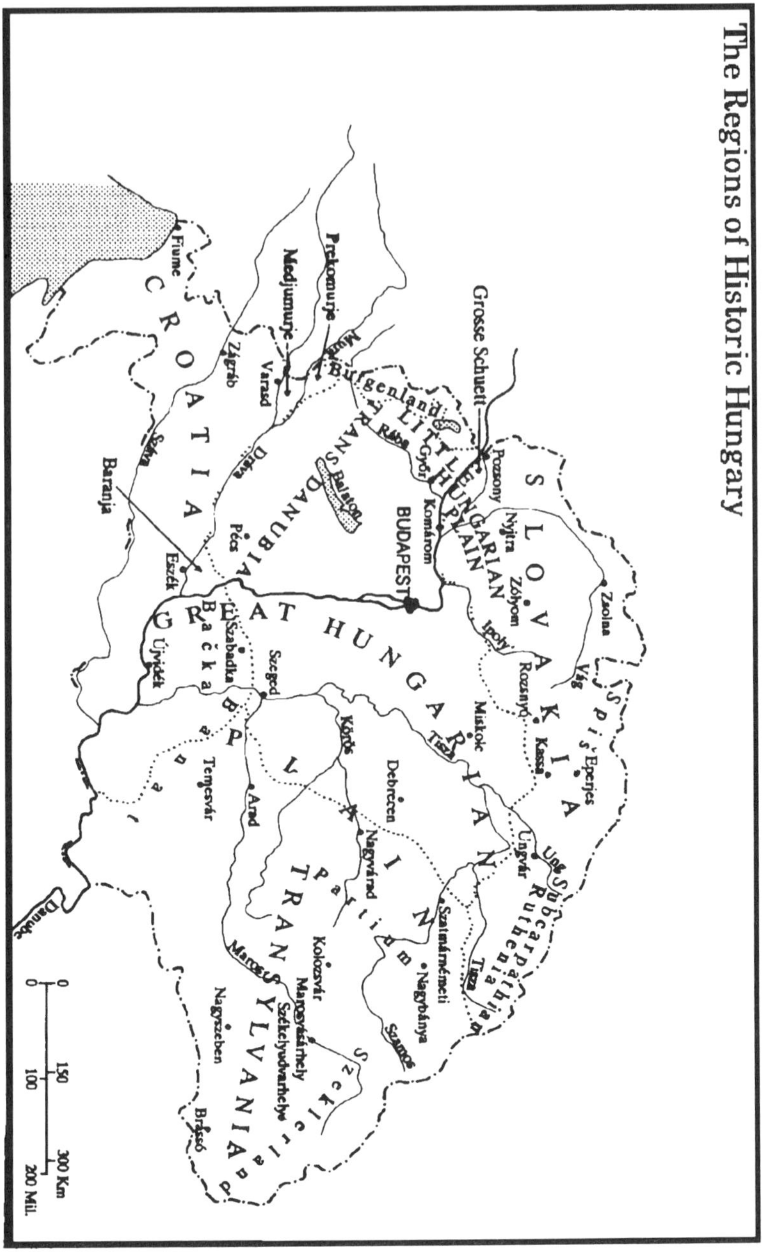
The Regions of Historic Hungary
SLOVAKIA
Grosse Schuett
Pozsony
Nyitra
Zólyom
Zsolna
Vág
Ipoly
Rozsnyó
Kassa
Eperjes
Spis
Miskolc
Tisza
Debrecen
Ungvár
Ung
Subcarpathia
Ruthenia
Szatmárnémeti
Nagybánya
Szamos
Nagyvárad
Partium
Kolozsvár
Marosvásárhely
Székelyudvarhely
Szeklerland
TRANSYLVANIA
Nagyszeben
Brassó
Maros
Arad
Temesvár
Banat
Körös
Szeged
Szabadka
Bačka
Újvidék
GREAT HUNGARIAN PLAIN
BUDAPEST
Komárom
Győr
Rába
LITTLE HUNGARIAN PLAIN
Burgenland
Mura
Prekomurje
Medjumurje
Varasd
Zágráb
CROATIA
Fiume
Száva
Dráva
Baranja
Eszék
Pécs
Balaton
TRANSDANUBIA
Danube
0 150 300 Km
0 100 200 Mil.

Name Index

Place Index

List of Contributors

Ivan T. Berend	Professor of History, University of California, Los Angeles, and Budapest University of Economic Sciences, Budapest.
Loránd Dombrády	Director Emeritus, Institute of Military History, Budapest.
György Lengyel	Department Chairman of Sociology at the Budapest University of Economic Sciences.
György Ránki	At the time of his death in 1988, he was Director of the Institute of History of the Hungarian Academy of Sciences and Director of Hungarian Studies, University of Indiana, Bloomington.
Tamás Stark	Scientific Researcher at the Institute of History of the Hungarian Academy of Sciences, Budapest.
Károly Szabó	Executive Director, Hungarian Foreign Trade Bank, Budapest.
Sándor Szakály	Department Chairman, Institute of Military History, Budapest.
László Virágh	Department Head at the Budapest Bank, Budapest.

Volumes Published by
Atlantic Research and Publications
"Studies on Society in Change"

No. 1 *Tolerance and Movements of Religious Dissent in Eastern Europe*. Edited by Béla K. Király. 1977.

No. 2 *The Habsburg Empire in World War I.* Edited by R. A. Kann. 1978.

No. 3 *The Mutual Effects of the Islamic and Judeo-Christian Worlds: The East European Pattern.* Edited by A. Ascher, T. Halasi-Kun, B. K. Király. 1979.

No. 4 *Before Watergate: Problems of Corruption in American Society.* Edited by A. S. Eisenstadt, A. Hoogenboom, H. L. Trefousse. 1979.

No. 5 *East Central European Perceptions of Early America.* Edited by B. K. Király and G. Barány. 1977.

No. 6 *The Hungarian Revolution of 1956 in Retrospect.* Edited by B. K. Király and Paul Jónás. 1978.

No. 7 *Brooklyn U.S.A.: Fourth Largest City in America.* Edited by Rita S. Miller. 1979.

No. 8 *Prime Minister Gyula Andrássy's Influence on Habsburg Foreign Policy.* János Decsy. 1979.

No. 9 — *The Great Impeacher: A Political Biography of James M. Ashley*. Robert F. Horowitz. 1979.

No. 10 Vol. I* — *Special Topics and Generalizations on the Eighteenth and Nineteenth Century*. Edited by Béla K. Király and Gunther E. Rothenberg. 1979.

No. 11 Vol. II — *East Central European Society and War in the Pre-Revolutionary Eighteenth-Century*. Edited by Gunther E. Rothenberg, Béla K. Király, and Peter F. Sugar. 1982.

No. 12 Vol. III — *From Hunyadi to Rákóczi: War and Society in Late Medieval and Early Modern Hungary*. Edited by János M. Bak and Béla K. Király. 1982.

No. 13 Vol. IV — *East Central European Society and War in the Era of Revolutions: 1775-1856*. Edited by B. K. Király. 1984.

No. 14 Vol. V — *Essays on World War I: Origins and Prisoners of War*. Edited by Samuel R. Williamson, Jr. and Peter Pastor. 1983.

No. 15 Vol. VI — *Essays on World War I: Total War and Peacemaking, A Case Study on Trianon*. Edited by B. K. Király, Peter Pastor, and Ivan Sanders. 1982.

No. 16 Vol. VII — *Army, Aristocracy, Monarchy: War, Society and Government in Austria, 1618-1780*. Edited by Thomas M. Barker. 1982.

No. 17 Vol. VIII — *The First Serbian Uprising 1804-1813*. Edited by Wayne S. Vucinich. 1982.

No. 18 Vol. IX — *Czechoslovak Policy and the Hungarian Minority 1945-1948*. Kálmán Janics. Edited by Stephen Borsody. 1982.

---

* Volume Numbers I through XXXI refer to the series, *War and Society in East and Central Europe*

No. 19 Vol. X *At the Brink of War and Peace: The Tito-Stalin Split in a Historic Perspective*. Edited by Wayne S. Vucinich. 1982.

No. 20 *Inflation Through the Ages: Economic, Social, Psychological, and Historical Aspects*. Edited by Edward Marcus and Nathan Schmuckler. 1981.

No. 21 *Germany and America: Essays on Problems of International Relations and Immigration*. Edited by Hans L. Trefousse. 1980.

No. 22 *Brooklyn College: The First Half Century*. Murray M. Horowitz. 1981.

No. 23 *A New Deal for the World: Eleanor Roosevelt and American Foreign Policy*. Jason Berger. 1981.

No. 24 *The Legacy of Jewish Migration: 1881 and Its Impact*. Edited by David Berger. 1982.

No. 25 *The Road to Bellapais: Cypriot Exodus to Northern Cyprus*. Pierre Oberling. 1982.

No. 26 *New Hungarian Peasants: An East Central European Experience with Collectivization*. Edited by Marida Hollos and Béla C. Maday. 1983.

No. 27 *Germans in America: Aspects of German-American Relations in the Nineteenth Century*. Edited by Allen McCormick. 1983.

No. 28 *A Question of Empire: Leopold I and the War of Spanish Succession, 1701-1705*. Linda and Marsha Frey. 1983.

No. 29 *The Beginning of Cyrillic Printing-Cracow, 1491. From the Orthodox Past in Poland*. Szczepan K.

Zimmer. Edited by Ludwik Krzyanowski and Irene Nagurski. 1983.

No. 29a *A Grand Ecole for the Grand Corps: The Recruitment and Training of the French Administration.* Thomas R. Osborne. 1983.

No. 30
Vol. XI *The First War between Socialist States: The Hungarian Revolution of 1956 and Its Impact.* Edited by Béla K. Király, Barbara Lotze, Nandor Dreisziger. 1984.

No. 31
Vol. XII *The Effects of World War I, The Uprooted: Hungarian Refugees and Their Impact on Hungary's Domestic Politics.* István Mócsy. 1983.

No. 32
Vol. XIII *The Effects of World War I: The Class War after the Great War: The Rise Of Communist Parties in East Central Europe, 1918-1921.* Edited by Ivo Banac. 1983.

No. 33
Vol. XIV *The Crucial Decade: East Central European Society and National Defense, 1859-1870.* Edited by Béla K. Király. 1984.

No. 35
Vol. XVI *Effects of World War I: War and Communism in Hungary, 1919.* György Péteri. 1984.

No. 36
Vol. XVII *Insurrections, Wars, and the Eastern Crisis in the 1870s.* Edited by B. K. Király and Gale Stokes. 1985.

No. 37
Vol. XVIII *East Central European Society and the Balkan Wars, 1912-1913.* Edited by B. K. Király and Dimitrije Djordjevic. 1986.

No. 38
Vol. XIX *East Central European Society in World War I.* Edited by B. K. Király and N. F. Dreisziger, Assistant Editor Albert A. Nofi. 1985.

No. 39
Vol. XX
Revolutions and Interventions in Hungary and Its Neighbor States, 1918-1919. Edited by Peter Pastor. 1988.

No. 40
Vol. XXI
East Central European Society and War, 1750-1920. Bibliography and Historiography. Complied and edited by László Alföldi. Pending.

No. 41
Vol. XXII
Essays on East Central European Society and War, 1740s-1920s. Edited by Stephen Fischer-Galati and Béla K. Király. 1988.

No. 42
Vol. XXIII
East Central European Maritime Commerce and Naval Policies, 1789-1913. Edited by Apostolos E. Vacalopoulos, Constantinos D. Svolopoulos, and Béla K. Király. 1988.

No. 43
Vol. XXIV
Selections, Social Origins, Education and Training of East Central European Officers Corps. Edited by Béla K. Király and Walter Scott Dillard. 1988.

No. 44
Vol. XXV
East Central European War Leaders: Civilian and Military. Edited by Béla K. Király and Albert Nofi. 1988.

No. 46
Germany's International Monetary Policy and the European Monetary System. Hugo Kaufmann. 1985.

No. 47
Iran Since the Revolution—Internal Dynamics, Regional Conflicts and the Superpowers. Edited by Barry M. Rosen. 1985.

No. 48
Vol. XXVII
The Press during the Hungarian Revolution of 1848-1849. Domokos Kosáry. 1986.

No. 49
The Spanish Inquisition and the Inquisitional Mind. Edited by Angel Alcala. 1987.

No. 50 *Catholics, the State and the European Radical Right, 1919-1945*. Edited by Richard Wolff and Jorg K. Hoensch. 1987.

No. 51 *The Boer War and Military Reform*. Jay Stone and Erwin A. Schmidl. 1987.

No. 52 *Baron Joseph Eötvös, A Literary Biography*. Steven B. Várdy. 1987.

No. 53 *Towards the Renaissance of Puerto Rican Studies: Ethnic and Area Studies in University Education*. Maria Sanchez and Antonio M. Stevens. 1987.

No. 54 *The Brazilian Diamonds in Contracts, Contraband and Capital*. Harry Bernstein. 1987.

No. 55 *Christians, Jews and Other Worlds: Patterns of Conflict and Accommodation*. Edited by Philip F. Gallagher. 1988.

No. 56 Vol. XXVI *The Fall of the Medieval Kingdom of Hungary: Mohács, 1526, Buda, 1541*. Géza Perjés. 1989.

No. 57 *The Lord Mayor of Lisbon: The Portuguese Tribune of the People and His Twenty-four Guilds*. Harry Berstein. 1989.

No. 58 *Hungarian Statesmen of Destiny: 1860-1960*. Edited by Paul Bődy. 1989.

No. 59 *For China: The Memoirs of T. G. Li, former Major General in the Chinese Nationalist Army*. T. G. Li. Written in collaboration with Roman Rome. 1989.

No. 60 *Politics in Hungary: For a Democratic Alternative*. János Kis, with an Introduction by Timothy Garton Ash. 1989.

No. 61 *Hungarian Worker's Councils in 1956*. Edited by Bill Lomax. 1990.

No. 62 *Essays on the Structure and Reform of Centrally Planned Economic Systems*. Paul Jonas. A joint publication with Corvina Kiadó, Budapest. 1990.

No. 63 *Kossuth as a Journalist in England*. Éva H. Haraszti. A joint publication with Akadémiai Kiadó, Budapest. 1990.

No. 64 *From Padua to the Trianon, 1918-1920*. Mária Ormos. A joint publication with Akadémiai Kiadó, Budapest. 1990.

No. 65 *Towns in Medieval Hungary*. Edited by László Gerevich. A joint publication with Akadémiai Kiadó, Budapest. 1990.

No. 66 *The Nationalities Problem in Transylvania, 1867-1940*. Sándor Bíró. 1992.

No. 67 *Hungarian Exiles and the Romanian National Movement, 1849-1867*. Béla Borsi-Kálmán. 1991.

No. 68 *The Hungarian Minority's Situation in Ceausescu's Romania*. Edited by Rudolf Joó and Andrew Ludanyi. Pending.

No. 69 *Democracy, Revolution, Self-Determination. Selected Writings*. István Bibó. Edited by Károly Nagy. 1991.

No. 70 *Trianon and the Protection of Minorities*. József Galántai. A joint publication with Corvina Kiadó, Budapest. 1992.

No. 71 *King Saint Stephen of Hungary*. György Györffy. A joint publication with Corvina Kiadó. Pending.

No. 72 *Dynasty, Politics and Culture. Selected Essays.* Robert A. Kann. Edited by Stanley B. Winters. 1991.

No. 73 *Jadwiga of Anjou and the Rise of East Central Europe.* Oscar Halecki. Edited by Thaddeus V. Gromada. A joint publication with the Polish Institute of Arts and Sciences of America. 1991.

No. 74 *Hungarian Economy and Society during World*
Vol. XXIX *War II.* Edited by György Lengyel. 1993.

No. 75 *The Life of a Communist Revolutionary, Béla Kun.* György Borsányi. 1992.

No. 76 *Yugoslavia: The Process of Disintegration.* Laslo Sekelj. 1993.

No. 77 *Wartime American Plans for a New Hungary.*
Vol. XXX *Documents from the U.S. Department of State, 1942-1944.* Edited by Ignác Romsics. 1992.

No. 78 *Planning for War against Russia and Serbia.*
Vol. XXXI *Austro-Hungarian and German Military Strategies, 1871-1914.* Graydon A. Tunstall, Jr. 1993.

No. 79 *American Effects on Hungarian Imagination and Political Thought, 1559-1848.* Géza Závodszky. Pending.